Parliament and the Crown
in the
Reign of Mary Tudor

JENNIFER LOACH

CLARENDON PRESS · OXFORD
1986

Oxford University Press, Walton Street, Oxford OX2 6DP
Oxford New York Toronto
Delhi Bombay Calcutta Madras Karachi
Kuala Lumpur Singapore Hong Kong Tokyo
Nairobi Dar es Salaam Cape Town
Melbourne Auckland

and associated companies in
Beirut Berlin Ibadan Mexico City Nicosia

Oxford is a trade mark of Oxford University Press

Published in the United States
by Oxford University Press, New York

British Library Cataloguing in Publication Data

Loach, Jennifer
Parliament and the crown in in the reign of Mary
Tudor.—(Oxford historical monographs)
1. England and Wales—Parliament—History
I. Title
328.42'09 JN525
ISBN 0-19-822936-4

Library of Congress Cataloging in Publication Data

Loach, Jennifer
Parliament and the crown in the reign of Mary Tudor.
(Oxford historical monographs)
Bibliography: p.
Includes index.
1. Great Britain. Parliament—History—16th century.
2. Great Britain—Politics and government—1553–1558.
I. Title.
JN525.L6 1986 942.05'4 85-25954
ISBN 0-19-822936-4

Set by Eta Services (Typesetters) Ltd.,
Beccles, Suffolk
Printed in Great Britain
at the University Press, Oxford
by David Stanford
Printer to the University

TO ALAN

Acknowledgements

This study was first presented as a thesis for the degree of Doctor of Philosophy in 1974. The reign of Mary and the parliamentary history of the sixteenth century have since attracted considerable scholarly interest and the use made of my thesis by other historians as well as the promptings of my friends encourage me to believe that there is value in the wider publication of my findings. I have taken account of studies that have appeared since 1974 but the views expressed in this book are essentially those of my thesis.

My early research was greatly facilitated by the generosity with which the section of the History of Parliament Trust under the direction of Professor S. T. Bindoff allowed me access to the biographies of early Tudor members of parliament on which they were then working. The staff told me of material about which I would not otherwise have known, and they—and, in particular, Alasdair Hawkyard—were always ready to discuss problems with me. Professor S. T. Bindoff himself was especially kind and patient, inviting me to a number of meetings of those working on the Marian section of the *History* from which I derived much benefit, although I did not always agree with the interpretation the Trust put upon certain documents. Had it been possible to write the chapter of the introduction to *The House of Commons, 1509–1558* that I was at one time commissioned to do, these questions of interpretation would have had a full airing: as it is, some of them are set out here in footnotes and appendices.

I must thank the Comptroller of the Duchy of Cornwall for permission to consult manuscripts in the Duchy Office, the Marquess of Anglesey for access to the Paget papers at Plas Newydd, and the Marquess of Bath for allowing me to use the Thynne manuscripts at Longleat.

I have incurred many debts in the writing of this work. The first, as always, is to my former tutor, Menna Prestwich. Amongst Oxford colleagues I wish to thank in particular Cliff Davies, who was also an examiner of my thesis, Alastair Parker, who read and commented on numerous early drafts, George Ramsay, Paul Slack, Keith Thomas, and Victor Treadwell. I am very grateful to George Bernard for references from the Talbot papers and for much other intellectual stimulus. Alan Fellows, Gary Hill, and Philippa Tudor have all generously helped my researches in the midst of their own. My debts to my colleagues in Somerville are great. In particular, I wish to thank Agatha

Ramm, Anne de Villiers, who provided me with information about early Stuart parliaments, and Christina Roaf, who has tirelessly helped me with the translation of Italian sources. Barbara Harvey has given endless and endlessly tactful encouragement. To my former superviser, Penry Williams, I am extremely grateful, not only for his assistance and guidance, but also for his willing and cheerful interest in Marian parliaments throughout what is now a very protracted period.

J. L.

Contents

Abbreviations and References

Arch. Étr.	Paris, Archives du Ministère des Affaires Étrangères.
APC	*Acts of the Privy Council*, ed. J. R. Dasent, vols. I–VII (London, 1890–1907).
BIHR	*Bulletin of the Institute of Historical Research.*
BL	British Library, London.
CJ	*The Journals of the House of Commons*, vol. I (London, 1846).
Complete Peerage	G. E. Cokayne, *Complete Peerage of England, Scotland, Ireland . . .* 8 vols. (Exeter, 1887–98).
CPR	*Calendar of the Patent Rolls* (London, 1924–39).
CSP Sp.	*Calendar of State Papers, Spanish*, ed. Royall Tyler, vols. XI–XIII (London, 1916–54).
CSP Ven.	*Calendar of State Papers, Venetian*, ed. R. Brown, C. Bentinck, and H. Brown, vols. IV–VI (London, 1864–98).
DNB	*Dictionary of National Biography*, ed. L. Stephen and S. Lee, 21 vols. (London, 1908–9).
EHR	*English Historical Review.*
Foxe	J. Foxe, *Acts and Monuments*, 6 vols. (London, 1841).
HLRO	House of Lords Record Office.
The House of Commons, 1509–1558	*The House of Commons, 1509–1558*, ed. S. T. Bindoff (London, 1982).
The House of Commons, 1558–1603	*The House of Commons, 1558–1603*, ed. P. Hasler (London, 1981).
HMC	*Historical Manuscripts Commission.*
LJ	*The Journals of the House of Lords*, vol. I (London, 1852).
Letters and Papers	*Letters and Papers, Foreign and Domestic, of the Reign of Henry VIII*, ed. J. S. Brewer, J. Gairdner, and R. H. Brodie (London, 1864–1932).
Machyn	H. Machyn, *The Diary of Henry Machyn*, ed. J. G. Nichols (Camden Society, os, LXXVII, 1859).
PCC	Prerogative Court of Canterbury.
PRO	Public Record Office, London.

Queen Jane and Queen Mary	*The Chronicle of Queen Jane and Two Years of Queen Mary*, ed. J. G. Nichols (Camden Society, os, LIII, 1852).
RO	Record Office.
RSTC	*A Short Title Catalogue of Books Printed in England, Scotland, and Ireland, 1475–1640*, ed. W. A. Jackson, F. S. Ferguson, and K. F. Pantzer, vol. II (I–Z) (London, 1976).
TRHS	*Transactions of the Royal Historical Society.*
SP	State Papers, Public Record Office.
STC	*A Short-Title Catalogue of Books Printed in England, Scotland, and Ireland, 1475–1640* ed. A. W. Pollard and G. R. Redgrave (London, 1969).
Vertot	R. A. de Vertot, *Ambassades de Messieurs de Noailles en Angleterre*, 5 vols. (Leiden, 1763).

Note on spelling of names. Where relevant, the spelling used here follows that of *The House of Commons, 1509–1558*.

Note on references to the Lords and Commons Journals. The references given here are to the printed volumes except where the manuscripts provide additional information. (The excessive use of capitals by the nineteenth-century editors has not, however, been followed.) Since several days are reported on a single printed page, reference is given to a date rather than a page-number.

1

The Crown in 1553

THE accession of Mary Tudor to the English throne was one of the most surprising events of the sixteenth century. At her brother's death on 6 July 1553 Mary appeared an isolated figure, her cause hopeless. The duke of Northumberland controlled the capital on behalf of his daughter-in-law, Jane Grey. He had substantial troops at his disposal and the hope of more, should they be needed, from the French king. The archbishop of Canterbury, the chancellor, most of his fellow privy councillors, many household officials, the mayor and aldermen of the city, twenty-two peers, several judges, leading London merchants, and the sheriffs of Middlesex, Surrey, and Kent had all given their formal consent to Edward's 'devise' whereby the succession was vested in the Suffolk line. Yet on 19 July, amidst bonfires and the ringing of bells, Mary was proclaimed queen in London. The manner of her triumph, and her own understanding of it, were to shape government policy for the next five years.

Mary was transformed from refugee to ruler by the action of gentlemen and nobles in the provinces—in East Anglia, Oxfordshire, Buckinghamshire, and the Thames Valley. Hers was a triumph of the counties against the centre; perhaps, as one commentator has put it, the last occasion before 1640 on which a local ruling establishment would 'so unambiguously set itself up against Westminster'.[1] It was made possible by an astonishing omission of Northumberland's: although the government had sought to conceal from the public the fact of Edward's critical illness, as, later, it did his death, no steps had been taken to secure the person of the princess who was, according to the statute of 1544 and to Henry VIII's will, his heir. Northumberland and the council were clearly startled

[1] 'The "Vita Mariae Angliae Reginae" of Robert Wingfield of Brantham', ed. D. MacCulloch, *Camden Miscellany* XXVIII (Camden Fourth Series, 29, 1984), 191–2.

when, on 4 July, before Edward's death, Mary suddenly left her residence, Hunsdon in Hertfordshire.[2] Via Sawston Hall in Cambridgeshire, the home of John Huddleston, and Hengrave Hall, Suffolk, she travelled to a former Howard property in Norfolk, Kenninghall.[3] There she learnt of Edward's death.[4] On 8 July she summoned to her assistance Sir George Somerset, Sir William Waldegrave, and Clement Heigham.[5] The next day she wrote to the council in London formally claiming the throne, and also to Sir Edward Hastings, ordering him to support her in Middlesex and Buckinghamshire.[6] Waldegrave and Heigham arrived, presumably in response to her letters, and so did Sir John Mordaunt, John Sulyard, Sir William Drury, and John Bourchier, earl of Bath, the step-father of young Richard Kitson, whose hospitality she had enjoyed at Hengrave.[7] The party then moved to another, and better fortified, Howard property, Framlingham in Suffolk. On 14 July Robert Brown, a baron of the exchequer, arrived at Framlingham with Sir Henry Bedingfield, and they were joined the next day by the earl of Sussex who had been persuaded by his second son, Henry, to assist Mary, by Sir Nicholas Hare, Sir John Shelton and a serjeant-at-law, Richard Morgan.[8]

Meanwhile, on 10 July, Jane Grey had been proclaimed in London.[9] Some other towns followed the lead of the capital, but many local authorities appear to have been reluctant to

[2] Antonio de Guaras, *The Accession of Queen Mary*, ed. R. Garnett (London, 1892), 89.

[3] S. Haynes, *A Collection of State Papers . . . left by William Cecil, Lord Burghley* (London, 1740), 118. This undated letter is there ascribed to 1551, but it clearly relates to 1553; *CSP Sp.* XI. 70.

[4] It is not known for certain who informed Mary. It was later, and perhaps surprisingly, claimed for Nicholas Throckmorton that it was he who sent the news by means of Mary's goldsmith (MS 'Life' quoted in *Queen Jane and Queen Mary*, 1–2) and the payment in March 1554 of a reward 'in consideration of his service to the Queen, especially at Framlingham' to Robert Reyns, citizen and goldsmith of London, lends some credence to the story (*CPR* 1553–4, 226). Wingfield's 'Vita' also claims that Mary was informed 'by her goldsmith, a citizen of London, newly returned from the City' (251).

[5] BL Lansdowne MS 1236, fo. 29.

[6] Mary's letter to the Council is printed in Foxe, VI. 385; her letter to Hastings in J. Strype, *Ecclesiastical Memorials* (London, 1721), III. ii. 1.

[7] *Queen Jane and Queen Mary*, 4–5; 'Vita', 254–5.

[8] *APC* IV. 429–32 (This is a list of gentlemen swearing fealty.)

[9] *Queen Jane and Queen Mary*, 8.

commit themselves in what was rapidly becoming a confused situation: in some towns, such as Ipswich and Coventry, both candidates were proclaimed by rival groups.[10] Northumberland's plan had presumably always assumed that it would be easy to secure Mary's person: her departure from Hunsdon had been a shock. Robert Dudley, sent after Mary, failed to seize her and on 14 July Northumberland himself left London with an army in pursuit.[11] At Ware, the duke met his sons and about 500 men-at-arms: Jane was proclaimed and Mary declared a bastard.[12] A total force of about 3,000 men moved to Cambridge, sacking Huddleston's house on the way.[13] At Cambridge the duke summoned the vice-chancellor of the university, Edwin Sandys, and ordered him to preach a sermon justifying Jane's accession, which Sandys did the following day.[14] But events were overtaking Northumberland. In Buckinghamshire, Sir Edward Hastings had proclaimed Mary as queen, and Sir John Williams did the same in Oxfordshire:[15] by 16 July the situation in these counties was considered by the council to be so grave that troops were dispatched.[16] In East Anglia there appears to have been little enthusiasm for the duke's cause. He set out for Framlingham on 18 July, but grew discouraged.[17] There was a retreat to Bury St Edmunds, where Jane was again publicly declared queen.[18] Northumberland himself returned to Cambridge, where he learnt on 19 July that the councillors in London had proclaimed Mary.[19]

---

[10] Jane was proclaimed at King's Lynn (*Queen Jane and Queen Mary*, 111). The city authorities were divided at Coventry (*Victoria County History of Warwickshire*, II. 442). For Ipswich, see 'Vita', 255–6.

[11] *HMC Bedingfield*, III. 237.

[12] *CPR* 1554–5, 42: pardon of Sir Andrew Dudley.

[13] 'The Narrative of Richard Troughton', ed. F. Madden, *Archaeologia*, XXIII (1831), 41.

[14] Foxe, VIII. 590.

[15] *Queen Jane and Queen Mary*, 8–9. Subsequent grants of charters to Aylesbury, Banbury, Buckingham, Higham Ferrers, and Wycombe which cite in justification the loyal behaviour of these towns during the crisis (*CPR* 1553–4, 44–5; 246–8; 100–2: 1554–5, 200–3: 1557–8, 371–4) suggest that it was in them that Hastings and Williams found support.

[16] *Queen Jane and Queen Mary*, 108.

[17] *CPR* 1553–4: pardon to Francis Jobson; 'The narrative of Richard Troughton', 32.

[18] *CPR* 1554–5, 42: pardon of Sir Andrew Dudley.

[19] 'Vita', 266.

Two factors explain Mary's triumph. One is the behaviour of the privy council after Northumberland's departure from London. The other is the support that Mary received both in East Anglia and, a fact less often noticed, in the Thames Valley, for it was the assistance that Mary found amongst provincial nobles and gentry that persuaded the councillors to abandon Northumberland. After Mary's triumph most councillors claimed that they had always had their doubts about the legality and justice of Northumberland's proceedings, but they had all nevertheless signed the letters patent bestowing the crown on Jane Grey and all of them except the earl of Arundel had signed an additional engagement promising to keep faith: they clearly believed at the time of Edward's death that Northumberland would be successful. The arrival on 11 July of Mary's letter claiming the throne shook their confidence,[20] which was further undermined the next day by the erroneous rumour that Robert Dudley had been defeated in battle by Mary.[21] The news that the crews of several ships at Yarmouth had been persuaded by Henry Jerningham to defect to Mary also worried the council; the Tower chronicler reports that at this information 'eche man then began to pluck in his hornes'.[22] On 14 July certain of the council asked for an interview with the Imperial envoys at which they adopted a far more conciliatory line than they had before.[23] The council's letters to the counties suggest a growing despair at the size of the revolt.[24] The first councillor to crack entirely may have been Paulet, who was escorted into the Tower on 16 July.[25] On 19 July Shrewsbury, Bedford, Pembroke, Arundel, Cheyne, Cheke, Paulet, Paget, Sir John Mason, and other councillors proclaimed Mary.[26] The Imperial ambassadors subsequently reported that the councillors had been moved by 'the popular rising, the

[20] *CSP Sp.* XI. 82: the envoys reported that when the letters arrived the council was at table and 'were greatly astonished and troubled'. The council seems to have thought at first that Mary's intention was to flee the realm: see the letter sent on 8 July to the authorities in Surrey (J. More-Molyneux, 'Letters illustrating the Reign of Queen Jane, *Archeological Journal*, XXX (1873), 276).

[21] Ibid. 86.

[22] *Queen Jane and Queen Mary*, 8–9: *APC* IV. 295.

[23] *CSP Sp.* XI. 88.

[24] *Queen Jane and Queen Mary*, 107–9; *APC* IV. 295.

[25] *Queen Jane and Queen Mary*, 9.

[26] Ibid. 11–12; Machyn, 37.

increase of the Lady Mary's forces and the fact . . . that seven of the best warships had surrendered to her'.[27] The plot to seize the Tower for Mary also seems to have played a part in the change of heart.[28] Thus it was the information that reached the council about Mary's support in the provinces that persuaded councillors to desert Northumberland rather than any belated scruples about his scheme.

The behaviour of Henry Fitzalan, earl of Arundel, is illuminating here.[29] Arundel had protested against the provisions of the letters patent, having, as he said, no desire to see perpetuated the power of a man who had earlier imprisoned and fined him, but in the end he signed. When Northumberland left London in his attempt to capture Mary the earl was said to have expressed his regret at not being able to go with him, 'in whose presence he coulde fynde in his harte to spende his bloode, even at his foote'.[30] Ten days later, however, it was Arundel who came to Cambridge to arrest the duke, replying to Northumberland's valid complaint that whatever he had done had been with the consent of the council only with the cold observation that 'my lorde . . . ye shoulde have sought for mercy sooner; I must do according to my commandement'.[31] Thus Arundel had been willing to be conciliated as long as Mary appeared powerless, but when he realized that her cause was not a lost one he turned with relief to a monarch more likely to be sympathetic to his desires.

The important question is therefore why Mary received support in the counties. To this the traditional answer has been that the gentlemen of the counties were profoundly disturbed by any tampering with the established line of the succession and that they in any case much disliked Northumberland's government. Certainly, some of those who supported Mary may have done so because they were out of favour with Northumberland. This is probably true of Sir Edmund Peckham, whose appearance on the council in Edward's reign had been

[27] *CSP Sp.* XI. 96.
[28] *Queen Jane and Queen Mary*, 8, 119.
[29] 'The Life of Henry Fitz Allan, last Earle of Arundell' ed. J. G. Nichols, *Gentleman's Magazine*, CIV (1833), 118–21.
[30] *Queen Jane and Queen Mary*, 7.
[31] Ibid. 10.

humiliatingly brief,[32] and of Sir John Williams, whose career in Augmentations had ended with accusations of peculation and debt.[33] But others amongst Mary's supporters had prospered under Northumberland. Sir Leonard Chamberlain, for instance, had held high office at the Tower, yet with Peckham he proclaimed Mary and he was involved in the plan to march on London and seize the armaments and munitions in the palace of Westminster.[34] Sir William Drury had been held in sufficient esteem for Northumberland to recommend him as knight of the shire for Suffolk in the parliament of March 1553.[35] Thomas Boys had been appointed captain of Deal Castle in 1550.[36] Mary's supporters were not, then, merely the 'outs' of the previous regime, and they were not men who had nothing to lose by a rash attempt to stop Northumberland. Indeed, all those involved must have shuddered at the risk they were running of total political and social upheaval: the great success of Northumberland's government had been, after all, to re-establish order, Clearly, too, some men did resent the interference with what had been decided by statute and by Henry VIII's will, a document for which contemporaries had considerable reverence. There is, for example, the story of Sir John Harington of Exton, Rutland, who went into his parlour after dinner one day during the crisis and got out a statute book, which he laid open on the table 'that every man myghte rede hit; And had noted the substaunce of the statute for the declaracion of the Quenes Maiesties ryght to the Crowne of Englond, after the deathe of Kynge Edward'.[37] Arundel, when persuading his colleagues to change sides, is reported to have declared, 'you knowe that by right of succession this Crowne discends upon Mary'.[38] None the less, Harington did not give Mary any active support, and Arundel changed sides not

---

[32] *DNB*; D. E. Hoak, *The King's Council in the Reign of Edward VI* (Cambridge, 1976).

[33] W. C. Richardson, *History of the Court of Augmentations 1534–1554* (Baton Rouge, 1961).

[34] *DNB*; *APC*, IV. 293. For the catholic tone of Chamberlain's will, made in 1560, see *The House of Commons, 1509–1558*, citing PCC 28 Loftes.

[35] BL Lansdowne MS 3, fo. 36.

[36] *CPR* 1551–2, 36.

[37] 'The narrative of Richard Troughton', 31.

[38] 'Life', 118.

because of Mary's legitimacy but because of the behaviour of the gentlemen in the counties.

It was not, in fact, primarily in terms of legitimacy and legality that contemporaries saw the struggle. The politicians and preachers who presented Jane's cause to the people did so in religious terms. Even before Edward's death the London preachers were reported to have been harping on such matters 'with a view to make the people ill-disposed towards the Princess',[39] whilst the explanation given by the dying king for his plan to supplant his sister was that if she were 'to possess the kingdom (which Almighty God prevent), it would be all over for the religion whose fair foundation we have laid'.[40] Jane's proclamation argued that Mary would have tried, had she been queen, to bring 'this noble, free realm into the tyranny and servitude of the bishop of Rome'.[41] Ridley, in a sermon at Paul's Cross, declared not only that Mary and Elizabeth were bastards but also that Mary wished to subvert 'the true religion'.[42] Northumberland's last words to his colleagues when he left London were a reminder that they were fighting for 'Goddes cause . . . the preferment of his worde and the feare of papestry's re-entrance'.[43] Letters sent by the council into the counties declared that Mary was stirring up rebellion 'to the greate parell and daunger of the utter subversyon of Godes holye worde and of the hole state of this realme' and that Mary's accession would have been followed by 'the bondage of this Realme to the old servitude of the Antichriste of Rome, the subversion of the true preaching of Goddes worde, and of thauncient lawes, vsages, and liberties of this realme'.[44] They went on to argue that Mary 'through the counsell of a nombre of obstinate papistes . . . forsaketh as by her seditious proclamations may appere the just title of supremacie annexed to thimperial Crowne of this Realme'.[45]

It is not surprising, therefore, to find it was the catholic gentry of East Anglia and the Thames Valley who actively

[39] *CSP Sp.* XI. 65.
[40] 'Vita', 247.
[41] The Queen's College, Oxford: Sel[ect Cases] b 228 (1).
[42] Foxe, VI. 389.
[43] *Queen Jane and Queen Mary*, 6–7.
[44] *HMC Finch*, LXXI, vol. I, 2; *Seventh Report* (More-Molyneux), 609.
[45] Guildford Museum and Muniment Room, Loseley correspondence 3/3.

supported Mary: protestants, whatever their doubts about
Northumberland's behaviour or their convictions about the
validity of her title, did not spontaneously join her. In Norfolk,
for example, where fourteen established magnate families have
been identified at the accession of Elizabeth[46] it was the two
most firmly catholic families who sent representatives to aid her
in the shape of Sir Henry Bedingfield of Oxborough, afterwards
Elizabeth's gaoler at Woodstock, and Sir Richard Southwell of
Wood Rising, whose vehement outburst against heretics later
in the reign—'to the rack with them, one of these knaves is able
to undo a whole city'[47]—is an indication of where his religious
sympathies lay, despite a career as surveyor of the court of augmentations. Bedingfields and Southwells were to provide support for the old religion for many decades to come. But families
such as the Heydons of Baconsthorpe and the Lestranges of
Hunstanton, families with protestant sympathies, did not help
Mary.[48] In Norfolk, therefore, there is nothing to suggest that
those who supported Mary were moved by anything other than
religious considerations. The same is true of the Suffolk gentlemen who arrived at Kenninghall and Framlingham: Foxe later
described Clement Heigham and John Sulyard as amongst the
most violent persecutors of protestantism in the county,[49] Sir
Thomas Cornwallis of Broome was to retire entirely from public life at Elizabeth's accession, whilst Richard Freston had
been in trouble for his religious views since 1538.[50]

The list of those swearing loyalty to Mary during these early
days, like the list of those receiving rewards for service at Kenninghall and Framlingham, contains catholic name after catholic name: William Dormer of Wing, whose daughter became
the countess of Feria and was himself described in 1564 as 'a

---

[46] A. Hassell Smith, *County and Court: Government and Politics in Norfolk, 1558–1603*
(Oxford, 1974), 52.

[47] Foxe, VI. 596; VII. 151; VIII. 585.

[48] It is possible to be fairly confident about who helped Mary at this time, since she
was assiduous in rewarding her supporters: there is a list in BL Lansdowne MS 156, fos.
90–94', of annuities given by Mary for service at Framlingham, which may be checked
against the patent rolls.

[49] Foxe, VIII. 493, 497, 630.

[50] A. Simpson, *The Wealth of the Gentry* (Cambridge, 1961): *Letters and Papers*, XIII. i.
964. Freston was Mary's cofferer.

hinderer of religion',[51] Francis Allen, Gardiner's secretary,[52] Anthony Browne, later Viscount Montagu and so on.[53] Indeed, when in 1561 Dr Sanders composed a list of catholic gentlemen who were suffering as a result of the accession of a protestant monarch it bore an uncanny resemblance to the earlier list of those rewarded in 1553: Browne, Waldegrave, Hastings, Sir Thomas Wharton, and Sir Thomas Mordaunt.[54] No nobleman sympathetic to protestantism supported Mary, and most of those who came to her aid were committed catholics. Thus the earl of Derby, for example, had opposed the religious changes of Edward's reign,[55] Lord Dacre, who marched south to join Mary, had voted in the House of Lords against the 1549 Prayer Book and was to remain a catholic in Elizabeth's reign,[56] and Lord Windsor, who assisted Hastings in proclaiming Mary in Buckinghamshire,[57] had persistently voted against the religious innovations of the previous reign. Thomas West, Lord Delaware, had opposed the Edwardian Prayer Books as he had earlier opposed the dissolution of the monasteries.[58] The earl of Bath, although he played little part in public affairs in Edward's reign, had voted against the bill for the marriage of priests.[59]

Mary's support was, therefore, drawn almost exclusively from the catholic and the conservative. Given this, it is difficult to argue that those who assisted her did so for any other reason than because they wanted a catholic ruler. If the appeal of her cause lay primarily in her legitimacy, or even in her opposition to Northumberland, the religious views of those who helped her should have been very much more varied. Her opponents had made sure that everyone realized where Mary's own sympathies lay. Their propaganda had been effective, for the news of

[51] His reward for service is in *CPR* 1554–5, 181, 211. The description comes from the bishops' letters of 1564, *Camden Miscellany*, IX. 32.

[52] His grant is in *CPR* 1554–5, 189. See also below, Ch. 3 n. 64.

[53] Grant in ibid. 314. See also below, p. 22.

[54] Catholic Record Society, *Miscellanea* I (1905) 44–5.

[55] *LJ* 5 Jan. 1549, 25 Jan. 1550, 6 Apr. 1552. The news that he was marching south to assist Mary is in *HMC Bedingfield* III. 297.

[56] *LJ* 15 Jan. 1549. He was described as a catholic in 1564: *Camden Miscellany* IX. 50. For his assistance to Mary, see *CSP Sp.* IX. 107 and the fealty oath in *APC* IV. 301.

[57] *Queen Jane and Queen Mary*, 8; 'Vita', 260.

[58] *DNB*: his reward for service is in *CPR* 1553–4, 82.

[59] *LJ* 10 Feb. 1552.

Mary's triumph was often greeted by the restoration of elements of the old faith: Richard Troughton recorded that at Grantham the proclamation of Mary on 21 July was accompanied by the singing of a Te Deum,[60] as it had been in London. Robert Parkyn in Chester-le-Street noted that when the news of Mary's accession reached Yorkshire 'priests were commanded by lords and knights catholic to say mass in Latin with consecration and elevation of the body and blood of Christ under form of bread and wine.[61] Politically aware men knew what the consequences of Mary's accession would be: the error that Northumberland's propagandists had made was to believe that, knowing those consequences, the governing classes would oppose her.

Thus Mary was not making the fatal error of which historians usually accuse her when she assumed that her triumph had proved that catholicism was still a political force. She may have mistakenly taken the behaviour of certain men in some areas as more typical of the whole country than it actually was, but her conviction that many noblemen and gentlemen would support the restoration of the old religion was not mistaken. She may have overlooked the possibility that men might still be sympathetic to protestantism, even though they did not actively support Northumberland in his hour of need, but their lack of action in a crisis which both sides had seen as a religious struggle was surely encouraging.

Mary's own faith in her ability to return England to the Roman obedience was undoubtedly strengthened by the manner of her triumph in July 1553. However, that was not the only consequence for the reign of the way in which she had come to the throne. Her triumph was, as we have seen, a triumph of the provinces against the capital, a triumph of 'backwoods' gentry and nobility against the professional politicians at Westminster. The spontaneous and courageous loyalty of Mary's household servants and of the gentlemen of Cambridgeshire, Norfolk, Suffolk, and the Thames Valley contrasted sharply with the fickle behaviour of the councillors who had

---

[60] 'The narrative of Richard Troughton', 44.
[61] 'Parkyn's Narrative of the Reformation', ed. A. G. Dickens, *EHR* LXII (1947).

sworn loyalty to Northumberland and then almost fallen over each other in their attempts to be the first publicly to espouse Mary's cause. This contrast Mary took to heart, and despite her willingness—indeed, her need—to forgive those who had acted against her, the only advisers she fully trusted thereafter came from outside the circle of professional politicians. (Stephen Gardiner, a politician to his fingertips despite his cloth, might have been an exception to this rule had he not backed the wrong man in the controversy over the queen's marriage.) Those who enjoyed Mary's confidence were the men who had been in her household during Edward's reign and had already suffered for their loyalty to her and to the old faith, like Henry Jerningham and Francis Englefield. Later, James Basset was to be a close adviser: it was Basset whom Paget asked to intervene with the queen on his behalf when he was in disgrace during 1556.[62] In spiritual matters Mary was to lean on Reginald Pole, who seems to have taken the strictures of catholic reformers against bishops accepting secular positions so seriously that he was not even a member of the council, and in matters with international implications, including, of course, the question of her marriage, Mary was often advised by the Imperial envoy, Simon Renard. Unlike Pole, Renard was a worldly and realistic man, but his unfamiliarity with England and its institutions, as well as his hysterical character, made his advice occasionally dangerous.[63] Mary also relied in some things upon her husband's greater political expertise. Perhaps it was largely temperament that prevented Mary from enjoying a close relationship with a minister such as Elizabeth was to have with William Cecil, but there can be little doubt that the attempted coup had strengthened Mary's antipathy for the Edwardian establishment.

None the less, Mary could not do without Edwardian councillors and civil servants. Paget was later to analyse her problems very acutely when he declared that she had been forced at her accession

to recognise the service of men of position who had followed her adverse fortunes and had helped her to come to the throne. There were a

[62] Plas Newydd, Anglesey, Paget Papers, Box II, no. 26.
[63] On Renard's character, see E. H. Harbison, *Rival Ambassadors at the Court of Queen Mary* (Princeton, 1940), 25–31.

good many of them; and as to begin with, though unable altogether to trust the former holders of office, who had been her opponents, she had had to make use of them, admit them to the Council and show them honour, the result was that England, which had always been a monarchy, was now governed by such a crowd that it was much more like a republic.[64]

Mary's council certainly contained a curious mixture of Edwardian administrators such as Petre and Paget, men whose fall and discomfiture they had sanctioned like Gardiner and the duke of Norfolk, and complete outsiders such as the minor East Anglian gentleman Sir John Huddleston.[57] Although they attended meetings only rarely, the placing on the council of Huddleston, Sir John Shelton, and Robert Strelley is significant, for they were representative of the men who had secured the crown for Mary.[66] Thus Mary's council was large compared with that of the previous two decades in part, as Paget noted, because of the circumstances of her accession.

Whether the size of the council was to hinder its efficient working is a matter of debate.[67] The use of committees, and the fact that actual attendance was always much lower than the council's nominal composition, alleviated some of the problems. The variety of opinions thus brought to the council table may have resulted occasionally in discord, but at other times it made for the careful exploration of a problem and all its possible solutions: the 'factiousness' sometimes attributed to the Marian council is, after all, only one way of describing wide-ranging discussion.

Certainly the council seems to have handled competently the difficult first months of the reign. The political atmosphere in

[64] *CSP Sp* XIII. 88.

[65] On Mary's council see A. Weikel, 'Crown and Council: A Study of Mary Tudor and her Privy Council' (Yale Ph. D. thesis, 1966), and G. A. Lemasters, 'The Privy Council in the Reign of Queen Mary I' (Cambridge Ph. D. thesis 1971). A list of councillors appears in D. M. Loades, *The Reign of Mary Tudor* (London, 1979), 474–80.

[66] There is no evidence to support Dr Lemasters' argument that admission to the privy council enabled these country gentlemen to play 'a vital role in linking authority in the centre with authority in the localities' (op. cit. 38) except in the rather obvious sense that they would have been somewhat better informed than their neighbours.

[67] A. Weikel, 'The Marian Council Revisited', in J. Loach and R. Tittler, ed. *The Mid-Tudor Polity c.1540–1560*, (London, 1980), 52–73.

the capital was highly volatile: when the queen's chaplain, Gilbert Bourne, preached at Paul's Cross on 13 August there was 'gret up-rore and showtyng at ye sermon' because he had prayed for 'soules departed' and declared that the imprisonment of Bonner, former bishop of London, had been illegal.[68] The council therefore summoned the mayor and aldermen and warned them that unless they could control the city its liberties would be forfeit.[69] When Thomas Watson preached the next Sunday the mayor and aldermen appeared accompanied by two hundred of the guard 'to se no dysquyet done'.[70] Mary further reduced religious tension by a proclamation of 18 August in which she said that although she herself professed that religion 'agreeable to God's word and the primitive church'—by which she meant, of course, catholicism—she 'mindeth not to compel any her subject thereunto until such time as further order by common assent may be taken therein': in the meantime there was to be no public preaching and no unlicensed printing.[71] On that same day Northumberland and his colleagues were arraigned at Westminster Hall. Their trials were quickly over, and Northumberland was executed on 22 August.[72]

By September London was relatively quiet, although inflammatory pamphlets were reputedly scattered in the streets urging 'noblemen and gentlemen favouring the word of God'—by which, this time, protestantism was meant—to beware the 'detestable papists' around the queen, and warning them of the projected Habsburg marriage.[73] The queen remitted the last instalment of the subsidy granted to Edward VI, a decision which was greeted by 'a mervaylouse noyes of rejoysinge',[74] and her request on 1 September for a loan of twenty thousand pounds was, the French envoys sagely reported, a move common when times were unsettled, for those who lent money then

[68] Machyn, 41: Wriothesley, 97.
[69] Ibid. 98.
[70] Machyn, 41.
[71] P. L. Hughes and J. F. Larkin, *Tudor Royal Proclamations* (New Haven and London, 1969) II, no. 390.
[72] Wriothesley, 99–101. *Queen Jane and Queen Mary*, 18–19.
[73] *CSP Sp.* XI. 173. See also Vertot, II. 183.
[74] *Queen Jane and Queen Mary*, 26.

had an interest in promoting calm.[75] The council was therefore able to deal with the coronation, which took place on 1 October, with a review of the government's financial situation, and with plans for the first parliament of the reign.[76]

[75] Wriothesley, 102.
[76] Vertot, II. 136.

2

Parliament: Summons and Preparation

IN 1593 Elizabeth I informed the House of Commons that just
as 'she had authority to summon the Parliament and to continue the same at her good pleasure and to dissolve it when she
thought good, so had she likewise to appoint unto them what
causes they were to treat of'. Parliament in the sixteenth century was, as Elizabeth here emphasized, an instrument of the
crown. The monarch decided when parliament should be
called: the needs of the crown led to the summoning of parliament. Mary held more frequent parliaments than any other
Tudor—five in five years—not because her feelings for the
institution were any warmer than those of her predecessors or
those of her successor, but because her policies were such that
they could be implemented only through parliament. If Mary
could have dispensed with parliament she probably would
have done so—when parliament refused to crown Philip she
searched hard for some other consent-giving assembly[1] but she
recognized that what had been done by parliament could be
undone only by parliament. Much of Mary's policy, and in
particular much of her religious policy, involved the undoing of
the past; parliament necessarily, therefore, played an important part in English affairs during her reign.

Each of the five parliaments of Mary's reign was summoned
to transact some specific piece of crown policy. The first dealt
with Mary's title to the throne, repealed Edward's religious
legislation, and granted her tonnage and poundage for life. The
second, the parliament of April 1554, was called primarily to
ratify the marriage treaty: the use of parliament in this context
is interesting, since it was unusual to present treaties to parliament for consideration, and it may be that Mary was here fulfilling the promise made to the Londoners at the time of Wyatt's
rebellion that she would not marry without the consent of the

[1] See below, 194–7.

realm.[2] Mary's third parliament was summoned in November 1554 to return England to the Roman obedience by the repeal of the Henrican reform statutes. In 1555 a fourth parliament was called, partly in order to grant a subsidy, partly, perhaps, because Mary's advisers had succeeded in convincing her that parliamentary ratification was essential of her restoration to the church of parts of its property was to be secure. The parliament of 1558 was assembled to provide another subsidy, essential after the declaration of war with France in June 1557.

Once the decision to summon parliament had been taken, chancery was instructed to issue the necessary writs. These were of three kinds: writs of election, for the Commons, writs of summons, for the Lords, and writs of assistance. It was by means of the last that the judicial element of the Upper House was summoned.[3] Writs of assistance were sent to the two chief justices,[4] the chief baron of the exchequer,[5] and the master of the rolls.[6] The judges were thus summoned, and so were the attorney-general and the solicitor-general. (Often the solicitor-general was also elected to the Commons—Richard Onslow was, indeed, to serve as speaker in 1566, when he was solicitor, and Coke did the same in 1593—but neither of the Marian solicitors sat in the Lower House during their tenure of office.[7]) It appears to have been considered improper for the attorney-general to sit in the Commons, and the practice was later forbidden; Mary's attorney, Edward Gryffyn, was a hard-

[2] Oxford, Bodley MS Rawlinson B 102, f 84ᵛ.

[3] E. R. Adair and F. M. Evans, 'Writs of Assistance, 1558–1700', *EHR*, XXVI (1921), 356–72.

[4] Chief justice of queen's bench: Sir Thomas Bromley, succeeded in 1555 by Sir Edward Saunders. Bromley was paid £80 in 1554 for his attendance at the two parliaments of that year. (*APC* V. 202.) Chief justice of common pleas: Sir Richard Morgan, succeeded in Oct. 1554 by Robert Broke. The chief justice of common pleas was paid £60 for his attendance at the two parliaments of 1554 (ibid.).

[5] David Broke, succeeded in Mar. 1558 by Clement Heigham. Broke was paid £40 in 1554. It is not clear whether Heigham vacated his seat in the Lower House, where he represented Lancaster, on receipt of his writ of assistance.

[6] Sir Nicholas Hare, succeeded in Nov. 1557 by Sir William Cordell. Cordell, who had been elected knight of the shire for Suffolk, took his seat in the Lower House and was in fact chosen as its speaker.

[7] William Cordell, succeeded in Nov. 1557 by Richard Weston. Cordell received £40 in 1554, and his clerk £10.

working figure in the Lords.[8] The queen's serjeants-at-law were also summoned by writs of assistance.[9] The legal assistants in the Lords had no vote, being present only to advise and to help with the drafting of bills, but their service was invaluable to the House,[10] as is implied by the scale of the fees they received. Oddly, the chancellor does not appear to have received any writ, even if he were a commoner, perhaps because as head of chancery he was responsible for the oversight of all other writs.[11] His role in the Lords was, of course, crucial, for he acted as speaker and presided over all debates. Although, under the 1539 act 'for the placing of the lords in parliament', the secretaries of state were entitled to receive writs of assistance,[12] all Mary's secretaries were also elected to the Lower House, and appear to have chosen to sit there.

Peers received writs of summons.[13] Some discretion seems to have been used in the dispatch of these writs: minors, and those incapacitated by poverty or mental instability were not summoned although peers held in confinement usually were.[14] The queen did not, apparently, regard summonses as a means of exercising political control; the issue of writs had become standardized in the reign of Henry VIII, or even before,[15] and the crown was in general more anxious to persuade peers to attend parliament than it was desirous of keeping them away.[16]

[8] His payment in 1554 was the same as that of the solicitor-general.

[9] On the role played by two serjeants, Sir James Dyer and Sir William Stanford, in the parliaments of these years, see L. Abbott, 'Public Office and Private Profit; The Legal Establishment in the Reign of Mary Tudor', in *The Mid-Tudor Polity c.1540–1560*, ed. J. Loach and R. Tittler (London, 1980), 142. The serjeants were well rewarded, Dyer receiving £26. 13s. 4d., for instance, for his attendance in the two parliaments of 1554, and Sir Edward Saunders £30.

[10] On this, see M. A. R. Graves. *The House of Lords in the Parliaments of Edward VI and Mary I. An Institutional Study* (Cambridge, 1981), Ch. 6.

[11] Ibid. 123.

[12] On this act, ibid. 127–30.

[13] See W. Dugdale, *A Perfect Copy of All the Summons of the Nobility . . .* (London, 1685).

[14] Graves, op. cit. 18, 29.

[15] H. Miller, 'Attendance in the House of Lords during the Reign of Henry VIII', *Historical Journal*, X (1962), 325–51; A. R. Myers, 'Parliament, 1422–1509' in *The English Parliament in the Middle Ages*, ed. R. G. Davies and J. H. Denton (Manchester, 1981), 154–9.

[16] M. A. R. Graves, 'Proctorial Representation in the House of Lords in the Reign of Edward VI: a Reassessment', *Journal of British Studies*, X (1971), 27. See also, however, the rejoinder by Vernon Snow, ibid. 36–46.

We do not know how many peers attended the first of Mary's parliaments since there is no extant Journal. The bishops may have been rather thin on the ground. Many of the Edwardian bishops were in prison by the time parliament met—Barlow of Bath and Wells was sent to the Tower on 15 September,[17] for instance, and Cranmer and Hooper were in custody.[18] Harley of Hereford and Taylor of Lincoln appeared on the first day of the session but were not allowed to take their seats.[19] The sees of Rochester and Bangor were vacant. The aged bishop of Salisbury was given a licence excusing him from attendance,[20] and it seems probable that King of Oxford, another old man— he had taken his first degree in 1507—did not come.[21] Gardiner was certainly present, and Thirlby was recalled from his embassy with the emperor in order to attend.[22] Aldrich of Carlisle, Bonner of London, Chambers of Peterborough, Day of Chichester, Goodrich of Ely, Heath of Worcester, Kitchen of Llandaff, Parfew of St Asaph, Salcot of Salisbury, and Sampson of Coventry and Lichfield were available, as, probably, were Tunstall of Durham and Veysey of Exeter.

In the remainder of Mary's parliaments the number of peers present was rather lower than the average of the previous reign. Of the forty-nine temporal and twenty-one spiritual peers summoned to the parliament of April 1554, twenty-four failed to attend. In November 1554 there were twenty-three absentees, in 1555 fifteen, and in 1558, twenty. Some of the original Marian bishops were very old, and with the appointment of younger men to the bishops' bench attendance amongst the spiritual peers improved, although this was balanced in 1558 by the absence of many secular lords on military business. The lay peers who failed to attend almost always seem to have had some valid excuse for their absence, such as sickness or old age: the earl of Shrewsbury was issued with a licence in 1555

[17] *A Chronicle of the Grey Friars of London*, ed. J. G. Nichols (Camden Society, os, LIII, 1852), 84.
[18] C. Wriothesley, *A Chronicle of England during the Reigns of the Tudors*, ed. W. D. Hamilton (Camden Society, ns, XX, 1877), 103.
[19] See below, 74.
[20] *APC* IV. 336.
[21] He attended no subsequent Marian parliament.
[22] *CSP Sp.* XI. 236.

because he was ill,[23] and other, less important, peers probably did not bother to secure formal permission. There is little evidence for disaffection as a factor in producing absence. Lord Mordaunt, for example, attended no Marian parliament for which there are records, but then he had also absented himself from all the parliaments of Edward's reign:[24] Mordaunt's son, John, was a Marian councillor and a devout catholic. Henry Clifford, earl of Cumberland, was a frequent absentee from parliament in both reigns, and the distance of his territories from London may account for this. Distance may also have been a factor in the frequent absence of Henry Neville, fifth earl of Westmorland, although in April 1554 Renard reported that Westmorland and Lord Abergavenny, whilst excusing their absence on grounds of ill health, were suspected of staying away for political reasons.[25] In the following autumn Westmorland was, indeed, thought to be plotting against Mary.[26] He claimed ill health as an excuse for his absence from the parliament of 1555,[27] and was afterwards suspected of having been 'privy' to Dudley's plotting.[28] However, in April 1557, Westmorland was responsible for recapturing Scarborough Castle for the queen from the rebel, Thomas Stafford;[29] he played a prominent part in the defence of the borders during the war with France and there is every reason to believe that he was a supporter of the catholic regime. Abergavenny's absences are, likewise, more probably to be explained by financial difficulties and a retiring temperament than by political disaffection—it was, after all, Abergavenny who, almost alone of the Kentish nobility, had stood firmly for the queen during Wyatt's revolt.[30] It is, in short, very difficult to prove that peers stayed away from parliament during this period because they were discontented, and the balance of the evidence suggests that

[23] E. Lodge, *Illustrations of British History* (London, 1791), 205, printing College of Arms, Talbot MS C157.

[24] *DNB*, and V. N. Snow, 'Proctorial Representation in the House of Lords during the Reign of Edward VI', *Journal of British Studies*, VIII (1969), 19.

[25] *CSP Sp.* XII. 202.

[26] Ibid. XIII. 134.

[27] *CSP Ven.* VI. i. 217–18.

[28] D. M. Loades, *Two Tudor Conspiracies* (Cambridge, 1965), 195.

[29] Ibid. 85–6.

[30] Ibid. 56–64.

their reasons for non-attendance had to do with their personal circumstances—such as the debts that seem to account for Lord Sandys' absences[31]—rather than their political or religious convictions.

Peers licensed to absent themselves from a parliamentary session could nominate proxies. Most chose privy councillors: Gardiner held five proxies in April 1554, for example, and eight in November 1554, whilst the earl of Arundel had six in both those parliaments. Sometimes peers seem to have been instructed which councillors they should appoint—Shrewsbury was told by Petre in 1555 to name Montagu and the bishop of Ely as his proxies,[32] which he did. It may be, too, that peers sometimes sent in blank proxy papers for the crown or a minister to complete, as John Tuchet, Lord Audley, had done in 1532.[33] Certainly the number of proxies held by councillors was a reflection of their standing with the crown, and it is interesting to note that Paget had no proxies in November 1554, probably as a result of his opposition to crown policies in the previous parliament (in which he had held three proxies). However, peers did not always nominate councillors—Lord Ogle, for instance, appointed Lord Lumley as his proxy in April 1554 and Lord North of Kirtling in November: for both peers it was the sole occasion in the reign when they held a proxy. Bishops always nominated other bishops but the Prior of St John of Jerusalem, Sir Thomas Tresham, chose a layman as his proxy in 1558.

It is difficult to understand the significance of proxies at this period.[34] There is no evidence about how, or indeed whether, proxies voted. What happened, for example, when an absentee peer named more than one proxy, as frequently occurred? In the 1560s Sir Thomas Smith was to declare that peers gave their votes first for themselves 'and then for so manie as he hath proxie', but he does not explain the procedure in the case of multiple proxies,[35] an omission that perhaps suggests that the problem had not yet arisen.[36] Indeed, neither D'Ewes nor

[31] L. Stone, *The Crisis of the Aristocracy* (Oxford, 1965), 485.

[32] Lodge, *Illustrations*, I. 204, printing Talbot MS C139.

[33] *Letters and Papers*, V. 734.

[34] On this see also Graves, *The House of Lords*, 72–5.

[35] T. Smith, *De Republica Anglorum*, ed. M. Dewar (Cambridge, 1982), 83.

[36] Peers gave their votes individually. See below, 60.

Robert Bowyer, clerk of the parliament from 1609 to 1621, seem clear on the point,[37] indicating that even in the early seventeenth century the problem was a rare one. This uncertainty about multiple proxies strengthens the case for arguing that proxy voting was unusual; there is, in fact, no evidence for it happening at all before 1581.[38] The tone of a letter written by Gardiner in 1547 certainly suggests that he was not acquainted with the procedure; discussing the validity of the consent given to a bill if the clerk had mistakenly noted 'that, in passing of this or that acte in the upper howse, I by name sayd, "Content", where in dede I was not there', he gives no consideration to the question of whether or not his proxy might have spoken for him.[39] When Gardiner himself died in the course of the 1555 parliament holding five proxies no attempt was made to provide substitutes, and no difficulty appears to have arisen. The balance of the evidence is against the existence of proxy voting at this period.

But if proxies could not vote, why did they exist at all? After all, the first few days of a parliamentary session were taken up in the Lords with the recording of proxy nominations: members of the council took the matter seriously enough to instruct absentees on their choice of proxies. The answer, and an inadequate one, must be that proxies were significant for the prestige they conferred on the holder, rather than because they conveyed any particular political or managerial advantage.

Indeed, the crown at this time seems to have exploited only rarely the managerial devices available to it. The House of Lords could have been 'packed' by new creations, for instance, and yet Mary at least appears to have regarded elevation to the peerage as a means of rewarding loyal service and not as a means whereby she could control the Upper House.[40] Sir John Williams was summoned to Mary's second parliament as Lord Williams of Thame, for instance, because of his loyalty at the

[37] See his MSS notes on the Lords Journals for 1566; *Catalogue of MSS in the Library of the Honourable Society of the Inner Temple*, ed. J. Conway Davies (Oxford, 1972), citing Petyt MS 537, vol. 6, fo. 111. See also, however, E. R. Foster, *The House of Lords, 1603–1649* (Chapel Hill and London, 1983), 21–2, on later practice.

[38] H. Miller, 'Attendance in the House of Lords during the Reign of Henry VIII', *Historical Journal*, X (1967), 345.

[39] *The Letters of Stephen Gardiner*, ed. J. A. Muller (Cambridge, 1933), 350.

[40] See *LJ*, *The Complete Peerage*, and *DNB*.

time of Northumberland's coup, and he was joined by Sir John
Brydges, created Lord Chandos of Sudeley in recognition of
his service during Wyatt's rebellion, and by William Howard,
who for the same service had been created Lord Howard of
Effingham. The elevation of Sir Edward North as Lord North
of Kirtling was not related to a specific act of loyalty, but North
was a member of Mary's council and a trusted servant. The
other two new creations of the reign—Anthony Browne as Viscount Montagu in September 1554 and Edward Hastings as
Hastings of Loughborough in January 1558—are readily
explained in terms of their fervent catholicism and their conspicuous devotion to the queen. (Mary also restored the third
duke of Norfolk, and the earls of Devon and Northumberland.)
There is nothing here to suggest that more than the normal—
and, indeed, rather sparing—use of royal patronage, and
nothing to indicate that the queen was attempting to create a
lay party in the Lords consisting of men who would back her
policies regardless of other considerations, a plan urged on
Elizabeth in 1559 by Sir Nicholas Throckmorton.[41]

Similarly, religious rather than political considerations were
foremost in Mary's choice of bishops. Her first parliament, with
most of the reformed bishops absent in prison, was very different from the first of her sister's parliaments, in which the
Marian prelates were to play an outstanding role, leading one
protestant to comment that 'they reign as sole monarchs in the
midst of ignorant and weak men, and easily overreach our little
party, either by their numbers or their reputation for learning'.[42] Not until 1 April 1554, just before her second parliament, did Mary's scruples allow the consecration of six new
bishops:[43] John White, warden of Winchester, to Lincoln,
Gilbert Bourne, Bonner's chaplain, to Bath and Wells, Henry
Morgan to St David's, James Brooks, master of Balliol, to
Gloucester, George Cotes to Chester, and Maurice Griffin to
Rochester.[44] They were described at the time as 'good and
catholic prelates, who, being amongst the most important

[41] 'Sir Nicholas Throckmorton's Advice to Queen Elizabeth on her Accession to the
Throne', ed. J. E. Neale, *EHR* LXV (1950), 9.
[42] *The Zurich Letters*, ed. H. Robinson (Parker Society, 1842), 10.
[43] R. W. Dixon, *History of the Church of England* (London, 1891), IV. 141.
[44] These elections were secretly confirmed by Pole (Lambeth Palace MS 922, fo. 3ʳ).

members of this parliament, can by their votes, and by persuading others to side with them, give great assistance' to the
cause of the old religion,[45] and Bourne and Griffin were indeed
to be assiduous in their attendance in the Lords.[46] John Holy-
man was consecrated as bishop of Bristol later in 1554; the
great Hebrew scholar, Ralph Baines, became bishop of
Coventry and Lichfield at the same time.[47] Neither played any
very prominent role in the Upper Chamber. In fact, although
most of Mary's bishops turned up in parliament when a religious matter was under discussion, only Gardiner, Thirlby,
and—to a lesser extent—Heath, were leading figures in the
Lords. It was, then, the Henrician bishops, with their administrative and conciliar experience, rather than the more scholarly
and retiring Marian ones, who eased the passage of government business through the Upper House.

The Commons, of course, were summoned by writs of election. These were addressed to the sheriff, except in the case of
the Cinque Ports, where the warden received the writs, and the
Duchy of Lancaster boroughs, for which the writs were issued
directly by the Duchy office. On receipt of the writ the county
sheriff arranged for the election of the knights of the shire to be
held on the next county day, and sent his precepts to the
enfranchised boroughs within the county, ordering them to
proceed to an election. The writs for the dozen and a half towns
and cities that were counties in themselves were sent directly to
the civic sheriff.

A result of this procedure was that the sheriff, if he so wished,
had ample occasion for tilting the balance in favour of his candidate. He might not warn the freeholders in sufficient time for
them to come for the election of the knights of the shire, he
might read the writ at an unusual hour, or he might grossly
abuse the voting system—in the Hampshire election of 1566,
for example, the sheriff was said to have spent three hours over
his lunch in the hope that the opposing party would grow
weary and leave before he was forced to count them.[48] After
the election at Anglesey in October 1553 Sir Richard Bulkeley

[45] *CSP Ven.* V. 471.
[46] Graves, *The House of Lords*, 68, 251–2.
[47] Dixon, op cit. 142.
[48] PRO Star Chamber 4/7/18.

complained to the exchequer court that he had failed to secure a seat because of the biased behaviour of the sheriff, Rhys Thomas.[49]

Although contested elections were rare at this time, another occurred at the beginning of Mary's reign in Staffordshire.[50] A local magnate, Henry, Lord Stafford, tried to secure his son's return for one of the county seats; he was challenged by a second local gentleman, Edward Littleton, who claimed that when, in response to the sheriff's request, the assembled free-holders had shouted out the names of their preferred candidates, only one name, that of Thomas Giffard, had been clear. Whether the second knight of the shire should be Henry Stafford or himself was, Littleton declared, uncertain, but 'when it was perceived the voices of the shire were against the said master Stafford', Lord Stafford had begun 'to find fault and pick quarrel by means of one Sir George Griffith, knight, and Humphrey Welles, who did as much as they could to have made sedition in that great assembly'. Littleton demanded that there should be a counted vote, and persuaded the sheriff that the credentials of the freeholders should be scrutinized, beginning with those of his rival. Stafford's supporters melted away as the day progressed—possibly because Stafford was not rich enough to provide them with a sufficient incentive to stay—and Littleton's party of 248 was victorious. The case was referred to the chancellor and also to the privy council, but Littleton's election was confirmed. Both men were ardent catholics, and the conflict must be seen as one between local factions, as at Anglesey, and not as one involving national politics. In the case of another contested election, that at Gloucester in 1555, the evidence is less certain.[51] After an unruly election, two local gentlemen, William Massinger and Arthur Porter, were returned, rather than the city's recorder as had usually been

[49] PRO E 159/333, discussed by P. S. Edwards, 'The Parliamentary History of Anglesey in the Mid-Sixteenth Century', *Welsh History Review*, X (1980), 65–6. I am grateful to C. S. L. Davies for this reference. See also *The Commentaries or Reports of Edmund Plowden* (London, 1816), I. 118–26.

[50] A. E. Andrew, 'Henry, Lord Stafford (1501–63) in Local and Central Government', *EHR* LXXVIII (1963), 227–9.

[51] *The House of Commons, 1509–1558*: constituency reports.

the case. Since Massinger and Porter were later to criticize some aspect of government policy in the course of the parliament[52] and since the recorder was Sir John Pollard, speaker of the House in October 1553 and again in 1555, the possibility exists that the contest was between those opposed to the Marian regime and those who supported it. But the electors may have believed that Pollard was safely returned elsewhere—he had sat for Oxfordshire in the three previous parliaments—or they may have merely been carrying on some internal feud since Massinger's younger brother was at this time locked in conflict with the mayor. Usually, however, the powerful men in a constituency seem to have been able to agree amicably on who should be returned. In Elizabeth's reign 97 per cent of county elections were not contested, or at least did not come to a poll.[53]

In boroughs the franchise varied widely from Gatton's solitary voter, the lord of the manor,[54] to Gloucester with a free citizen vote of between four and five hundred, but even where the franchise appeared fairly wide real power usually lay with the mayor and council. In Chichester, for example, one member was named by the guild merchant (that is, the mayor, aldermen, and free citizens) and the other by the commoners, but the guild in fact nominated the commoners' candidate.[55] Where power really lay in Exeter as late as 1589 was very clearly revealed when the council met and 'thoughte and considered what persons shall be moste fitt to be proposed to the Freholders at the nexte Countie daye [and] by them to be chosen'.[56] Many of those returned were lawyers or gentlemen, some of them only remotely associated with the borough. This 'gentry invasion of the boroughs' was undoubtedly aided by the heavy cost of parliamentary representation: one of the members for Exeter was paid £10 in wages in 1558, for example, and was reimbursed £47 for expenses and £2. 13s. 4d. for the loss of his horse.[57] Exeter was rich enough to bear such bur-

---

[52] See below, Appendix D and 152–8.
[53] *The House of Commons, 1558–1603.*
[54] See, for example, PRO C 219/23/123, C 219/24/155.
[55] *The House of Commons, 1509–1558*: constituency reports.
[56] Exeter RO, Act Book, V, fo. 96.
[57] Exeter RO, Act Book, II, fo. 145.

dens, but it none the less did not keep the resolution passed in
October 1554 that 'from hensforthe ther shallbe no burges for
the parlement chossed for thys cytte unles he be a Cyttessen
Innbytent and allso a Fremane of the same', for by the following September it had weakened enough to swear in Sir John
Pollard as a freeman 'in consideracon that he is appoyntid to be
one of the burghes of the parliament'.[58] One or two boroughs,
despite the heavy cost, continued to preserve their indepen-
cence. Cambridge, for example, paid out a great deal of money
in 1555: five shillings for the carrying of a letter to London for
the burgesses, £4 in wages, twice, forty-five shillings for a
present that the burgesses had been instructed to give,[59] as
well, presumably, as the customary charges for the enrolling of
the writ and the recording of the names. Despite this, the corporation resisted the attempt of their high steward, the duke of
Norfolk, to put in 'his servant', Sir Nicholas Lestrange, at the
next election, telling the duke that only residents of the town
were eligible for election.[60] Hard-pressed boroughs may also
occasionally have been assisted by their own residents: in 1555,
for instance, John Bell, a mayor of Reading, who was owed two
shillings a day for the fifty days he had spent at Westminster,
agreed to 'take but only xxs.'[61] None the less, frequent and
costly parliamentary sessions like those of the 1550s undoubtedly increased the attractions of outside candidates offering to serve without charge.

Such candidates might offer themselves, or be offered by a
patron. The earl of Rutland, for example, nominated one of the
members for Lincoln throughout this period. In January 1558
the corporation agreed not only to the nomination, but also decided to give the earl a tun of claret 'for his goodness hereto-
fore'. In October 1553, both parliaments of 1554, and in 1555,
Rutland's secretary, Robert Farrer, was returned, and in 1558
his mace-bearer, Francis Kempe.[62] Occasionally, however, such
offers met with a rebuff: Grantham informed William Cecil
apologetically before the elections to Edward's second parlia-

[58] Ibid. fos. 135ᵛ, 143.
[59] C. H. Cooper, *Annals of Cambridge* (Cambridge, 1853), 99.
[60] Ibid. 140.
[61] J. M. Guilding, *Reading Records* (London, 1892), I. 249–50.
[62] *HMC Lincoln Corporation*, XIV. viii. 47–9. See also below, p. 209.

ment, for instance, that he could have only one of the two
nominations he sought, since the other had been promised to
Rutland.[63]

The greatest patron of all, of course, was the monarch.
Manors in the hands of the queen, Duchy of Cornwall
boroughs, stannery towns: all could be used to provide seats for
government officials and crown servants. How systematically
such patronage was used is difficult to say, for there are men
such as Francis Allen, Gardiner's secretary and clerk to the
privy council, whom one might have expected to find in every
parliament but sat in fact once only. On the other hand, it is
certain that much use was made of the Duchy of Lancaster
boroughs; the system by which writs were issued directly by the
Duchy office and sent to the sheriffs by Duchy officials allowed
considerable influence to be brought to bear. Thus, for instance, in September 1555 Sir William Petre wrote to the earl
of Shrewsbury who, as president of the Council of the North,
exercised some general supervision in such matters, 'for the
matter yow wrote me to haue one of the counsayle ther in Mr.
Chaloners [Sir Thomas Chaloner's] place, my lords haue not
yet resolued, nor moued the Queenes Ma*jestie*';[64] quite what
was at issue here is not clear, but although the return for
Knaresborough records the election of Chaloner,[65] a letter sent
to Shrewsbury on 22 October notes the choice of George
Eden.[66] This same letter reports that John Holmes and Thomas
Poley, the Members for Ripon, were 'appointed by Mr Con-
troller', that is, by Sir Robert Rochester, chancellor of the
Duchy and comptroller of the household. However, crown
officials such as Shrewsbury and Rochester were not the only
patrons to take an interest in these seats, for in October 1554
Henry Clifford, earl of Cumberland, informed John Holmes
that he had 'devised a place' for him 'either amongst the burgesses of Boroughbridge or Knaresborough';[67] in the event,
Holmes sat for Boroughbridge, and a year later for another

---

[63] BL Lansdowne MS 3, no. 38.

[64] Lodge, *Illustrations* I. 204, printing College of Arms, Talbot MS *C*139.

[65] PRO C 219/24/59°.

[66] Talbot MS P268. Another letter to Shrewsbury, dated 13 Oct. 1555, reported
that 'Mr. W.' was angry with the earl because he had not been returned as knight of the
shire (Talbot MS C155). I am very grateful to George Bernard for these references.

[67] *HMC Third Report*, 37.

Duchy seat, Ripon. The earl advised him to 'shew yourself as (well) catholique as conformable to the kings and queen's majestys' pleasure and their godly reformation', advice that was perhaps particularly valuable to Holmes, who had been one of Northumberland's secretaries. (He had also been, between 1550 and the end of Edward's reign, a feodary of the Duchy.)

Moreover, the crown was not only a much greater patron than any other individual or institution, it also possessed a number of tactical advantages. For a start, the monarch, obviously, knew when parliament was going to be summoned, and could plan accordingly. The period between the decision to summon parliament being taken and the formal opening might be very brief—in the autumn of 1554, for instance, the writs were not sent out until 3 October for a meeting of 12 November.[68] This was perhaps even more rushed than usual,[69] but in 1555 a part of the council decided on 30 August to summon parliament,[70] the writs were sent out on 3 September and parliament opened on 24 October.[71] In remote areas the time between the arrival of the writ and the date by which the elections had to take place could be very brief; indeed, at Lincoln the writ for the first parliament of Elizabeth's reign arrived so late that there was not another county day before the opening of parliament.[72] It may be that the shortness of the period between the arrival of the writ and the election served to reduce the amount of controversy over the choice of candidates: it certainly ensured that, if influence were to be brought to bear, those who knew first of the impending meeting, that is the crown and its close associates, were in an advantageous position.

The most general way in which the crown could attempt to influence elections was by letters sent out with the writs. Such 'circular letters' were employed by Edward's government in 1553 to urge the return of men 'of gravity and knowledge in their own countries and towns ... men of knowledge and ex-

---

[68] PRO C 219/23.
[69] Forty days was the commonly accepted minimum period.
[70] SP 11/6/16.
[71] PRO C 219/24.
[72] *APC* VII. 39.

perience',[73] but none appears to have been used before the first parliament of Mary's reign, although a letter of thanks to the gentlemen of Cornwall suggests that some individual directive had been sent to them.[74] There is no evidence that any instructions were given before the elections to the parliament of April 1554. However, in August of that year the Imperial ambassador reported that letters had been drawn up on the model of those used under Henry VII in the hope of securing the election of good and catholic members,[75] and Francis Yaxley told Cecil that 'for the better elecion of the Knight*es* and burgesses her mai*es*tie hath addressed forth her *lett*res to the Sheriefes of the Sheres'.[76] The import of these letters was passed on with the writ by the sheriff; the sheriff of Lincolnshire, for instance, when sending the writ to Grimsby, informed the corporation of the queen's desire that it should choose an inhabitant, one 'of the wysest, grave and catholycke sort, syche as in deyd meyne the trew honor of god *with* the prosperyte of the comen welthe'[77] whilst his letter to Stamford, unfortunately very damaged, urges the electors to choose 'Inhabitaunt*es* and of the wy ... Catholycke sort'.[78] The form of the royal instructions may have varied, since the city of York received 'a speciall lettre from the Queenes majesty and hir honorable consell in theis North partes' with its writ[79] (which was, of course, sent to the city directly and not through a sheriff) whilst the city of Hereford was informed by Bishop Heath—who was a councillor— that the queen desired the return of men 'of good Catholique religion': Heath urged Hereford to elect the men who had sat in the previous parliament but his recommendation was ignored.[80] No letters appear to have been sent in 1555, although Philip before his departure abroad had suggested that 'only Catholics and persons not subject to suspicion' should be

[73] BL Royal MS 18 C. 24, fo. 290ᵛ.

[74] *APC* 1552–4, 344.

[75] *CSP Sp.* XIII. 67. There does not appear to be any record of such letters being sent by Henry VII.

[76] BL Lansdowne MS 3, no. 44.

[77] *HMC Grimsby Corporation* XIV. viii. 255: 19 Oct. 1554.

[78] PRO C 219/23, fo. 77ᵛ.

[79] *York Civic Records*, ed. A. Raine (Yorkshire Archaeological Society, CX, 1946), V. 109: 16 Oct, 1554.

[80] *HMC Hereford Corporation*, XIII. iv. 319–20: 13 Oct. 1554.

elected.[81] Perhaps individual councillors repeated the king's words, however, for Heath again asked Hereford for the return of such 'as be grave men and of good and honest haviour and conversacion, and specially of Catholique religion'.[82] The unruliness of this fourth parliament may have led the crown away from its policy of non-intervention, for at the end of 1557 a letter very similar to those used in the elections to Edward VI's second parliament was sent out, asking for the return of men 'of gravitie and knowledge in theyr owne Countires and towns fitt for theyr vnderstanding and qualities to be in soche a greate counsell'.[83] Another letter directed that those elected should be men 'geven to good ordre, Catholick and discrete'.[84]

On two occasions at least, therefore, Mary issued a general directive that those elected should be local men faithful to the old religion. Although the letter sent in 1557 added, as its Edwardian predecessor had done, that if the privy council or individual councillors made a specific recommendation that recommendation should be followed, the Marian council does not appear to have intervened in county elections to the extent that Northumberland's colleagues had done: in early 1553 names had been put forward for election as knights of the shire in Northamptonshire, Bedfordshire, Surrey, Cambridgeshire, Berkshire, and Oxfordshire.[85] (These recommendations had not always been accepted, which may explain the absence of such advice in Mary's reign.) Overall, it is difficult to believe that circular letters had any great impact on the pattern of elections. The letter sent in 1554 certainly produced some response, for the sheriff of Northumberland in his return stated that Sir Thomas Grey and Cuthbert Horsley were 'graue and Catholike personnes',[86] and the return for Lancaster noted that the election there had been made 'punderinge and consederinge not only the contentes of the sayd wrytt but also the Quenes most gracious lettres vnto the sayd Sheref in that behalf

[81] *CSP SP.* XIII. 239.
[82] *HMC Hereford Corporation*, XIII. iv. 320: 18 Sept. 1555.
[83] SP 11/12/2.
[84] Bodley, Tanner MS 90, fo. 211.
[85] BL Royal MS 18 C. 24, fo. 290ᵛ.
[86] PRO C 219/23, fo. 95.

addressed and vnto vs by hym shewed and declared'.[87] The return for Stamford, although very damaged, also notes that the
sheriff's demand for residents of the wise and 'catholycke sort'
had been observed.[88] However, in neither of these elections did
compliance with the crown's directive involve any real shift of
allegiance on the part of the voters, for Lancaster, as a Duchy
borough, was always vulnerable to crown influence, whilst
Grey and Horsley had been returned for Northumberland in
the parliament of October 1553 without any royal prompting.
It seems improbable that the pattern of election was substantially altered by the circular letters.

The monarch had yet another advantage over all other
patrons. This was the power of enfranchising new boroughs:
Boroughbridge, Aylesbury, Banbury, Droitwich, Abingdon,
Higham Ferrers, Castle Rising, Aldborough, and St Ives all
sent representatives in Mary's reign for the first time in the sixteenth century. Was the crown attempting to 'pack' the Commons with these creations? In some cases, a local magnate may
have been responsible; Castle Rising, for instance, was almost
certainly enfranchised at the request of the young duke of
Norfolk, whose client, Sir Nicholas Lestrange, found a seat
there. It is possible that Paulet was responsible, as lord of the
manor, for the enfranchisement of St Ives.[89] Aylesbury secured
representation through a charter which the corporation had
sought as a means of strengthening itself against the lord of the
manor, Sir Thomas Packington.[90] In these instances, and perhaps in the case of the three single-member constituencies—
Abingdon, Banbury, and Higham Ferrers—it is improbable
that we are dealing with royal 'packing'. However, the increase
during the reign in Duchy of Lancaster patronage is surely significant, given the careful way in which, as we have seen, this
patronage was manipulated. The new boroughs provided seats
for 'useful' men: Ripon, for example, which was never represented during this period by a true townsman, returned courtiers like Thomas Poley, lawyers such as William Rastell and
Thomas Seckford, and, in 1558, the brother and the servant of

[87] Ibid. fo. 69.
[88] Ibid. fo. 77ᵛ.
[89] See the constituency report in *The House of Commons, 1509–1558*.
[90] R. Tittler, 'The Incorporation of Boroughs, 1540–1558', *History*, LXII (1977), 29.

the archbishop of York.[91] Similarly, Knaresborough was represented throughout the reign by lawyers and civil servants. Given the considerable use made by the government of these new seats, it seems improbable that government need was not a major factor in their creation.[92]

What is striking about such efforts by the crown is that they appear to have been aimed primarily at creating or securing seats for those who wanted them, or who were thought to be particularly valuable to the government: there is nothing to suggest that Mary's government ever sought actively to prevent the return of specific individuals. Of course, the monarch may have made her wishes known in ways too subtle to have left any trace in the records, but it is surely of importance that some identifiable and articulate opponents of Mary's religious policy, such as Ralph Skinner, found seats, and that men who had been hostile to the government's proposals in one parliament do not appear to have found any difficulty in securing a place in the next. It seems likely that all intervention in elections at this time, whether by the government or by private individuals, was of this positive sort. Thus, when one of the burgesses elected in Sandwich was replaced by an outsider close to the Lord Warden in both 1555 and 1558, the motive was obviously to secure a seat for Cheyne's sons-in-law, not to prevent some unknown townsman from taking his seat at Westminster.[93]

Whilst the process of summoning and selection went on, the crown was busy with other preparations. Often an informal committee of the privy council was set up to consider how government policy was to be implemented: in February 1554, two months before the next meeting of parliament, a committee consisting of the chancellor, the treasurer, the bishop of Durham, Paget, Petre, Baker, and Hare was formed 'to consider what lawes shal be establisshed in this Parliament, and to name

---

[91] See the constituency reports.

[92] On this topic in general, see J. Loach, 'Parliament: A "New Air"?', in *Revolution Reassessed: Revisions in the History of Tudor Government and Administration* ed. C. T. Coleman and D. Starkey (Oxford, forthcoming).

[93] In 1555 Roger Manwood, elected for Sandwich, was replaced by Sir John Perrot (for whom see below, 211–13). Manwood was found a seat at Hastings (PRO C 219/24). In 1558 John Manwood was replaced by Nicholas Crispe.

men that shall make the bookes thereof'[94]—the 'books' being draft bills. Some councillors seems to have been given particular responsibilities in such matters. In October 1553, just before parliament opened, Paget complained to Renard about how busy he was deliberating on 'the articles concerning religion' to be brought before parliament,[95] and he and Petre were much involved a year later in the details of the reconciliation with Rome.[96] Paget was also preoccupied in 1558, when the legislative programme was largely concerned with the needs of war.[97] The proposals for the parliament of 1555 were submitted in outline to Philip,[98] who was out of the country, partly, perhaps, to mollify the queen who, when she heard some rumour that Philip might return to England, had thought of proroguing parliament. This plan was disliked by the council, which claimed that 'for necessite of money that is to be demaunded in the parlament and other wyse can not be provided the prorogation of that should be much dispendiose'.[99]

The council also considered the choice of speaker for the House of Commons. Although in theory the speaker was elected freely by the Lower House, a note from Northumberland to the chamberlain in Edward's reign had made the reality clear: the duke had suggested that the king should be consulted 'to the intent that he [the speaker] might have secret warning thereof, as always it hath been used, because he may the better prepare himself towards his preposition, otherwise he shall not be able to do it to the contentation of the hearers'.[100] At the beginning of the session one of the councillors sitting in the Commons would suggest the name previously decided upon, a task which usually fell to the treasurer, and it was customary for the man nominated to appear both surprised and reluctant, whilst expressing his surprise and reluctance in a flow of carefully prepared rhetoric. In their close links with the

---

[94] *APC* IV. 398. (A similar committee was set up before Elizabeth's first parliament: *APC* VII. 28.)

[95] *CSP Sp.* XI. 270.

[96] Plas Newydd, Anglesey, Paget Papers, Box I Miscellaneous, no. 7: F. G. Emmison, *Tudor Secretary: Sir William Petre at Court and Home* (London, 1961), 184.

[97] Plas Newydd, Anglesey, Paget Papers, Box II, no. 33.

[98] SP 11/6/16, 1/6/19, 11/6/22.

[99] BL Cotton MS Titus B. II, fo. 162.

[100] P. F. Tytler, *England under the Reigns of Edward VI and Mary* (London, 1839), II. 163.

Duchy of Lancaster, two of the Marian speakers followed a medieval tradition:[101] John Pollard, speaker in 1553 and 1555, was deputy chief steward of the south for the Duchy, and Robert Broke, speaker in April 1554, held a similar office in the north.[102] All the speakers of the reign were lawyers. Pollard, 'excellent in the laws of this realm',[103] had been appointed justice of Brecon, Radnor, and Glamorgan under Edward VI,[104] and this position was confirmed by Mary;[105] in 1557 he also became justice of Denbigh, Monmouthshire, Cheshire, and Flint.[106] Broke became chief justice of common pleas in October 1554, whilst Clement Heigham, speaker of the second parliament of 1554, became chief baron of the exchequer in March 1558. William Cordell, speaker of the last parliament of the reign, was solicitor-general until, in November 1557, he became master of the rolls.[107]

Because the speaker was a crown nominee, and paid by the monarch, he could usually be relied upon to assist the government in securing as easy a passage as possible for bills in the Lower House. Through councillors sitting in the Commons, who had special places close to his chair, the speaker could receive instructions and ask advice: it was behaviour of this kind that was to arouse Sir Anthony Kingston's wrath in 1555.[108] However, it would be erroneous to believe that the speaker was a mere royal pawn: he was the mouth-piece of the Commons in disputes with the crown, and Pollard undertook this task so enthusiastically in November 1553 when he led a deputation to ask the queen to marry within the realm that Mary became very angry.[109] He was obviously forgiven, however, as he served as speaker again later in the reign.

---

[101] J. S. Roskell, *The Commons and their Speakers in English Parliaments, 1376–1523* (Manchester, 1965), 338.

[102] Somerville, *The History of the Duchy of Lancaster* (London, 1953), I. 432, 427.

[103] *CJ* 5 Oct. 1553. The speaker, who sat in Marian parliaments for Oxfordshire and Chippenham, must be distinguished from Sir John Pollard, member for Barnstaple and Exeter: it was the latter and not, as Professor Loades suggests (*Two Tudor Conspiracies*, 212), the speaker, who was subsequently indicted for his part in the Dudley conspiracy.

[104] *CPR* 1551–2, 211–12.

[105] Ibid. 1553–4, 61.

[106] Ibid. 1557–8, 468.

[107] *DNB.*

[108] See below, 139.

[109] See below, 79–80.

The preparations being made by the government were echoed in some constituencies. As Professor Elton has pointed out, 'a meeting of Parliament acted as a signal to all the interests in the realm—especially those one may call organised—to prepare their grievances for an airing'.[110] In York, for example, the mayor normally seems to have assembled the aldermen and part of the common council and

> willed theym if any thyng they could devyse to be sewed above by the seyd burgesses for the worship, amendment and profite of this Citie they wold cast theyr headdes togider and articlat such thynges as they thought good to be done by the same Burgesses.[111]

There was, indeed, great bitterness in the city when, in 1553, Mr Langton, a baker, sent a bill into the Commons without the permission of the council[112]—this was, no doubt, the bill for the bakers of York read on 28 October and 3 November—and the city members were instructed to put in an answer to the bill.[113] It then appears to have lapsed, which may explain why, at the beginning of January 1554, Langton was reported to be saying abusive things about the city's government and swearing that he would shout their misdeeds through the streets of London.[114] At Lincoln the city council decided on 7 October 1553, two days after the formal opening of parliament, that articles 'for the weal of the city' should be devised and sent to the city burgesses at London.[115] The corporation of London decided on 5 April 1554 that a bill should be drawn up constraining foreigners to pay taxes;[116] a bill requiring inhabitants of towns to pay the same taxes as citizens was read in the Commons on 11 April. In 1558 the city of Exeter paid for the drafting of a bill to permit the taking of apprentices in the city, contrary to the provisions of the 1555 act;[117] a proposal that received only one reading in the Commons.

[110] G. R. Elton, *Reform and Renewal* (Cambridge, 1973), 77.

[111] *York Civic Records*, V. 110. See also 129, 168.

[112] Ibid. 94.

[113] Ibid. 95.

[114] Ibid. 98.

[115] *HMC Lincoln Corporation*, XIV. 47.

[116] Corporation of London RO, Repertory 13, i, fos. 145, 147ᵛ. For a fuller account of the measures in which London was interested in this period see *The House of Commons, 1509–1558*, I. 143.

[117] Exeter RO, Act Book, II, fo. 158ᵛ.

The cities of London and York were in fact so anxious about what went on in parliament that they paid various officials to look after their interests. For example, on 7 November 1553 London paid the speaker £6. 13s. 4d. for his 'lawfull favor to be borne and shewed in the parlyament howse towardes this Cytie and theyre affayres theire'.[118] The city also paid the clerk of the Commons to hold a watching brief: he was given £5 in 1553 for the previous two parliaments, and forty shillings in June 1554 with the somewhat reluctant comment 'albeyt that nothing passyde for the Cytie in the last parlyament'.[119] After the next two parliaments he received gifts of forty shillings, and an unspecified amount in 1558 for 'his good will and favor' in the last parliament.[120] In 1558 the city of London also gave the clerk of the parliament, Spelman, forty shillings for his good will in the previous parliament and at other times.[121] Similarly, the city of York, finding that both its members were sick, wrote to the recorder in 1558 instructing him 'to lerne from tyme to tyme of Maister Speaker if ought to put in agaynst this Citie that he may forsee therefor as occasion serueth'.[122] The close relationship between the representatives of London and York and the speaker was in fact formally recognized in the Chamber by the reign of Elizabeth, since those members occupied seats near to the speaker's chair, 'on the ryght syd next to the counsellors'.[123]

From the careful instructions given by York to its representatives both before and in the course of the parliament two things emerge. The first is the importance attached by the city to 'the parliament time' as an occasion on which all sorts of business might be done, much of it outside the Chamber. The members were told to find out about cases pending in the exchequer, to seek a reduction in the city's tax assessment, to petition the new archbishop about fish garths.[124] They were instructed to seek the

---

[118] Repertory 13. i., fo. 92.
[119] Ibid. fos. 103, 167.
[120] Ibid. fo. 252; 13. ii, fo. 353; 14, fo. 13ᵛ.
[121] Ibid. 14, fo. 32.
[122] *York Civic Records*, V. 167.
[123] J. Hooker, 'The order of kepinge of a parlament yn these dayes', fo. 13ᵛ.
[124] *York Civic Records*, V. 93.

advice of eminent men about these matters and, accordingly, they asked the earl of Shrewsbury in 1553 whether they should 'putt in a bill into the parlament howse for restitucon of our sayd liberties'.[125] Parliamentary meetings were obviously seen as providing opportunities for the transaction of a great deal of business in London. The other point that emerges from the correspondence between York and its representatives is how little interest the city took in matters that did not directly concern it. In the first parliament the passage of three bills in the opening session was reported[126]—these were the bills restoring Edward Courtenay and his mother and the bill repealing new treasons—but no other political measure of the reign, save the subsidy bills, was apparently reported back during the session.

It was not only the crown and civic authorities that laid plans; many trades had proposals that they wished to see implemented. On 12 October 1553, for instance, the city of London agreed that a bill drawn up by the leather curers repealing an Edwardian act regulating the trade should 'be put into the parliament howse'.[127] The leather trade formed a well-organized pressure group, and on 14 November the city authorities found it necessary to decree that not more than four curriers and two cordwainers should 'at once resorte vnto the parlyamente howse',[128] and to say in 1555 that no bill or suit 'shalbe exhibytye or made by any of the parlyamente howse concernyng leather without the knowledge and permission' of the mayor and councils.[129] A very large amount of legislation clearly had its origins in consultations of this sort between interested parties. The preamble to a bill passed in 1554 for the making of 'russels' mentions as originators of the proposal the two burgesses for Norwich, John Corbet and Alexander Mather, both clothiers of the town.[130] In 1558 one of the burgesses for Worcester, Robert Youle, was paid an additional sum of money for expenses incurred 'in his suit for the redress of

---

[125] Ibid. 94.
[126] Ibid.
[127] Corporation of London RO, Repertory 13. i, fo. 85.
[128] Ibid. fo. 94ᵛ.
[129] Ibid. fo. 323ᵛ.
[130] 1 & 2 Philip and Mary, c. 14.

the weight of cloths':[131] it was in the parliament of that year that Worcester succeeded in securing an amendment to the Edwardian statute regulating the cloth trade, a previous attempt in 1555 having failed.[132]

Individuals might also seek to improve their personal fortunes through statute. On 28 September 1555 Thomas Kerry, who represented Leominster in the parliament that opened a month later but lived just outside Hereford, wrote to the mayor of Hereford about a bill he wished to promote. He sent a copy of the proposal and asked that

I may receave by your Burgenses (whom I truste you will instructe depely in this case) the same fayre writene in parchement under your hands and comon seale to thentent the said Burgenses, and suche as I shall require to be my good lordes and masters herein, may the bolder and rather exhibite the same to the parliament howse, and overthrowe suche as shall blyndely obiect any matier against yt.[133]

This bill was presumably that for the rebuilding of four mills for corn and cloth-making outside Hereford, which was passed in the Lords on 5 December despite the objections of Rutland and Fitzwalter.[134] Perhaps the most obvious private interest-groups were those wishing to reverse the misfortunes that had befallen their families in the shape of acts of attainder. A high proportion of the private acts passed in Mary's reign were of this nature—there were nine of them in the first of her parliaments alone. The very fact that such bills were normally introduced with the queen's signature already upon them[135] shows that some considerable planning had been necessary. On some occasions men may specifically have sought election in order to promote bills touching their families: thus, in 1542, Sir Gilbert Talbot, knight of the shire for Worcestershire, secured an act confirming his right to the manor of Grafton, and in 1545 Sir Ralph Sadler, sitting for Preston, was undoubtedly

---

[131] *The House of Commons, 1509–1558*, citing Worcester Guildhall Audit of Accounts, 1540–1600.

[132] 4 & 5 Philip and Mary, c. 5, adjusting 5 & 6 Edward VI, c. 6.

[133] *HMC Thirteenth Report*, IV. 322–3.

[134] 2 & 3 Philip and Mary, c. 14. *LJ* mistakenly records the objectors as Lords Russell and Fitzwalter.

[135] For earlier procedure, see S. E. Lehmberg, *The Later Parliaments of Henry VIII* (Cambridge, 1977), 247.

responsible for the act passed in that parliament legitimating his children.[136] Such clear evidence of personal involvement is not common for Mary's parliaments: however, the complicated saga of the Howard lands[137] reminds us that considerable efforts were made by interested parties during this period to manipulate parliament both before and after its assembly.

It is important, then, to realize that men went to parliament with their minds full of the affairs of their locality, their trade or their family, and often returned still preoccupied by such matters. Much of their time whilst they were in the Chamber was taken up by these things, and even more of their time outside the Chamber. They went prepared to listen to what the government proposed and with no directives on how to respond. But they did not go only to listen to what the government proposed.

[136] 33 Henry VIII, c. 41; 37 Henry VIII, c. 30.
[137] See below, 64–72.

Parliament: Meeting and Management

PARLIAMENT began with a mass. A foreign observer has left a
vivid account of the service with which the parliament of
November 1554 began.[1] Both the king and the queen attended
dressed in velvet and ermine, with their swords of state carried
by the earls of Pembroke and Cumberland and their caps of
maintenance by the earls of Shrewsbury and Arundel.[2] They
were followed by four mace-bearers with silver maces, 'six
heralds with their velvet coats adorned with the arms of
England' and four pursuivants 'with damask coats after a different pattern'. There were 'trumpeters blohyng', Machyn
records, and 'the juges in ther robes', thirteen bishops, and the
lords in 'great scarlet mantles lined with ermine'. Only those
who had a vote in the Upper House were entitled to the scarlet
robes, and the foreign writer noted that 'the Duke of Norfolk,
who has not attained his majority, and the Lord Warden, who
is only a lord because of his office as Lord Warden of the
Cinque Ports, and not on account of any title of his own, were
not so attired, but accompanied their Majesties notwithstanding'.[3] The monarchs were met at the porch of Westminster
Abbey by the clergy and escorted to their places under a balda-
quin, where they remained whilst mass was said. Afterwards
White, bishop of Lincoln, preached a sermon in which he said
that

those who had separated from the primitive Church ... did not
harbour thoughts of peace, any more than did the introducers of new
religions and new dogma, or the seditious or those who were dis-

---

[1] *CSP Sp.* XIII. 81–2.

[2] Machyn, 74.

[3] It is of interest to note, in the light of the so-called 'decline' of retaining, that the
earl of Pembroke was accompanied by 300 retainers, 44 of them being gentlemen
clothed in velvet and gold chains, and the rest in blue cloth 'with a devise representing
a serpent on one sleeve'. Lord Talbot had a similar retinue, as did many of the other
nobles present.

obedient to the King, the Queen and their magistrates ... [He] finally exhorted the King, Queen and lords assembled to attend Parliament, urging them to frame 'bonas leges quae respiciant cultum et honorem dei' and the firm establishment of our true catholic religion, always having a thought for the public weal and the policy, defence and increase of the realm.[4]

Thirlby's sermon was to the point, since parliament was to be asked to return England to the Roman obedience, and it seems that this opening sermon was sometimes used, discreetly, to indicate something of the crown's intentions for the forthcoming session. After the service the king and queen with the rest of those present returned to the parliament house, where the speaker of the House of Lords, the chancellor, read a speech setting out government policy; in 1554 this lasted two hours. It is from these speeches, briefly recorded in the Lords' Journals but often described at greater length by outside observers, that some impression of the government's legislative 'programme' may be obtained. The members of the House of Commons were then instructed to go to their own Chamber and elect their speaker. The name already decided by the council would be suggested and agreed upon, and the speaker would, either immediately or within a few days, be presented to the monarch, in whose presence he would make an elegant oration; in November 1554, for instance, Clement Heigham made a speech 'comparing a body politick to a body natural'. These speeches ended with a request for 'free speech in the House, privilege from arrest and troubles for the Common House, and their servants, and to have access to the King and Queen, for the cases of the House.' In 1558 the speaker, William Cordell, also asked that if he made any mistakes in reporting what had been said and done in the House, this should not be to the detriment of the House; this request, or something similar, was probably customary.

Only the first of these privileges, freedom of speech, led to difficulties in Mary's reign. The House had access to the monarch, although the deputation of November 1553 that wished to ask Mary not to marry a foreigner had to wait for a few days for an appointment. Freedom from arrest was largely a matter for members' servants. Occasionally members sought

protection from royal courts, such as the exchequer[5] or Star
Chamber.[6] Once the House sent to the Tower for a day
someone who, objecting to the way in which a certain member
was performing his duties as under-sheriff of Berkshire, had
assaulted him.[7] It also gave consideration to the claim of one
member to have been slandered by another.[8] Jurisdiction over
its members by the House led to the examintion of John Story,
who had spoken directly to the queen in the presence of the
speaker, thus usurping his function; in this instance the House
did not feel punishment of the offending member was necessary.[9] Freedom of speech was, however, a privilege more difficult to define. Sir Anthony Kingston clearly stepped over the
generally recognized mark in 1555, and was committed to the
Tower for his 'contemptuous behaviour'.[10] The young
Thomas Copley, in 1558, spoke irreverently of the monarch in
a debate on the bill for the confirmation of letters patent, by
saying that he 'feared the Queen might give away the crown
from the right inheritors', a remark which must have expressed
the fears of some of his more timorous elders. Anxious, perhaps,
to forestall royal intervention, the House committed Copley to
the charge of the serjeant-at-arms and informed the queen of
what had happened, asking, however, for mercy on the
offender. The queen returned a frosty answer, and Copley was
not immediately forgiven.[11] In general, however, the reign was
not marked by tension over the interpretation of questions of
privilege.

Sometimes, after the election of its speaker, the House of
Commons had to turn its attention to disputed election cases.
Most of these in Mary's reign concerned members who had
been returned for two constituencies, but in the first parliament
there was controversy over the election at Looe of a notable
protestant divine, Alexander Nowell, which may have had
political or religious undertones. A committee consisting of

---

[5] William Allen, member for Calne, *CJ* 21 Apr. 1554.
[6] Gabriel Pleydell, member for Marlborough, *CJ* 6 Dec. 1555.
[7] *CJ* 23, 24 Apr. 1554.
[8] Ibid. 18 Feb. 1558. See Ch. 10 n. 115.
[9] *CJ* 20 Nov. 1555.
[10] See below, 139.
[11] Ibid. 5, 7 Mar. 1558.

Secretary Bourne, Sir Richard Southwell (another member of Mary's privy council), Sir John Tregonwell (a lawyer and government official knighted and favoured by Mary), the fervent catholic John Story, and two members of less certain loyalties, John Marshe and John Gosnold (Edward's solicitor-general), decided on 12 October that Nowell should be expelled, since, as a prebendary of Westminster, he had a voice in Convocation.[12] In 1558 a protestant writer was to suggest that Nowell's expulsion, and that of two other members whom he does not name, was due to their religious sympathies,[13] but there is no evidence to support this view, nor is there any reason to believe that the members of the committee had been given any directive by the queen. In the same parliament there was a dispute over the return of John Foster for Plympton; his case was considered by two separate committees but their decisions are not known.[14]

It has been argued that, the crown could at this period control the composition of the Commons through the granting of licences for absence—members were, in theory, required to obtain such licences from the speaker if they left Westminster whilst parliament was still in session. During Mary's reign, however, there is no evidence that any member was encouraged to absent himself. Those who were given licences to depart seem on the whole to have been either men summoned home by family sickness or lawyers wishing to attend the assizes;[15] in 1558, too, a large number of members were afflicted by the prevalent disease.

Indeed, the main concern of the crown appears to have been to secure a large attendance. Members of the House of Commons were not, as a group, very assiduous in the pursuit of their duties. Figures are not available except from division lists, which may reflect a House unusually swollen by controversy, but even they do not suggest high attendance: in a division of April 1554 321 members were present in the Lower House,[16]

---

[12] *CJ* 12 Oct. 1553.

[13] BL Harley MS 419, no. 50, fo. 146.

[14] *CJ* 12, 27 Oct. 1553.

[15] For example, Richard Onslow, licensed to go to the Worcester assizes on 22 Feb. 1558, and Ellis Price, licensed on 25 Feb. 1558 'to be absent for the Queen's Affairs for Musters'.

[16] *CJ* 19 Apr. 1554.

but in January 1555 there were only 193.[17] In November 1555 277 men were in the House for a division,[18] but a week later there were 319.[19] On 18 February 1558 217 members were present. Sir John Neale calculated that the largest number of members present in a division in the early parliaments of Elizabeth's reign was 276 out of a total membership of 411.[20] Tudor governments tried to deal with the problem by threats and by legislation. In January 1548 two members had been instructed to 'draw a bill for the absence of Knights and Burgesses of Parliament', and a bill was read a week later.[21] A bill on the same lines received two readings in November 1548.[22] During Mary's second parliament the problem of a thin Commons obviously arose, for a call of the House was ordered at the end of April 1554:[23] a call of the House rarely seems to have been taken save when attendance was low. The House was called three times in the next parliament,[24] when at least 106 members absented themselves,[25] and after the last call a bill was introduced, read three times, and sent to the Lords.[26] Lack of time prevented its passing in the Upper House, but the bill was reintroduced on the first day of the next parliament, and it was read three times before it was dropped in favour of a slightly different bill which was, however, lost.[27] The House was called in the first session of the 1558 parliament,[28] and a bill for the attendance of members was discussed on three occasions in November 1558.[29] On 17 April 1559, after stern warnings had seen sent out to sheriffs urging them to ensure that absentees returned to Westminster, a bill was read

---

[17] Ibid. 16 Jan. 1555.
[18] Ibid. 25 Nov. 1555.
[19] Ibid. 3 Dec. 1555.
[20] J. E. Neale, *The Elizabethan House of Commons* (London, 1949), 398.
[21] *CJ* 8, 15 Jan. 1548.
[22] Ibid. 8, 9 Nov. 1548.
[23] Ibid. 25, 27 Apr. 1554.
[24] Ibid. 17 Nov. 1554, 11 and 14 Jan. 1555.
[25] See below, p. 45.
[26] *CJ* 14, 15 Jan. 1555.
[27] Ibid. 21, 24, 26, 30 Oct. and 8 Nov. 1555.
[28] Ibid. 26 Jan. 1558.
[29] Ibid. 9, 10, 11 Nov. 1558.

again in the Lower House.[30] The problem was not to be solved in the sixteenth century, however.

Mary took a step that is probably unique in parliamentary history when she instituted legal proceedings against those members who had absented themselves without licence from her third parliament. On 21 December 1554 Renard had reported that the holiday was near but that members of the Commons had 'been forbidden to scatter'.[31] Foxe adds that on 22 December 'all the whole parliament had strict commandment, that none of them should depart into their country this Christmas, nor before the parliament were ended: which commandment was wonderful contrary to their expectations; for as well many of the lords, as also many of the inferior sort had sent for their horses, and had them brought hither'.[32] Doubtless the government was particularly concerned about attendance because neither the great bill of repeal nor the legislation dealing with the guardianship of the expected heir to the throne had yet been passed: parliament was, in fact, to sit on 24, 26, 27, 28, and 29 December. However, numbers had so obviously shrunk that a call of the House was ordered on 11 January. It was then decided that another call should be taken on 14 January. This clearly produced an unsatisfactory result, and the normal measure was adopted of introducing a bill 'for absence of knights and burgesses of the parliament'.[33] It was after the dissolution that Mary acted in an unprecedented way, taking out writs of *venire facias* against one hundred and six members[34] (see Appendix A). They were charged with having left parliament before 12 January without a licence, in direct defiance of the royal command. The cases dragged on throughout the remainder of the reign, many being uncompleted at Mary's death.[35] The case against John Harford was, however, dropped in Michaelmas 1558 when he claimed that he had in fact obtained a licence—there is no trace of it in the Journal— and the case against a Shrewsbury merchant, George Leigh,

[30] Ibid. 17 Apr. 1559; Neale, *The Elizabethan House of Commons*, 398.
[31] *CSP Sp.* XIII. 126.
[32] Foxe, VI. 579.
[33] See above, 44.
[34] PRO KB 29/1188, fo. 48r-v. (See Appendix A.)
[35] PRO KB 27/1176, 1177, 1179, 1180, 1181, 1182, 1184, 1185, 1186, 1187.

was also abandoned, although no reason was given for this. In Michaelmas 1556 the great lawyer Edmund Plowden was able to show that the charge against him was technically invalid, and it was dropped. Twenty-five others were fined.

Strype, commenting on these events, argued that the motive behind the prosecutions was political,[36] and other historians have gone further, suggesting that the members who left did so deliberately, that they 'seceded' because they disliked the policies urged by the crown. Both theories are improbable. The 'seceders' include men of great devotion to the church, such as Edmund Plowden, who would certainly have been favourably disposed towards the religious legislation still before parliament. Indeed, if these departures were a protest against the reunion with Rome it is very surprising that the one member known to have objected openly to the petition asking for the reconciliation, Sir Ralph Bagnall, was not amongst those who left.[37] It might also have been expected that Richard Grafton, the publisher of Tyndale's translations, who had lost his position as Royal Printer at Mary's accession, would have joined such a protest movement.[38] But there is, in fact, no aura or persistent religious opposition about this group as a whole. Of the 'seceders' only one, Nicholas Adams, also had a mark by his name on the Bodley list as standing in 1553 'for the true religion', although there were five other men whose names had been so marked sitting in the third parliament.[39] Whilst it is difficult to say anything definite about what the religious views of these members were at the time of their offence—wills drawn up twenty years later, for example, are of little value—it is interesting that those categorized by their bishops in 1564, that is, a decade after the indictments, fall into no single religious group. Some, such as Adams, Cheyne, Depden, and John Horde, are described as 'favourers' of the 1559 settlement, but

---

[36] J. Strype, *Ecclesiastical Memorials* (London, 1721), III. ii. 262. Strype copied a list in Coke (*Fourth Part of the Institutes*, London, 1644, 17–19), which follows KB 29/1188 except for the omission of Thomas Roydon, but for some reason he thought that only the first thirty-seven names were relevant, and ignored the remainder.

[37] See below, 107–8, 221–2.

[38] *DNB.*

[39] See below, 83–90.

Hodson, Lawrence, and Wigston were thought to be 'mislikers' of the established religion.[40] Henry Vernon was even regarded as the leader of a 'hurtful knot' of 'adversaries to religion'.[41]

Michael Graves has suggested that the seceders were staging 'a protest against the regency bill',[42] this is, against the bill dealing with the guardianship of the child Mary believed herself to be expecting.[43] He also argues that 'the odds are in favour of a collaboration' between these men and the nine peers—including Arundel, Cumberland, Pembroke, Sussex, and Bedford—whom he believes stayed away from parliament in order to avoid giving their consent to the bill.[44] The question of the conduct of the peers will be considered later,[45] but it may here be noted that there is no evidence of any contact between the members of the two Houses who were opposed to the bill, and the suggestion even of clientage links between them rests on very tenuous arguments. Mr Graves notes, as a thing significant in itself, that thirteen of the seceders were returned from Devon and Dorset 'including members from Tavistock (where the returning officer was Bedford's official), Bridport, Dorchester, Poole, and Weymouth'.[46] The constituency reports of the History of Parliament Trust, together with the biographies of the relevant members, do little, however, to support the notion that these members were particularly close to the disaffected peers.[47] John Evelegh, burgess for Tavistock, 'could have been' the nominee of the earl of Bedford, according to this source, but only because he is an outsider and a member of Lincoln's Inn, as was the earl. Since John Moynes, who sat for Bridport in November 1554, sat for Melcombe Regis in 1559 at the nomination of the second earl of Bedford, 'it is possible that he owed his election at Bridport to Russell patronage': he was, however, a resident and freeman of the town, who may have been elected simply as a man of the locality. Of Dorchester, the Trust notes that the trend at this time 'was towards

---

[40] *Camden Miscellany IX*, 69–70, 38, 19, 45, 56, 7, 46, 45–6.

[41] Ibid. 42, 43.

[42] Graves, *The House of Lords*, 196–8.

[43] See Ch. 6.

[44] Graves, op. cit. 197.

[45] See below, 119–22.

[46] Graves, op. cit. 292 n. 134.

[47] All that follows is taken from *The House of Commons, 1509–1558.*

electoral independence', and Christopher Hole is particularly mentioned as a man who owed his return to no outside influence. Poole, both of whose representatives left early, was at this period a borough with no history of interference. Both the members for Weymouth also left early but, once again, there is nothing to connect their election with noble influence, and the earl of Pembroke's power in the borough does not seem to have begun before 1559. Graves goes on to mention the Cornish members, and the six seceders who 'come from the earl of Arundel's county of Sussex'. When they are examined, the members from Sussex do not, however, appear to have been closely connected with Arundel. John Ashburnham, one of the knights of the shire, owed his election to his own 'standing and connections'. Walter Roynan was a townsman of Chichester. In Shoreham and Steyning Howard influence was normally great, but the death of the third duke and the accession of a minor had left it dormant: the burgesses for Steyning were both townsmen, and William Mody, a servant of the recently deceased Lord Delaware, was returned for Shoreham probably because he had served the borough well enough in the previous parliament. Of Arundel, the Trust notes that 'all the Members [during the reigns of Edward and Mary] were nominees of the earls, apart from John Burnet[48] and Richard Bowyer in November 1554, who were townsmen with municipal and parliamentary experience'. The links between the Wiltshire members and the earl of Pembroke, mentioned by Graves, similarly shrink on close examination, and it is therefore very difficult to accept his theory that these men were puppets, used by the peers 'to sing their song of protest for them'.[49]

Even the notion that the seceders were opponents of the regency bill is difficult to sustain. The bill in its final form was far from being as favourable to Philip as Mr Graves suggests— hence the Imperial disappointment. Moreover, the members of the Commons who were worried about power accruing to Philip if Mary were to die whilst her child was a minor, far from absenting themselves in chagrin, fought the matter out on the

---

[48] Burnet was not a seceder.
[49] Graves, *The House of Lords*, 197.

floor of the House, and won.[50] The bill did not pass the Commons until 14 January; given its slow progress, given the great changes that it had undergone, a member opposed to it might still on 12 January, the day on which members were formally noted as absent, have nurtured hopes of shaping it to his liking.

Whether the measure to which these absentees are believed to have been opposed is thought to be the bill for reunion with Rome or the regency bill, should the queen not have been relieved to see critics of her policy removing themselves rather than actively standing in her way? Even Strype was forced to concede that the departures were 'inwardly well enough liked by the Queen and her popish Cabal'.[51] One would have expected licences for absence to have been granted readily to anyone known to dislike the bills under the discussion.

The reason for the departure of so many members was surely the proximity of Christmas, linked with anxiety about the weather. Thirty-six of them left with their fellow members, which suggests a desire to travel in company, rather than any coherent stand on principle. It is interesting that for almost half of these men it was their first experience of parliament, which might indicate a lower degree of political commitment than the average, and a correspondingly higher commitment to the delights of hearth and home. A large number of them were also townsmen, traditionally averse to London and the delights of the court.

If it had not been for Strype's comment, later historians would undoubtedly have continued, like Coke, to regard the whole episode as part of the *lex et consuetudo parliamenti*. This is where it belongs. The queen, angry at so many members having disregarded an express commandment that they should not leave and perhaps further annoyed because the legislative programme, so lightly abandoned, was in fact one of considerable importance, decided on an unusual gesture. She clearly did not regard the men involved as untrustworthy: Sir Thomas Moyle became sheriff of Kent in 1556, Sir William Wigston sheriff of Warwickshire and Leicestershire in 1557, and John

---

[50] See below, 117–19.
[51] Strype, *Ecclesiastical Memorials*, III. ii. 263.

Knill sheriff of Radnorshire in the same year. Thomas Keys, who sat for Hythe in 1554, became serjeant porter of the palace of Westminster and Thomas Mathew, burgess for Penryn, was given an appointment in the exchequer. Only seven of the twenty-three seceders who sat in the parliament of 1555 appear on the list of members who opposed some aspect of royal policy.[52] Neither the conduct of the men themselves, therefore, nor the attitude of the crown towards them implies that the episode was anything more than one round in the centuries-long battle to secure the daily attendance of members of the House of Commons.

There is, then, little evidence to suggest that the crown took any continuing interest in the day-to-day composition of the House of Commons beyond a general desire to keep up attendance. Far more important for control of the Lower House was the role of the privy councillors. Hooker was later to note that the councillors in the House sat in a prominent position—'vpon the lower rowe next to the Spekers'[53]—where their actions could be observed and imitated by less confident members and by those anxious to win royal favour. On 14 November 1558, when a number of lords came down from the Upper House to consult the Commons about the grant of a subsidy, they sat in these prestigious seats, and the speaker and the non-noble councillors had to content themselves with lower positions.[54] The assistance of the councillors could be crucial—in 1555, for instance, when the controversial first fruits bill ran into difficulties Cardinal Pole summoned the councillors who had seats in parliament one by one, and each promised him his own vote and agreed 'to exert themselves with the others for the approval of the measure with less difficulty both with the Lords and the Commons'.[55] It has often been argued that Mary had too large a council, but one advantage of its size must have been that there were more councillors available to sit in parliament: it is certainly interesting to note that the most obstreperous House

---

[52] Carey, Chiverton, Crowche, Jobson, Peyton, John Phelips, and Thomas Phelips.
[53] J. Hooker, 'The order of kepinge of a parlament yn these dayes', fo. 13ᵛ.
[54] *CJ*; see below, 170.
[55] *CSP Ven.* VI. i. 426. See below, 135–8.

of Commons of the reign, that of 1555, was the one in which fewest councillors sat (see Table 1).

Table 1. Number of Privy Councillors in Parliament

Date	Commons	Lords
1553	18[a]	15[b]
Apr. 1554	17[c]	15[d]
Nov. 1554	17[e]	15[f]
1555	10[g]	13[h]
1558 (1st session)	13[i]	14[j]

[a] Baker, Bedingfield, Bourne, Cheyne, Cornwallis, Drury, Englefield, Hastings, Huddleston, Jerningham, Mordaunt, Edmund Peckham, Petre, Rochester, Southwell, Strelley, Waldegrave, Wharton.

[b] Estimated in the absence of the Journal: Arundel, Bath, Bedford, Derby, Gardiner, Heath, Norfolk, Paget, Pembroke, Rich, Shrewsbury, Sussex, Thirlby, Tunstall, Winchester. I have excluded Lord Delaware because of his great age, and Lord Wentworth, who was probably in Calais.

[c] As above, but without Englefield, Peckham, and Strelley (who had died). Robert Peckham sat in his father's place, and Mason was added. (Heigham did not become a councillor until after parliament ended.)

[d] As above, but without Bedford, who was in Spain; Lord William Howard was added.

[e] Baker, Bourne, Cheyne, Drury, Englefield, Hastings, Heigham, Huddleston, Jerningham, Mordaunt, Edmund Peckham, Petre, Rochester, Shelton, Southwell, Waldegrave, Wharton.

[f] Bedford attended this time, but Norfolk was dead.

[g] Baker, Bourne, Drury, Englefield, Hastings, Jerningham, Mordaunt, Petre, Rochester, Wharton.

[h] Not Bedford, nor Shrewsbury, because of illness.

[i] Baker, Bedingfield, Bourne, Cheyne, Cordell (who became a councillor in Dec. 1557), Cornwallis, Englefield, Heigham, Jerningham, Mason, Petre, Waldegrave, and Wharton.

[j] Arundel, Bath, Derby, Hastings, Heath, Howard, Montagu, Paget, Pembroke, Rich, Shrewsbury, Thirlby, Winchester, and Clinton.

Note: The list of councillors is taken, with a few alterations, from that in Loades, *Mary Tudor*, 475–80. The number of councillors in the Lords does not agree with that in Graves, *The House of Lords*, 249 n. 29, partly because Pole was never, in fact, a member of the privy council.

The 1555 parliament also witnessed the death of perhaps the most experienced parliamentary manager amongst Mary's advisers, the bishops of Winchester. The Venetian ambassador noted that the Commons grew bolder after Gardiner's death, and claimed that he 'had been feared and respected in an extraordinary degree by everybody'. He was, Michieli wrote, the possessor of 'knowledge so extensive and minute, both of the business and of all the persons of any account in this kingdom, and also of the time and means by which to please and flatter, or to overawe and punish them'.[56] Noailles also noted that after Gardiner's death 'la noblesse qui est assemblée icy, et jusqu'aux plux petitz parlent plus licentieusement . . . contre ladicte religion qu'ilz n'ont faict devant'.[57] Persecuted protestants believed that Gardiner used his power to evil effect; John Rogers, the first Marian martyr, told the bishop that 'the whole parliament-house is led as you list; by reason whereof they are compelled to condescend to things both contrary to God's manifest word, and also contrary to their own consciences: so great is your cruelty'.[58] He went on to declare: 'ye have called three parliaments in one year and a half, that what ye could not compass by subtle persuasion, ye might bring to pass by tyrannical threatening'. A pamphlet printed in 1557 claimed that some members of the Commons had been bribed to subdue their opposition to Philip's coronation, and goes on to allege that 'one quarrel or another' was picked against those who refused the bribes, whereby 'they were brought quorum nobis, and then to lay ether treason or heresie (as they call it) to ther charges'.[59] (This was probably the origin of Burnet's later claim that Gardiner had bribed the Commons in the parliament of April 1554 'by giving the most considerable of them pensions: and had £200 and some £100 a year, for giving their voices to the marriage'.[60]) A speech written on Elizabeth's accession also declared that it was Gardiner who had prevailed upon Mary to write letters to the sheriffs asking for the return of catholic members, he 'himself beside commendyng many, and in a manner by name, commaunding sum to serue for the turne as he thought best. Whereby he still placed in the the hous right many'.[61] Anyone who spoke against a government bill was, this writer claims ominously, summoned and 'shopt vp for sunburnyng.'

Not surprisingly, historians have accepted these views of

[56] *CSP Ven.* VI. i. 251.
[57] Arch, Étr., IX. fo. 540: (Vertot, V. 204).
[58] Foxe, VI. 604.
[59] *The lame[n]tacion of England* (n.p., 1557), fo. 8.
[60] G. Burnet, *The History of the Church of England* (Oxford, 1865), II. 447.
[61] *A Speciall grace . . . vpo[n] the good nues and Proclamation . . .* (n.p., 1558), sig. C 1ᵛ–2.

Gardiner's activities, and have gone on to claim that he was 'a potent force for good or ill' in parliamentary affairs.[62] It is clear that the Edwardian government, when it prevented Gardiner from sitting in the Lords and from exercising his customary electoral patronage, believed that he was a serious opponent.[63] He was a towering figure, and a more colourful and charismatic one than most of the rather grey if worthy men by whom Mary was surrounded: his personal impact on those who came into contact with him was correspondingly significant. Yet his electoral influence, and even his clientage group in the Commons, was not very considerable. Six or seven of the men sitting in the Commons in these years were servants or close associates of the bishop—Francis Allen was his secretary,[64] Thomas Martin his chancellor, and Jacques Wingfield and Oliver Vachell performed a number of functions for him. James Bassett probably owed his election for Downton in April 1554 to his friend the bishop, but his subsequent returns as knight of the shire for Devon were due to his own standing. John Bekinson and Thomas White, who also represented Downton during this period, were presumably acceptable to Gardiner, but there is no reason to believe that they were particularly close to him. The return for Downton of John Norris, an usher of the privy chamber, may have owed more to the queen's influence than the bishop's. Others who sat for constituencies in which the bishop's official was the returning officer may simply have been respected townsmen: Richard Bethell, for example, who represented Winchester in October 1553, had been mayor the previous year. Thus, although Gardiner had a little group of clients in the Lower House,[65] their number was not great, and they were conspicuous only for their silence and absence from committees. It seems, therefore, that Gardiner's role was that of manager rather than faction-leader: his influence had of necessity to be exercised outside the Chamber rather than within it. The same is probably true of other councillors: it was

[62] For example, Graves, *The House of Lords*, 190.
[63] See *The Letters of Stephen Gardiner*, 424. It is, however, improbable that Gardiner, when writing of 'Winchesters faction, as som terme it' (ibid. 405), has in mind 'a parliamentary following', as Mr Graves claims (op. cit. 189).
[64] But see above, 27.
[65] I have taken here the names listed by Graves on p. 290 n. 86; the biographical details are from *The House of Commons, 1509–1558*.

not so much their personal patronage networks that gave them power in parliament as their ability to influence the timid and inexperienced.

One way in which they could do this was through their control of committees. Little is known about the committal stages of bills in this period,[66] but councillors appear to have been named as a matter of course to many of the joint committees of the two Houses. On 4 December 1554, for instance, the attorney and the solicitor brought to the Commons a list of certain of the Upper House who wanted 'a number of this House to confer with them for parliament matters', and the 'whole council of this House' together with twenty-one knights or burgesses were nominated on 6 December, according to the Lords' Journal, a committee consisting of the treasurer, the steward, the earl of Pembroke, the bishops of Durham, Worcester, and Lincoln, and the Lords Wharton, Paget, and North went to confer with some of the Commons 'for the drawing of a bill touching the repeal of certain statutes'. The great bill of repeal was, therefore, the product of a committee heavily dominated by privy councillors.[67]

It was also, of course, a product of consultation between the two Houses. Joint conferences were a common occurrence at this time. All were formally initiated by the Lords. On 29 November 1554, for instance, it was reported to the Commons that the lord chancellor, four earls, four bishops, and four barons had been appointed to a committee and wanted some of the Commons to join them, a request that was immediately met: together they devised a supplication asking that England should return to the Roman obedience. (The way in which the delegates from the Upper House were drawn in equal numbers from the three grades of peers suggests that these conferences bore a close relationship to the 'intercommuning' of fourteenth century parliaments.[68]) The subsidy bill of 1558, although not that of 1555, was also a product of a conference between Lords and Commons.[69]

---

[66] For Elizabethan practice, see Neale, *The Elizabethan House of Commons*, 360–5.

[67] For another example, see below, Ch. 8 n. 7.

[68] J. G. Edwards, *The Commons in Mediaeval English Parliaments* (Creighton Lecture for 1957, London, 1958), 22.

[69] See below, 160–1.

There was also, of course, contact between the Houses over the redrafting of various bills and provisos. The most common cause of complaint was a failure to cancel sufficiently clearly some abandoned part of a bill.[70] Sometimes one House would redraft a proviso added to a bill by the other, as the Lords did on 7 March 1558, in the course of the musters bill.[71] In general provisos added by the second House seem to have been accepted without debate, for when a bill returned to the House from which it originated the new provisos were usually given three purely formal readings.[72] At the end of the second parliament of the reign, however, there was a dispute between the two Houses over an amendment to the bill for the attainder of Wyatt and his fellow rebels, and the matter was not settled before the dissolution.[73]

In the House of Commons bills usually, but not invariably, received only three readings, sometimes being discussed over several days without a formal reading. However, bills were occasionally read four times—the bill enabled Mary to dispense with the last instalment of the subsidy granted to Edward is one example[74]—and, more rarely, five or six: the bill touching leases made by married priests was read on 8 December 1554 for the fifth time, and the bill concerned with prisoners' bail was read for the sixth time on 12 January 1555. Just under one half of the bills discussed by the Commons are recorded as having been committed.

It is difficult to be certain, at this period, about how precisely the House of Commons voted on a bill. The question is important, for Sir John Neale pointed out that by that latter part of Elizabeth's reign the system was such as to militate against those proposing some change in the status quo, members being reluctant to leave their hard-won seats in the Chamber to vote in a division.[75] Moreover, Sir Goronwy Edwards has suggested that the very development of the division came about 'largely in the course of opposition to contentious government bills which accompanied the varied vicissitudes following upon the

[70] e.g. *LJ*, 4 Jan. 1555.
[71] See below, 163.
[72] e.g. *LJ*, 17 Ap. 1554.
[73] See below, 102–3.
[74] Read for a fourth time on 29 Nov. 1553.
[75] Neale, *The Elizabethan House of Commons*, 383.

breach with Rome, and particularly in the course of 'reformist' opposition to bills promoted by the pro-catholic and pro-Spanish government of Queen Mary'.[76]

There is no contemporary account of voting under Mary. Sir Thomas Smith, writing in the 1560s, described two methods of voting in the House of Commons. First, in reply to the speaker's question, 'they which allowe the bill crie yea, and as many as will not, say no: as the crie of yea or no is bigger, so the bill is allowed or dashed': this is the system of voting by voices. If, however, the vote by voices is not clear, 'they divide the house, the speaker saying, as many as doe alowe the bill goe downe with the bill, and as many as do not sitte still. So they divide themselves, and being so divided they are numbred who make the more part'[77]: this is voting by numbers.

Hooker, writing about five years later, describes the system slightly differently. He said that the speaker asked:

'as many as will have this byll passe yn manner and forme as you have herde say yea' then those which lyke the byll say yea: 'as many as will not have this byll passe lett them say no' then they which lyke it not say no / If vpon this question the whole howse or the more do say yea thin the byll is to be sent vnto the lordes but if they say no thin the byll is dashed / If the voyces be doubtful then shall he cause the howse to be devyded and then all they which are of the negatyve part must aryse and depart out yn to an vtter howse. wherevpon the speker shall choysse too or iiij to nomber them, first which are of thaffermatyve part as they do sytt: That donne they which are with out to be called yn and to be nombred as they come yn.[78]

There is a discrepancy between these two accounts, for Smith has the affirmative voters leaving the Chamber and Hooker the negative; in the printed version of Hooker's account, however, published about 1575, the description of voting declares that 'the affirmatiue part must arise, & departe into the vtter rowme'.[79] It may be that Hooker was simply mistaken in his first, manuscript, version of the work, or that the tradition was not yet clearly established. However, by the end of the century

---

[76] J. G. Edwards, 'The Emergence of Majority Rule in the Procedure of the House of Commons', *TRHS* Fifth Series, XV (1965), 186.

[77] *De Republica Anglorum*, 83–4.

[78] Exeter RO, Book 60h, fo. 15^{r-v}.

[79] *The order and vsage of the keeping of a Parlement in England* (n.p., n.d.), fo. 27^{r-v}.

the convention had apparently been settled that it was the party of change that left the Chamber.

The purpose of the division was to provide a counted vote: the House was divided because it was then easier to count. There are, therefore, two questions to be considered about voting under Mary: how frequently a counted vote was taken after a vote by voices, and whether a counted vote is the same thing as the division described by Hooker. The first counted vote of the reign to be recorded in the Journal was on 19 April 1554 when 'upon the question for the bill the House did divide', with 201 members for the bill and 120 against it. On 16 January 1555, upon division of the House', a bill was rejected by 120 votes to 73. On 25 November 1555 'by division of the House' a bill was passed by 152 votes to 125, and on 3 December 'per divisionem domus' a bill was passed by 193 votes to 126. Three days later came the rejection of the exiles' bill 'per divisionem domus', when the clerk was clearly very agitated and forgot to record the votes. The last division of the reign came on 18 February 1558 when 'per divisionem' a bill was rejected by 111 votes to 106. In the first parliament of Elizabeth two divisions are recorded.[80]

There were, then, at least six times in the reign of Mary when the House proceeded to a division. But it would be unwise to assume that a division in Mary's reign meant what it did when Hooker was writing. Sir Goronwy Edwards has argued convincingly that the division as Hooker knew it could not come about until the Commons had moved to St Stephen's, where there was a 'house' and an 'outer-house', and that this move occurred around the middle of the reign of Edward VI.[81] However, there are several pieces of evidence which suggest that the counted vote existed before the change of meeting-place made true divisions possible. There is the story of Chapuys, the Spanish ambassador, that in 1532 during the passage of the annates bill Henry devised a plan whereby 'those among the members who wished for the King's welfare and the prosperity of the Kingdom, as they call it, should stand on one side of the House, and those who opposed the measure on the

[80] *CJ* 17 Apr., 1 May 1559.
[81] Edwards, 'The Emergence of Majority Rule', 180–2.

other'.[82] Sir Goronwy Edwards declares that this was not a division, which of course it was not, in the sense in which Hooker uses the term, but the only possible motive for such action must have been to facilitate the task of judging which party was the larger; a similar procedure was followed sometimes in elections, as a stage between voting by voices and a counted vote. In 1551 the Venetian ambassador reported that if a vote by voices did not produce a clear result, 'the Speaker counts it one by one'.[83] William Thomas, who had sat in the parliament of 1547, wrote that 'the Judgement in ye parliament cases, is gyving by devyding the persons, all yt say yea on the one syde of ye house and all that say nay on ye other syde'.[84] In 1554 the Venetian ambassador reported that when the vote by voice was uncertain 'the Ayes are told to move to one side and the Noes to remain in their places; and both sides being counted, the greater number conquers'.[85] Surely what all these accounts suggest is that the two groups simply moved within the Chamber, or even that the Ayes alone moved to one side, as described by the Venetian ambassador.

There is no clear evidence, therefore, that a division had yet come to mean, as it did by Hooker's time, that part of the House moved into an antechamber: it seems quite possible that the House still divided within the Chamber, and had not yet taken advantage of the architecture of its new meeting-place to make simpler the task of counting votes. If a division did not, as yet, involve anyone moving outside the Chamber it becomes easier to understand what happened in the famous scene over the rejection of the exiles' bill in 1555. According to the Venetian ambassador, Sir Anthony Kingston and his friends

---

[82] *Letters and Papers*, V. 896.

[83] *CSP Ven.* V. 343.

[84] MS Bodley 53, fos. 81ᵛ–82. This is a contemporary English translation of the work: another version was published in 1861 as *The Pilgrim*, ed. J. A. Froude (London), and the relevant passage is on p. 30. The History of Parliament Trust drew my attention to this work. There is a difficulty about this account, for Thomas goes on to describe the chagrin of More and Fisher when they found themselves in the minority on such an occasion: More and Fisher could be found together only in the Upper House. Probably Thomas is simply confusing the procedure of the Lords, which was perhaps unknown to him, with the procedure in the Commons with which he was familiar.

[85] *CSP Ven.* V. 554.

saw that there was present in the House a majority in favour of rejecting the bill and therefore wanted to force an immediate vote before the government could bring in more of its supporters, as, it would seem, had been done only a few days earlier over another controversial bill. Kingston insisted on a division and put himself with some friends at the door of the House 'to prevent anyone who had the wish to do so from quitting it'.[86] Presumably the point of shutting the door was to stop any government supporter from going out to seek assistance, or to prevent the timorous from escaping the necessity of making their views public. Another account of these events, which will be considered in detail later,[87] stresses the delaying tactics of the Speaker and government supporters as well as the insistence of Kingston that the question should be put, but there is nothing in either account to suggest that the division yet involved anyone moving out of the Chamber. (Indeed, even in Smith's description of a division, written a decade later, there is no clear evidence that members actually left the Chamber, although this had obviously become the practice by 1571, when Hooker sat in the Commons.[88]) Thus there is little to support either Sir Goronwy Edward's suggestion that the procedural development of the division took place at this time or his argument that the development was precipitated by conflict over religion, since less than half of the recorded divisions of the reign occurred over religious bills.

In the House of Commons bills were read by the speaker's clerk; bills were read in the House of Lords by the clerk of the parliament. Three readings were again the norm, and there were far fewer exceptions than occurred in the Commons.[89] About half the bills discussed in the Lords are recorded as having been committed. After a bill had received a sufficient number of readings it might be rejected unanimously, as was the bill for the duke of Norfolk's patentees on 28 November

---

[86] Ibid. VI. i. 283.

[87] Bodley MS Tanner 391, fo. 68; see below, Appendix C.

[88] *De Republica Anglorum*, 84.

[89] In 1555 both the lay and spiritual subsidy bills received only one reading, but this was unusual. (5 Nov. 1555, lay; 30 Nov. clerical.) See below, Ch. 8 n. 10, for 1558, and for 1549 *LJ* for 5, 6, 12 Mar. and for 1553, *LJ* for 15, 16, 18 Mar. See also ibid., 17, 18 Dec. 1566.

1555, or it might be rejected only by a majority of the House, as the heresy bill was on 1 May 1554. A bill might be agreed to unanimously, or passed by a majority, as a bill for leather curing was on 5 May 1554. A variant of the last was for a bill to be passed, but for a minority of peers to express their dissatisfaction formally, as the earls of Arundel, Shrewsbury, and Rutland did, together with the bishops of Worcester and Chichester, in the case of a bill regulating the wine trade on 16 April 1554. Peers registered formal protests against just under one third of the bills passed by the last four Marian parliaments, the number of peers registering a protest against any one bill ranging from one to nine. It is not always clear why individual peers objected to certain pieces of legislation, and it is obvious that some peers, such as Lord Lumley, made more use of the procedure than did others. The process was facilitated by the fact that peers' votes were cast individually—as Justice Saunders pointed out in the course of a disputed election case, 'the majority of voices in the Upper House may be easily known, because they are demanded severally, and the clerk of the House reckons them',[90] or, as Sir Thomas Smith put it, 'in the Upper House they give their assent and dissent ech man severallie and by himself'.[91]

In both Houses, however, a large number of bills never reached the stage of a vote, having been lost through lack of time, or lack of enthusiasm and interest. Because of the difficulty of identifying bills of which the only record is a cryptic entry in one of the Journals—a difficulty compounded in some instances by the introduction in a single sessions of several bills dealing with a similar matter—precise figures are impossible to produce, but it is interesting that far more bills were lost in the Commons than in the Lords. This is in part a reflection of the much greater size of the Lower House, since it is likely that the majority of abortive bills were introduced by the initiative of an individual. Mr Graves is undoubtedly correct in also drawing attention to the greater political skill and experience of members of the House of Lords, and to the valuable service provided

---

[90] *The Commentaries or Reports of Edmund Plowden* (London, 1816), 126. Sir Goronwy Edwards discusses this in 'The Emergence of Majority Rule', 187–9.

[91] *De Republica Anglorum*, 83.

for the Upper House by its legal assistants.[92] Overall in the reign a larger number of statutes originated in the Commons than in the Lords—61 to 46: this was the reverse of the pattern of the latter years of Henry VIII's reign, as described by Professor Lehmberg,[93] and a change from the reign of Edward, when 64 per cent of acts began, according to Mr Graves's figures, in the Lords.[94] This may be explained by a fact to which Professor Elton has drawn attention:[95] the number of acts passed for private persons—these almost always began in the Upper House—was small in Mary's reign compared with that of her predecessor and successor. Whether the change amounts, therefore, to what Mr Graves has described as 'a clear shift of emphasis in the bicameral relationship' is difficult to decide.[96] It has been suggested that the changing habits of privy councillors are largely responsible for the difference[97] rather than, as Graves suggests, the growing instability and inefficiency of the Lords in the face of Mary's unpopular policy; it is certainly interesting that whereas only seven privy councillors sat in the Commons in the first session of Edward's first parliament, compared with thirteen in the Lords,[98] the balance for much of Mary's reign was, as we have seen, equal.[99] The government may, therefore, have felt easier about introducing major pieces of legislation into the Commons because a larger number of privy councillors sat there to aid their passage. None the less, the great bill of repeal, perhaps the most important measure of the reign, and various other important bills, including that for the surrender of first fruits, were first introduced into the Lords.[100]

---

[92] Graves, *The House of Lords*, 176–7.

[93] Lehmberg, *The Later Parliaments of Henry VIII, 1536–1547*, 257.

[94] Graves, *The House of Lords*, 178.

[95] G. R. Elton, 'Tudor Government: the Points of Contact. I: Parliament', *TRHS*, Fifth series, XXIV (1974), 194.

[96] Graves, *The House of Lords*, 178.

[97] C. G. Ericson, 'Parliament as a Representative Institution in the Reigns of Edward VI and Mary' (London Univ. Ph.D. thesis, 1974), 47.

[98] Ibid.

[99] See above, Table 1.

[100] All the acts of this period for the continuance of expiring statutes (HLRO, Original Acts, 1 Mary 2, 18; 1 Mary 3, c. 11; 1 & 2 Philip and Mary, c. 16; 2 & 3 Philip and Mary, c. 21; 4 & 5 Philip and Mary, c. 9) began in the Lords, and this practice was not changed until the latter part of Elizabeth's reign. (S. Lambert, 'Procedure in the House of Commons in the early Stuart Period', *Historical Journal*, XXIII (1980), 779–80.)

By intervening in elections, by creating new peers and electing new bishops, by its choice of speaker and his manipulation of events in the Commons, and by the intervention of privy councillors the monarch at this period could, if she so wished, very often bend parliament to her will. If these and similar tactics were unsuccessful members of both Houses might be summoned to the queen's presence and persuaded or bullied into doing what she wished; in 1555, for example, when the bill for first fruits had run into difficulties, the queen 'sent for several members of either House and addressed them so gravely and piously that the act of renunciation, having been read three times in the Lords, at length on the third they passed it, and only one or two non-contents';[101] Henry VIII had done much the same when parliament had criticized his divorce proceedings.[102]

Moreover, the crown had ample means outside the Chamber of influencing what went on within. The history of parliament is obviously intermingled with that of patronage, although it is impossible to draw causal connections between crown favours and men's behaviour in parliament; the Imperial ambassador, who was convinced of the English love of gold, handed out pensions and gold chains to courtiers and government officials,[103] many of whom were also members of parliament, but the attitude of the assembly towards Philip remained hostile. It may be, however, that threats hanging over their heads had more effect on men than did favours bestowed on them. The heavy fines imposed on those who had supported Jane Grey, fines that worried Paget as he believed that it was impossible to 'keep both men's hearts and their goods',[104] were used as a political weapon, and Renard considered the queen's clemency towards the earls of Huntingdon and Rutland and the remission of Suffolk's fine of £20,000 were astute tactics.[105] Moreover, as members of the Lower House pointed out in 1555,[106] many

---

[101] *CSP Ven.* VI. i. 256–7.
[102] *Letters and Papers*, V. 989.
[103] *CSP Sp.* XII. 315–16; XIII. 454–6.
[104] Ibid. XI. 333. See also 236.
[105] Ibid. 356, 366.
[106] *CSP Ven.* VI. i. 229.

crown officials, both past and present, owed the crown large sums of money. An attempt in the parliament of 1558 to secure an act that would have made it possible to recover money from the estates of officials who had died foundered on the rock of organized opposition,[107] but other efforts to recover debts were more successful. There were, after all, two senses in which such efforts could strengthen the crown; it might recover the debt— very useful in a country which had once, as Paget declared, been 'so well off as to be able to supply its friends and neigh- bours' but was now 'sorely embarrassed itself, and the Queen unable to find money for her household expenses and her offi- cers' pay'[108]—or, by holding the threat of recovery over the heads of men of questionable loyalty, the crown might per- suade them into obedience. Crown debts, like attainted estates, could be used as a sort of probation system.

It would be tedious to set out all the ways in which the crown could influence men's behaviour and attitudes, and thereby influence what went on in parliament. In any case, it is imposs- ible to prove that men acted as they did because of favours received, or because they feared what would happen if they behaved differently. All that needs to be said, perhaps, is that parliament was only part of the total structure of government in England, and that we must beware of looking at what went on in the Chamber too much in isolation. The behaviour of those in the Chamber was often influenced, moreover, by matters outside the monarch's control. Personal quarrels and antagonisms, such as that between Bonner and Gardiner,[109] and differences over trading matters like that which provoked Thomas Wild, burgess for Worcester, to slander his fellow- member, John Marsh, before the London Drapers' Com- pany,[110] are probably as important in any attempt to explain why men did what they did in parliament.

Crown business in any case never dominated the whole of a parliamentary session. Much time was given to other matters about which the government was totally indifferent, although such matters might themselves create tension and hostility

---

[107] See below, 164–5.
[108] *CSP Sp.* XIII. 90.
[109] Foxe, V. 154–61.
[110] *CJ* 18 Feb. 1558.

between those sitting. A prime example in Mary's reign of such an issue is that involving the Howard lands. At the end of the reign of Henry VIII, Thomas Howard, third duke of Norfolk, and his son, the earl of Surrey, had been accused of treason. Surrey was executed, but Norfolk was saved by Henry's own death on 28 January 1547. However, just before Henry died, he had given his assent to acts of attainder passed on the two men.[111] Since he was by then very feeble, Henry did not appear in person to assent to the bills, but commissioned the chancellor, St John, Hertford, and Russell to report his assent to parliament. Contention soon arose about the legality of this commission, which, it later transpired, had not been signed by the king's own hand, but set up only under the dry stamp. In July 1547 the master of the rolls, Sir Robert Southwell, was ordered with other legal experts to examine the attainder act relating to the duke.[112] In January 1552 it was scrutinized again, by the chancellor and three judges, Montagu, Baker, and Hales.[113] At the beginning of Mary's reign members of Serjeants' Inn were consulted, although they do not seem to have ruled on the validity of the act.[114] However, the duke of Norfolk, released from the Tower by Mary, brought a bill into parliament in 1553 to declare invalid the act of attainder. (It was during the discussions on the bill that Paget admitted that the commission had not been signed with the king's own hand.[115]) Since bills had to be signed either by the king in person or by letters patent assigned under the great seal, Norfolk's measure declaring invalid the act of attainder was passed.[116]

[111] There is a short discussion of the attainder process in H. Miller, 'Henry VIII's Unwritten Will: Grants of Land and Honours in 1547', in *Wealth and Power in Tudor England*, ed. E. W. Ives, R. J. Knecht, and J. J. Scarisbrick (London, 1978), 92–3. Mr Gary Hill, of The Queen's College, Oxford, is at present engaged in a study of these land transactions to which I am much indebted.

[112] *APC* II. 106.

[113] Ibid. III. 194, 208.

[114] J. Dyer, *Reports of Cases in the Reigns of Henry VIII, Edward VI, Queen Mary and Queen Elizabeth* (Dublin, 1794), I. 93a.

[115] According to Dyer, Paget made this statement in the Commons. There is no record of it in the Journal, and it is more likely that he made the declaration in the Lords: the Lords' Journal has, of course, disappeared.

[116] HLRO, Original Acts, 1 Mary 2, 27. See PRO C 65/163/34, and H. Miller, 'Henry VIII's Unwritten Will', 92–3.

Because the act of attainder was thus annulled, rather than reversed, the question of the legality of grants made from Howard property after its confiscation was a tortuous one. Originally, Henry VIII's intention had apparently been to use the confiscated lands to support the nobility that had fallen on hard times, 'sum by atteyndours, sum by there owne misgoueraunce and riotous wastinge and sum by sickness and sundry other meanes', but, at Norfolk's own request, he had finally decided to keep the land for the support of his heir, Edward.[117] However, after Henry's death the need of both Somerset and Northumberland to reward their supporters led to the alienation of most of the Howard land. Some property changed hands several times in the political upheavals of the period. To take but one example of these complications: Sir Ralph Vane (or Fane, or Phane) was, at Paget's instigation, granted the house and park at Sheffield, the park and house at Horsham, St Leonard's Forest, and other properties. But Vane supported Somerset too long, and fell. His lands were dispersed and some of the former Howard property went to one of Northumberland's followers, Sir John Gates. Gates was later attainted for his part in promoting the cause of Jane Grey, and his lands reverted to the crown.[118] The political turmoil of the period and the fluidity of the land market meant, therefore, that a great many people were directly touched by the question of what happened to Howard land.

Those involved seem to have been preparing for concerted action from the time of the debate at Serjeants' Inn. On 30 November 1553, when the duke's bill, having passed the Lords, came before the Lower House for the first time, it was reported that:

Taverner, and others, in the name of all such as have letters patents of grant of the said duke's lands, require, they may have a copy of the bill exhibited, and also their interest saved; and thereupon put in their bill: And for that there be no names expressed, the bill being uncertain, to whom the copy should be delivered. It is ordered, that the bill be again delivered.[119]

---

[117] *APC* II. 15–20.
[118] Ibid. 19.
[119] *CJ*.

In the afternoon of the following day, Taverner and his colleagues again 'exhibited a bill for preservations of their interests in the late duke of Norfolk's lands, and prayed a copy of the bill; which copy is granted unto them; and further, that they be here ready furnished tomorrow with their counsel at nine of the clock.' On 2 December the bill was given a second reading, and the counsel for the patentees, Mr Cholmley and Mr Riches, asked to be heard. It was ordered that 'the House will proceed to the body of the bill; and the patentees to be here at two of the lock, if they have further to say; and Mr Speaker to write for the records, or copies of such things, as may make for furtherance of the matter.' On Monday, 4 December, the duke of Norfolk himself came into the house and asked that it should pass his bill, 'shewing, that, for the causes betwixt him and the patentees, he would abide the order of certain Lords, and other, to whom the matter was compromitted; and if the arbiters did not agree, then the Queen to make a final end, as it should please her highness.' The bill was then given a third reading. On the next day the Journal records 'arguments upon the bill', and its passing.[120]

Although the duke had won his point and the act of attainder had been declared void, he did not perhaps obtain all he had hoped. On 29 November, whilst the bill was still before the Lords, the Imperial ambassador had reported that the duke was also claiming back all his property,[121] and there is no doubt that this is what he really wanted. But the 'patentees', those who had received grants of the land, or who had bought it from the first grantees, were determined to restore nothing without compensation. Norfolk was therefore forced, during his appearance in the Commons, to agree that the claims of the patentees should be considered by a group of arbitrators. On 1 April 1554 this group—Gardiner, Arundel, the bishop of Norwich, Paget, Sir Robert Rochester, Sir Edward Hastings, Petre, and Sir Edward Waldegrave—entered a judgment in chancery. Their judgment was that patentees whose lands were recovered by the duke should receive compensation, but only if the grant

[120] *CJ*, 5 Dec. 1553.
[121] *CSP Sp.* XI. 401.

mentioned the commissioners—Wriothesley, Paulet, Russell, and Hertford—whom Henry had, by whatever means, empowered to report to parliament on 27 January 1547.[122] Many of the patentees were therefore left without compensation, and when the question of Howard property came up again in parliament they made their discontent known.

Parliament was forced to consider the Howard lands again in 1555. The third duke had died and his heir was a minor. A bill introduced on his behalf recalled that in 1553 the third duke had agreed to accept the decision of the arbitrators, or a majority of them. 'concernyng the right, titles and interes*t*es of all and singular p*er*sones that deymed demanded or pretended to haue any of the [Lands] of the same late Duke by the lettres patentes of the late kyng Harry the eight', or Edward VI, during the time that the duke was in the Tower—that is, the duke had agreed to buy back some of the land, and had also agreed to pay the crown for the manors and other properties that had come into the crown's possession in exchange for parts of Norfolk's estate that had been granted away. The young duke could not raise the money to do this without selling other lands and touching his capital: as he was under age, a statute was needed to allow him to do this. (In its final form, it allowed him to sell with the consent of Gardiner, Arundel, and the bishop of Ely.[123])

This bill was read twice in the Lords on 6 November 1555 and was passed the next day. It received a first reading in the Commons that same day, 7 November, and then held fire until 19 November, whilst the discontented owners or former owners of Howard property set out their griefs. On 9 November, 'Mr. West, and other patentees of the late duke of Norfolk, by humble petition exhibited a bill for their assurance; and required a copy of the duke's bill, which was granted.' The bill put forward by the petitioners claimed that although, during the passage of the act reversing the third duke's attainder, the duke's officer in the House had promised that earlier land changes should be respected, they had found themselves thrust

---

[122] The judgment itself has disappeared, but its purport can be worked out from the 1555 petition.

[123] See PRO C 65/164/23, or House of Lords Original Acts, 2 & 3 Philip and Mary, 23.

out. Arguing that it was quite improper to pass acts that 'bothe give and take awaye', they asked for their position to be protected.[124] However, the bill read on 9 November was declared to be too general, 'by not naming of the patentees', and was redelivered: an amended bill was read on 14 November. It received a second reading on 21 November, after the fourth duke had himself appeared in the House in an attempt to expedite his own bill dealing with the land sales. The duke's bill was in fact passed after its third reading, and so too, on 25 November, by 152 votes to 125, was the patentees' bill. However, after three apparently straightforward readings in the Upper House, the patentees' bill was rejected by all present on 28 November.

Clearly, therefore, both in 1553 and in 1555 there was considerable sympathy in the House of Commons for those to whom Howard land had, in good faith, been granted. (The Upper House seems to have been more moved by the plight of the duke himself.) This is hardly surprising, for many of the men sitting in the Commons possessed Howard property themselves, or were closely related to those who did. The spokesman for the patentees in 1553 appears to have been Roger Taverner, brother of the great reformer, Richard Taverner—Roger, Richard, and another brother, Robert, were all named in the 1555 petition. Roger Taverner was not a member of parliament in 1553, although he was to sit for Launceston in the next parliament. The names of the other patentees involved in this first petition are not known, but it must have been supported in parliament by John Caryll, attorney-general of the duchy of Lancaster, who was knight of the shire for Sussex, for Caryll owned the reversion to the former Howard manor of Shortesfyld, in Sussex,[125] by Thomas Farnham, representing Leicester, who owned a former Howard property in Southwark,[126] by Sir Henry Hussey, who sat for Lewes and held former Howard land in Washington, Sussex,[127] and by John Michell, sitting for

---

[124] SP 46/8, fos. 59–62. I am most grateful to Mr Hill for a transcript of this document.

[125] *CPR* Edward VI, V. 261. Caryll also sat in 1555.

[126] Ibid. V. 206. Farnham sat for East Grinstead in 1558.

[127] Ibid. V. 157. Hussey sat for Gatton in 1555.

Horsham, who had bought the Howard property of New Park, Bedding, from his brother-in-law, Edward Lewknor.[128] The member for Rochester in 1553, Sir Thomas Moyle, had acquired Wilmington, Kent, through Lord Paget.[129] Richard Weston, sitting for Saltash, had bought some former Howard land in Essex and Bedfordshire in conjunction with Anthony Browne.[130] Sir John Guildford, elected in 1553 for both Romney and Winchelsea, was named in the 1555 petition. Sir Edward Warner, sitting for Grantham, had received a grant of Castleacre under the provisions of Henry's will.[131]

The chief mover of the 1555 petition was William West, a most unsavoury character who had once attempted to murder his uncle, Lord Delaware. Delaware, 'the best howse keper in Sussex', died, presumably of natural causes, in October 1554,[132] and amongst his possessions were the former Howard properties of Stoke Park and Knapp, Sussex. William West, as one of the executors of his uncle's will, thus became involved in the struggle over the Howard land. He was not a member of parliament, but two of the others named in the petition were: Sir Edmund Rous, who sat for Dover,[133] and Henry Peckham, representing the family borough of Wycombe.[134] Other members of the 1555 parliament who possessed some former Howard property included Sir Martin Bowes, member for London, who had bought East Wickham in Kent in June 1553,[135] the burgess for Shoreham, Thomas Hogan, who had been involved in some complicated dealings in Howard property in 1549 and still possessed the manor and ironworks at Sheffield,[136] and Francis Shirley, the other burgess for Shoreham, who held the manor of East Grinstead.[137] Sir William

---

[128] Ibid. V. 73, 102.
[129] Ibid. I. 46, 53. Moyle represented Rochester again in Apr. 1554, and Lynn in Nov. 1554.
[130] Ibid. V. 145. Weston sat for Lancaster in Nov. 1554 and for Maldon in 1555.
[131] *APC* II. 16.
[132] Machyn, 71.
[133] *CPR* Edward VI, III. 21.
[134] See below, 215–17.
[135] Ibid. V. 306–7.
[136] Ibid. III. 321, 332, 354. See also *APC* II. 382.
[137] R. J. W. Swales, 'Local Politics in the Parliamentary Representation of Sussex, 1529–1558' (Bristol Univ. D. Phil. thesis, 1964), 84.

Brooke, one of the members for Rochester, had acquired 'The
Angel' at Thetford.[138]

When so many members of both Houses had an interest in
Howard lands, it is hardly surprising that bills dealing with the
property had a long and contentious passage. The third duke
had been forced to agree that those with valid grants should be
compensated when he recovered his lands—Mary gave him
nearly two thousand pounds per annum to help—but the way
in which the transactions were carried out seems to have caused
great resentment, even amongst those whose grants were not
disregarded for the technical reasons set out in the arbitration
award. An example of this is the case of Richard Fulmerston,
who had been granted Downham Marsh by Northumberland
after the duke had acquired it through an exchange.[139] Fulmerston had once been the servant of Henry, the executed earl of
Surrey,[140] and from 1558 to 1568 he was to be the treasurer of
the fourth duke of Norfolk. He sat for Bedwyn in 1553, and in
both parliaments of 1554, and in 1558 for Horsham, a Howard
borough. In July 1554, however, he wrote to Sir John Thynne
in depressed terms, explaining that he was much preoccupied
with the Norfolk land transactions, which, he declared, 'tow-
chetch the substance of my hole lyvinge'. He explained to
Thynne that the matter had been submitted to the judgement
of some of the council, and

... they haue amongest others ordered for me, that I shall haue my
land agayne, at the Duk*es* redempc*i*on, that I delyuerd in exchange
for his, and then he to haue agen that was his, and further, for suche
land*es* as I bought, he to haue his land agan and I the money that I
hau paid for the same/ Wheruppon the saide Duke by his counsall
and I haue hadde metyng*es* for goings through accordingly, and haue
showed to them my *letters* patentes and ther conveyaunc*es*, of suche
land*e* as were his.[141]

Amongst these was a property Fulmerston had bought from the

138 Ibid. V. 281.
139 *CPR* Edward VI, III. 350, 365. See also II. 298.
140 *Letters and Papers*, XXI. ii. 553, 555.
141 Longleat, Thynne Papers, II, fo. 201.

duke of Somerset, 'of the late Monkes of Thetforde' for which he had paid £200 and some sheep, a bargain which he wanted Thynne to confirm. This Thynne did.[142] Fulmerston was obviously worried at the valuations of the various properties involved in the exchange.

For men less contented or optimistic than Fulmerston, the affair of the Duke of Norfolk's land seems to have been a last blow. After the failure of his attempt to secure the former Howard property William West became involved in Dudley's plotting;[143] the Venetian ambassador described him in June 1556 as 'factious and scandalous'.[144] When he was tried he 'woulde not aunswere to his name of William West, esquier, but as Lord De La Ware, and to be tried by his pieres';[145] he was nevertheless condemned, although not executed.[146] As late as 1592 Sir Edmund Rous remembered these experiences with bitterness: writing to Burghley he explained about the reversal of Norfolk's attainder and declared 'on the accession of Queen Mary, the said Duke was enlarged' and the patentees turned out, although the patentees went to some pains to prove the attainder valid. The whole thing, Rous argued, was an act of oppression.[147] The man on whom the Norfolk land-dealings had the greatest effect, however, was Henry Peckham, who was subsequently executed for his part in the Treasury plot.[148]

Thus, bills concerning individuals or small groups could occupy as much parliamentary time as those which, for instance, levied a subsidy on all the property-owning class, and could provoke bitter feelings amongst those involved. Such legislation often emanated from the aristocracy. The matrimonial difficulties of Henry Radcliffe, second earl of Sussex, for instance, produced a flurry of discussion. In November 1553 both Lords and Commons read a bill 'against the adulterous living of the late countess of Sussex'; this bill appears to have been lost through pressure of time. On 9 November 1555 the Lords read another bill debarring the countess from her jointure unless 'she

[142] Ibid. fo. 206.
[143] Loades, *Two Tudor Conspiracies*, 214–15.
[144] *CSP Ven*. VI. i. 474.
[145] Wriothesley, 135.
[146] He was pardoned in Apr. 1557. (*CPR* Philip and Mary, III. 538).
[147] *HMC Salisbury*, II, no. 12.
[148] See below, 215–17.

shall repair into the realm within a time limited and make her purgation before the bishop of her diocese'. This passed the Lords on 13 November, with the bishops of St David's and Bangor registering protests; however, despite the fact that the bill was apparently already signed by the queen,[149] the Commons rejected it on 28 November. This abortive bill, which was intended to cut the countess off from both jointure and dower, was replaced by another in 1558 which permitted her to hold certain manors under very strict conditions, although she was still not allowed any dower; this slightly more generous bill was passed.[150] Other bills of this sort dealing with the family problems of the aristocracy include that for the marquis of Northampton's marriage,[151] and the long debate in 1554 about the Willoughby inheritance.[152]

Although, as Professor Lehmberg has said, it would be totally erroneous to believe that bills were 'rammed intact through browbeaten Houses',[153] it is obvious that the organization of parliament at this period favoured the crown: resistance had to be both determined and considerable before government bills would be rejected, although they were frequently amended. However, foreign observers who believed that parliament always did what the crown wanted[154] failed to notice an important fact: the crown introduced only bills that it believed had a good chance of being accepted. When the majority of parliament was thought to be unwilling to agree to Philip's coronation, for example, the queen wisely decided to make no formal proposal.[155] Where government proposals were accepted, they were accepted because parliament approved of them or was largely indifferent, rather than because of the procedural advantages available to the monarch. Privy councillors sitting in either House, the alliance between them and the speaker,

---

[149] On 25 and 28 Nov. *CJ* so describes it. The 1558 bill was signed.
[150] HLRO, Original Acts, 4 & 5 Philip and Mary, 13. This bill, unlike the two preceding ones, originated in the Commons.
[151] HLRO, Original Acts, 1 Mary 2, 30.
[152] See below, 123–4.
[153] S. E. Lehmberg, 'Early Tudor Parliamentary Procedures: Provisos in the Legislation of the Reformation Parliament', *EHR* LXXXV (1970), 10.
[154] For example, Soranzo: *CSP Ven.* V. 554.
[155] See below, 196–7.

control of committees: all these made easier the smooth transaction of business, but they could not prevent the occasional
outburst of criticism or the loss from time to time of a government bill.

The emphasis laid by some historians on 'management' rests
on the assumption that without it the parliaments of this period
would have been bloody battles between crown and subjects.
The evidence of Mary's reign suggests that such an assumption
is unwarranted. Although Mary did not regard the summoning
of parliament with any obvious enthusiasm, she took the event
seriously—so seriously, indeed, that she insisted upon a regular
attendance by members of the Lower House. Men of the governing classes were anxious to sit in parliament but their pre-
occupations when in the Chamber often appear very different
from those of their monarch. Management was therefore necessary in order to get business done. That business, however,
seems to have been universally recognized as including matters
of private interest as well as those affecting the country as a
whole.

4

The Parliament of October 1553

MARY's first parliament began on 5 October 1553. The queen, accompanied by the lords spiritual and temporal dressed in their parliament robes, went to Westminster Abbey to hear mass and to listen to a sermon by Heath, at this time still bishop of Worcester.[1] She returned in procession with the earl of Westmorland bearing before her the cap of maintenance and the earl of Devon, shortly to be restored to the dignities stripped from him by the queen's father, carrying the sword.[2] Gardiner, as chancellor, outlined the government's plans, telling the assembled estates that parliament had been summoned primarily to repeal what he described as the iniquitous laws that had separated England from the Roman church.[3] The House of Commons was then instructed to choose its speaker, and John Pollard duly elected. In the midst of the pageantry there was one discordant note, however, for the bishop of Lincoln, John Taylor, and John Harley, bishop of Hereford, withdrew from the mass, and one of them at least was stripped of his parliament robe and imprisoned in the Tower.[4] This probably left the protestant bishops unrepresented in the Lords.[5]

Soon after Edward's death two lists had been composed of problems confronting the new government. The first included amongst its priorities the summoning of parliament, a survey of justices of the peace and an attempt 'to restreyne the number of them', the calling in of grants for retainers, consideration of the Irish problem, the recovery of debts owed to the crown, and an

[1] Wriothesley, II. 103.
[2] Machyn, 46.
[3] CSP Ven. V. 431.
[4] Foxe (VI. 394) says that the bishops withdrew from this mass: his account is based on BL Harley MS 419, no. 50, fo. 146. The examination of Taylor is recorded in A Chronicle of the Grey Friars of London, 84–5. Taylor later sought refuge with one of the members of this parliament, Sir Thomas Smith (Dewar, Sir Thomas Smith, 7).
[5] See above, 18.

attempt at retrenchment by the reduction of military establishments and the expenses of the court—it was hoped that household costs might be reduced to something like their level at the end of Henry VII's reign—as well as some attempt to deal further with the coinage and an effort 'to restore the lawes to their full auctoritie'.[6] The second memorandum, composed by Petre at the beginning of August, was on similar lines, the main addition being the proposed reform of various church matters, such as the problem of the prebends' and bishops' land seized since the death of Henry VIII: the list again included questions of law and order, and it stressed the need to curb royal expenditure.[7] Petre and Gardiner appear to have been entrusted with the task of surveying the financial situation and devising remedies.[8] To Paget fell the task closest to the queen's own heart; he told Renard at the beginning of October that he was very busy since Mary had asked him to consider the articles concerning religion to be brought before parliament.[9] Although Mary knew that parliament was likely to question her about her marriage plans she appears at this stage to have believed that she could fend off any full discussion of the matter,[10] and apparently no specific tactics were decided upon by the council, which was in any case bitterly divided on the issue.

A major difficulty about assessing the ease with which the government was able to implement the measures discussed in these lists is the loss for this parliament of the Journal of the House of Lords. The loss is the more serious because many contemporary commentators believed that it would be in the Upper House that opposition would be voiced both to religious proposals and to any plan for a foreign marriage: Pole, for instance, wrote to Mary predicting that the main objections to reunion with Rome might be expected from the nobility, which had benefited from the dispersal of former ecclesiastical property.[11] The Imperial ambassadors urged that the great personages of the realm should be sweetened with honours and

[6] SP 11/1/3.
[7] SP 11/1/5.
[8] Emmison, *Tudor Secretary*, 161.
[9] *CSP Sp.* X. 270.
[10] Ibid. 254.
[11] *CSP Ven.* V. 421.

pensions.[12] Mary herself, when considering the possibility of appointing new bishops to sit in the Upper Chamber in time for this parliament (a plan she subsequently dropped), recognized the possibility that her proposals might not be welcomed by the peers.[13]

The first measure to be discussed in the Lords appears to have been a bill 'for avoiding treasons and praemunire' which was sent down to the Commons on 12 October. This bill, which was already signed by the queen, an indication both of its importance and of her willingness to see it enacted, repealed all definitions of high treason other than those set out in the act of 1352:[14] it was not retrospective, however, and therefore left untouched the position of those accused of participation in Northumberland's conspiracy. The bill also repealed all new felonies and all definitions of praemunire created since the first year of Henry VIII's reign. It seems to have encountered no opposition in the Upper House,[15] but there were at once difficulties in the Commons.

The extent of the hostility to the bill is puzzling. According to Renard it was believed that the real purpose of the measure was to restore the authority of the pope in England, which raised the whole question of the future of former ecclesiastical property.[16] However, the bill in its final form does not mention church property, nor, explicitly, the pope, although the repeal of the act that had made it treasonable to deny that Henry VIII was head of the English church showed plainly that Mary intended to come to terms with Rome. The queen herself, writing to Pole, confirms Renard's reports; she explained that the Commons would not hear of 'the abolishing, specially of that law that gave the title of the supremacy of the church in the realm of the crown, suspecting that to be an introduction of the pope's authority into the realm, which they cannot gladly hear of'.[17] Clearly the whole question of the royal supremacy and

---

[12] *CSP Sp.* XI. 247, 270, 455–6.
[13] Ibid. 236.
[14] HLRO, Original Acts, 1 Mary, sess. i, 1.
[15] Renard reported on 12 Oct. that parliament was going well (*CSP Sp.* XI. 292).
[16] Ibid. 305.
[17] BL Cotton MS Titus B. ii, fo. 148. This is a translation of Mary's letter of 28 Oct., printed in A. M. Quirini, *Epistolae Reginaldi Poli* (Brescia, 1744–57), IV. 119.

England's relations with the pope was openly debated, and one observer even believed that a bill had been passed 'that men might reason whether the Quene were Supreme Hedd, or whether the bushoppe of Rome might not lawfully have the same agayn, with certayn other mattyers'.[18] Finally, however, the Commons passed the bill on 19 October.

Two days later Mary brought the first session of parliament to an end by giving her formal consent to this bill, to another restoring the earl of Devon, and to a third for Courtenay's mother, the marchioness of Exeter.[19] It is not easy to understand why she did this, for it meant that all remaining bills, including that for tonnage and poundage, had to be reintroduced: a year later, when the royal consent was given to a bill repealing the act of attainder passed against Reginald Pole, the session was not brought to an end.[20] Perhaps the explanation is that Mary was not yet fully familiar with parliamentary procedure, but her action inevitably suggested that Courtenay's position was of great importance to her.[21]

In the interval before the second session 'many earls, lords, knights, gentlemen and divers others of the court and country' went to listen to the debates in convocation.[22] These had begun on 18 October, and on 20 October some of the peers had sent a request to the queen that they might be enabled to hear the discussion.[23] However, as one commentator noted, although 'there came moche pepulle', they were 'never the wyser', and the council finally sent word 'that there should be no more disputation', but that matters should be discussed 'by the hole parlament'.[24]

The whole parliament met again on 24 October. On 31 October an important bill was introduced into the Commons to repeal 'divers acts touching divine service and the marriage of priests'. In its final form the bill repealed the act of 1547

---

[18] *Queen Jane and Queen Mary*, 32.
[19] HLRO, Original Acts, 1 Mary, sess. i, 2 and 3.
[20] See below, 106.
[21] *CSP Sp*. IX. 314.
[22] Later published by the protestants as *The trew report of the dvsputacyon in the conuoca-cyo(n) hows* (Basil, n.d.). There is also a Latin version, that claims to have been printed in Rome (*STC* 19891). Much of the debate appears in Foxe (VI. 395–411).
[23] Foxe, VI. 397.
[24] *A Chronicle of the Grey Friars of England*, 85. See also *CSP Sp*. XI. 322, 332.

against those who spoke irreverently of the sacrament (an act which had permitted communion in both kinds), the act enabling the ruler to appoint bishops, the 1549 act of uniformity, the act removing restrictions on the marriage of priests, the act for the abolition of images, the act setting out forms of consecration and ordination, the 1552 act of uniformity, the act reducing the number of holy days that were to be observed, and the 1552 act for clerical marriage.[25] From 20 December 1553 religious services were to be conducted and the sacraments administered as they had been in the last year of Henry VIII's reign. This bill was discussed in the Commons on 3, 4, 6, and 7 November, before being passed on 8 November. Noailles reported that it 'a demeuré huict jours en merveilleuse dispute'[26] and Mary herself wrote that it had been passed only after 'contentione, disputacione acri, et summo labore fidelium':[27] indeed, although no division is recorded, it seems that a substantial minority of the House was opposed to the bill, for Noailles commented that 'la tierce partie de ceulx du tiers estat' was 'de contraire oppinion',[28] and Gardiner told Renard that 'out of 350 voters only 80 had gone against'—these, he declared, were not 'men of importance'.[29]

Meanwhile the Lords were considering a bill that declared valid the marriage between Henry VIII and Catherine of Aragon. The question of this marriage had been raised during the earlier session: some statutory proposal was thought to be desirable to prevent the validity of the marriage, and hence of Mary's claim to the throne, from appearing to rest solely on the judgment of the pope.[30] Whether any specific measure had then been introduced is not certain. Noailles wrote on 17 October that 'en la chambre desditz millords ... a esté aussy proposé de casser tous les arrestz qui ont esté par cy-devant donnez sur le divorce du mariage du feu roi Henry dernier et de la royne Catherine mere de ladicte dame; ce qui n'est toutesfois

[25] HLRO, Original Acts, 1 Mary, sess. 2, 2, repealing 1 Edward VI, c. 1 and c. 2, 2 & 3 Edward VI, c. 1, c. 21, 3 & 4 Edward VI, c. 10, c. 12, 5 & 6 Edward VI, c. 1, c. 3, c. 12.
[26] Arch, Étr., XII. fo. 102ʳ⁻ᵛ; (Vertot, II. 247).
[27] Quirini, *Epistolae Reginaldi Poli*, 121.
[28] Arch, Étr., XII. fo. 102ᵛ (Vertot, IV. 247).
[29] *CSP Sp*. XI. 349.
[30] Ibid. 298, 308, 310.

encoures venu jusqu'à l'aultre chambre'.[31] Any bill dealing
with the marriage would, of course, have lapsed when the first
session ended. The bill that subsequently became law reached
the Commons on 26 October and was passed there three days
later.[32]

The topic of royal marriages was in everyone's mind. Mary
tried to stave off any debate about her own plans—on 29
October she had secretly pledged herself to an alliance with
Philip—but the Commons wanted to send a deputation to address her on the subject. By feigning illness she delayed the
audience for three weeks,[33] but the temper of the House was
rising, and certain members of parliament told the French ambassador that 'si elle ne les satisfaict d'honneste responce, selon
leur volunté et intention', they would 'rompre eulxmesmes le
parlement, et s'en aller chascun en sa maison'.[34] Finally, on 16
November, the deputation was admitted.

The speaker delivered what Renard described as 'a long and
carefully composed discourse, full of art and rhetoric, and illus-
trated by historic examples'.[35] He pointed out that the succession was still uncertain, and it therefore behoved Mary to
marry speedily, but he tried to persuade her not to marry a foreigner; to do so would displease the people, would be financially disastrous for the realm as a whole, and might, when the
queen died, lead to a succession struggle—the very thing they
wished to avoid—for a foreign consort might attempt to seize
the throne for himself. These references were so clearly made
with the Spanish proposals in mind that Mary lost her temper.
Instead of answering through the chancellor, as was customary,
she spoke herself, declaring that it was not proper or respectful
for parliament to address the sovereign in such a way. She
added, according to Noailles, that 'elle tenoit de dieu la couronne de son royaulme, et que en lui seul esperoit de conseiller
de chose si importante'; she had no immediate intention of
marrying, but if she were to do so it would not be to the detri-

---

[31] Arch Étr., XII. fo. 92ᵛ (Vertot IV. 221).
[32] HLRO, Original Acts, 1 Mary, sess. 2, 1.
[33] *CSP Sp.* XI. 343.
[34] Arch Étr., IX. fo. 106ᵛ (Vertot, II. 256).
[35] *CSP Sp.* XI. 363–4.

ment of her realm.[36] (The following day the councillors in the
Commons rather ominously asked for copies of the articles on
which the speaker had addressed the queen.)

Noailles believed that many of those who heard the queen's
reply were dissatisfied. He was doubtless correct, yet only four
members of the Commons attended the meeting in London on
26 November at which the first moves were made towards what
was later known as Wyatt's rebellion: they were Sir Peter
Carew, Sir Edward Rogers, Sir Nicholas Throckmorton, and
Sir Edward Warner.[37] After the failure of the rising another
three members of the 1553 parliament, Sir Thomas Dyer, Sir
Ralph Hopton, and William Smethwick, were questioned.[38]
Although it is of interest that such well-informed and astute
men believed that a rebellion against the proposed Spanish
marriage would gain widespread support, the fact that so
few members of the House were involved in the plot suggests
that Noailles's belief that the majority of the Commons was
restless and rebellious should be taken with a pinch of salt. Indeed, events in parliament were proceeding smoothly enough.
A bill against 'such as disturb divine service or preachers',
necessary because the relevant Edwardian act had been
amongst those so recently repealed, was introduced into the
Commons on 28 November and passed two days later.[39] There
is no reason to believe that the bill ran into problems in the
Upper House, although a proviso was added to protect anyone
against punishment by both magistrate and ordinary. However, another bill, aimed at those 'who say not their service or
come not to the church' and already passed by the Commons,
was lost in the Lords, according to Renard because peers felt
that for the present it was enough to punish those who had
offended against some specific existing law.[40] In their turn a
majority of the Commons on 5 December rejected a bill that

[36] PRO Transcripts 31/3/21: 24 Nov.
[37] There are two versions of the indictment, one containing the names of Carew and
Rogers, another adding those of Throckmorton and Warner (Loades, *Two Tudor Conspiracies*, 16–17).
[38] See Ch. 10 nn. 38, 47, and 35.
[39] HLRO, Original Acts, 1 Mary, sess. 2, 3.
[40] *CSP Sp.* XI. 419.

had come from the Lords 'for the confirmation of the bishopric of Durham, and of Durham Place' to Cuthbert Tunstall and his successors. This bill would have recreated the great medieval bishopric dismembered by Northumberland, and even restored to the bishop the magnificent London house of which he had been deprived in 1536.[41] On 1 December the Lower House added to the bill a proviso guaranteeing the Princess Elizabeth in her possession of Durham Place, but four days later the Commons rejected the entire bill, presumably because it heightened barely submerged anxieties about the whole issue of former ecclesiastical land.

The remainder of the session was taken up with what Noailles described as 'choses politicques pour ce royaulme'.[42] Bills were introduced, probably at the initiative of the government, to deal with counterfeit coin and to prevent sheriffs from becoming justices of the peace.[43] Another successful bill gave Mary the same powers to dissolve the Cromwellian revenue courts that Edward had possessed at his death. These powers were to allow Mary in January 1554 to amalgamate by letters patent the courts of augmentation and of first fruits and tenths into the exchequer, as the revenue commission of 1552 had suggested. However, the savings that thus ensued were not as great as the commissioners had envisaged, for the bill as finally passed preserved all stipends, pensions or annual payments due on the day of Edward VI's death. (The interest of augmentations officials was protected in the main body of the bill, that of the officials of the other courts in a separate schedule. As Professor Elton has suggested, this may well have been added after the bill had been committed on 29 November to Sir John Baker, a privy councillor who was also chancellor of both the courts of first fruits and tenths and of the exchequer.[44]) Other bills of particular interest to the crown included that for tonnage and poundage, one making valid legal transactions which

---

[41] C. Sturge, *Cuthbert Tunstal* (London, 1938), 204. Elizabeth had taken possession of Durham Place in 1551 (*CPR Edward VI*, 91).

[42] Vertot, II. 270.

[43] HLRO, Original Acts, 1 Mary, sess. 2, 6, 8.

[44] HLRO, Original Acts, 1 Mary, sess. 2, 10; G. R. Elton, *The Tudor Revolution in Government* (Cambridge, 1952), 230–51.

had taken place between 6 July and 1 August, and a bill which
made it a felony for twelve or more men to assemble with the
purpose of changing the law about religion or throwing down
enclosures.[45]

Private interests also took up a considerable amount of parliamentary time. A bill was passed to prevent the excessive importation of foreign-made hats and both the physicians of
London and Merton College, Oxford, received statutes of incorporation.[46] Bills dealing with the leather industry, the
maintenance of tillage and increase of corn, the introduction of
a single system of measurement, and the question of what artificers dwelling in towns might be permitted to sell were all lost,
though many of them were to be successful in subsequent
parliaments. Naturally, after the upheavals of the previous
decades, the new reign began with a spate of bills for the restitution in blood of families that could claim they had suffered
for the catholic cause. The most important of these were for
the duke of Norfolk and for his grandson, Sir Thomas Howard,
but Matthew Arundel, Thomas Stanhope, Sir Marmaduke
Constable, and the daughters of Sir Miles Partrich were also
successful with their petitions.[47] So too was Sir Edward
Seymour, son of the late Protector.[48] The complicated and
continuing matrimonial tangles of the marquis of Northampton produced another private act.[49] Of these measures dealing
with individuals the most significant for the crown was the bill
which confirmed the attainder of the duke of Northumberland
and his associates. To this bill the Commons added a proviso
declaring that 'goods, chattels or debts' that had been 'granted,
given or bargained' away at the time when the treason was
committed were not to be among the things forfeited to the
crown.[50]

In general, the government could feel content with the way
in which the meeting had gone: a great deal of useful business

---

[45] HLRO, Original Acts, 1 Mary, sess. 2, 17, 4, 12.
[46] HLRO, Original Acts, 1 Mary, sess. 2, 11, 9, 22.
[47] HLRO, Original Acts, 1 Mary, sess. 2, 27, 19, 25, 26, 28, 29.
[48] HLRO, Original Acts, 1 Mary, sess. 2, 21.
[49] HLRO, Original Acts, 1 Mary, sess. 2, 30.
[50] HLRO, Original Acts, 1 Mary, sess. 2, 15.

had been done. For Mary herself the situation was less happy. On the day of the dissolution a dog with a shaven crown, representing a tonsured priest, was thrown into the presence chamber,[51] a reminder of the hostility to Rome which had been revealed during the discussions on the bill for the repeal of new treasons. It had also been made clear to the queen that a large number of those who had attended parliament were opposed to the Spanish marriage to which she was now committed. Her doubts and fears were reflected in the speech that the chancellor made at the dissolution, in which he declared that although the queen was by nature merciful she would strive against that nature if she found that those in authority were not fulfilling their duties, and would not hesitate 'to do justice as well upon the nobles as upon the meanest'.[52] On the following day Mary's betrothal was made public.

In the Bodleian Library there is a list of knights and burgesses for this parliament, in the form of a Crown Office List, with the heading 'they which stode for the trewe religion arre signed thus +'.[53] There are crosses against sixty names. On the list is one other comment, beside the name of John Throckmorton, burgess for Old Sarum; this notes that he was 'with the last acte & agaynst the furste'. These comments are not easy to interpret. Both catholics and protestants, of course, thought of their own as being 'true religion', and both used the phrase.[54] However, the use of the term in the 1547 Injunctions perhaps links the phrase more closely with reformers, and it was constantly used in that sense by John Knox.[55] A study of the later beliefs of those whose names are marked on the list tends to support this interpretation of the phrase, although, of course, the men on the list may have had quite different views in the 1550s from

---

[51] *CSP Sp.* XI. 418.

[52] BL Harley MS 6069, fo. 113. See also *CSP Sp.* XI. 418.

[53] Bodley MS e Museo 17. See Appendix B.

[54] Northumberland spoke, on the scaffold, of catholicism as 'true Religion'. (*Queen Jane and Queen Mary*, 18–19.) Pole, when addressing Parliament in Nov. 1554 about the recent past, described it as a time in which 'all lyghte of true religion seamed utterly extincte'. (John Elder's 'Letter', ibid. 157.)

[55] *Iniunccions geue(n) by the moste excellent prince* (London, 1547), sig. A 2; J. Knox, *A faythfull admonition* (Kalykow, 1554) sig. C 3ᵛ; *The first blast . . .* (n.p., 1558) fo. 30ᵛ.

those they revealed in the 1560s and 70s.[56] None the less, on balance it seems probable that it is to protestantism rather than catholicism that the list refers.

When did the men named 'stand' for true religion? To what incident does the list refer? There were a number of religious bills discussed in this parliament: the bill for the repeal of treasons and praemunire, the bill for the repeal of the nine Edwardian statutes, the bill against those disturbing divine service, the bill lost in the Lords against those who 'say not their service', and the bill for the recreation of the bishopric of Durham. An obvious interpretation of the list would be that it records a vote or a division. The clerk did not record any divisions in the course of this parliament, and there are known to have been votes in the Commons only on the bill repealing the nine statutes and on the Durham bill. On 8 November Gardiner told the Imperial ambassador that the bill for the repeal of the nine statutes had been opposed by eighty out of the three hundred and fifty members present:[57] this number does not coincide with the sixty names marked on the Bodley list, and the error is large enough to cast doubt on the link between this debate and the affair to which the list refers. The other occasion on which a vote is known to have been taken is 5 December, when the bill for the bishopric of Durham was

---

[56] Many of the men whose names are marked were described by their bishops in 1564 as 'favourers' of the 1559 settlement. Amongst these are John Lyttleton (*Camden Miscellany IX*, 5, 7), Clement Throckmorton (ibid.), William More (ibid. 56, and see below, 284–6), and Sir John Hercy (ibid. 72). A few also left wills strong enough in tone to reveal more than mere social convention. Richard Blackwell, for example, declared in 1567 that 'by grace we are made safe without the deeds of the law' (*The House of Commons, 1509–1558*, citing PCC 6 Babington) and Sir Thomas Russell thought that the passion of Christ was 'sufficient for the salvation of my soul without any work or works, and my belief is that there is but one God ... and one mediator ... that immaculate lamb Jesus Christ ... so that I accept none in heaven or in earth between me and God' (ibid., citing PCC 8 Pyckering). Gosnold, who had served on the Edwardian commission investigating the case of Bishop Tunstall (*CPR* Philip and Mary, I. 76, 377), asked before his death to be buried with 'as lytell pomp as may be' (*The House of Commons, 1509–1558* citing PCC 11 More) and was described by the first Marian martyr, John Rogers, as 'that worthy man ... who laboured for me' (Foxe, VI. 599). Sir Walter Mildmay's devotion was to lead him in the next reign to found Emmanuel College, Cambridge, specifically to provide a true preaching clergy. Ralph Skinner was to further the protestant cause as dean of Durham (see below, 217–18).

[57] *CSP Sp.* XI. 349.

rejected. It is highly improbable that the men who 'stode for the trewe religion' were the minority who voted in favour of the bill, but if these sixty men were the majority who opposed it, the House was unusually empty.[58] It is not, then, easy to link the Bodley list with either of the religious bills on which a vote is known to have been taken.

Perhaps the list does not refer to a vote, but rather to the positions adopted by those named in the course of some debate? There is no evidence of controversy in the Commons over the bill against those disturbing divine service or that against those who did not go to church, but many commentators, as we have seen, reported bitter arguments over the treasons bill and many of them suggested that the cause of contention was the royal supremacy. If it were to this debate that the Bodley list refers it would solve the problem of the presence on the list of one or two men of conservative religious views, for it was perfectly possible, as the Henrician bishops had shown, to combine an adherence to the royal supremacy with orthodox doctrines. Some of the more conservative figures on the list were, it is true, not wholly committed—Thomas Gawdy, one of the members for Arundel, for example, who was much involved in the heresy persecutions in Essex in Mary's reign, went on to a distinguished legal career under Elizabeth.[59] The presence on the list of Sir Thomas Cornwallis, described by a recent historian as 'a Marian courtier whose hopes were blasted by a Protestant succession',[60] requires some explanation, for as late as 1569 he was found 'to embrace the Catholique faithe nowe termed papistical', without being in 'any weye touched with any disloyalty towards his Prince'.[61] As sheriff of Norfolk and Suffolk in 1553 Cornwallis had played an important part in Mary's triumph over Jane Grey;[62] he was to serve her again in Wyatt's rebellion,[63] and to act as one of the commissioners sent to interrogate Elizabeth at Ashridge.[64] Thus, Cornwallis's inclusion on

[58] See above, 43–5.
[59] J. Strype, *Ecclesiastical Memorials* (London, 1721), III. i. 440; *DNB*.
[60] A. Simpson, *The Wealth of the Gentry* (Cambridge 1961), 143.
[61] Ibid. 173.
[62] 'Vita'. 255–6.
[63] Machyn, 52.
[64] *Queen Jane and Queen Mary*, 63.

the list suggests that some issue other than doctrinal protestantism was raised by the bill or bills opposed by those whose names are marked on the Bodley list.

At the time of the debates on the treasons bill, Renard declared that what he called 'a conspiracy' had been discovered amongst those in possession of former church property, 'who would rather get themselves massacred than let go'.[65] Without taking Renard's words too literally, it may be that anxiety about former church lands, however inappropriate in the light of the bill's specific purpose, unites those on the Bodley list. Some of the men named had accumulated considerable estates from such property: John Gosnold, for example, as solicitor of the court of augmentations, had done very well,[66] and so had Clement Throckmorton, a surveyor of the same court.[67] Robert Beverley had bought extensive properties in Bedfordshire and Hertfordshire in 1548 that had once belonged to the church,[68] whilst Richard Fulmerston had purchased land that was once the property of Holy Trinity, Pontefract, and friary land in Thetford.[69] Of course, many of those sitting in this parliament but not on the Bodley list also owned former church property: Henry Polstead, member for Bletchingley, for instance, had purchased very large amounts of monastic and chantry land in Edward's reign,[70] Sir Thomas Holcroft, who sat for Cheshire, had been involved in the dissolution of the monasteries and bought quantities of their land,[71] and Richard Mytton, knight for Shropshire, had bought land around his principal seat, Halston, from the dissolved monasteries.[72] Sir Thomas Smith, who sat for Grampound, is not marked on the list, yet he had purchased land belonging to the Royal Free Chapel in the Church of All Saints, Derby, and the

[65] *CSP Sp.* XI. 305.

[66] *CPR* Edward VI, I. 145; II. 215.

[67] *CPR* Edward VI, I. 56; IV. 85; V. 28–30; W. C. Richardson, *The History of the Court of Augmentations 1534–1554* (Baton Rouge, 1961), 322 n. 30.

[68] *CPR* Edward VI, I. 387–8.

[69] Ibid. III. 350; T. W. Swales, 'The Redistribution of Monastic Lands in Norfolk at the Dissolution', *Norfolk Archaeology*, XXXIV (1966), 20. See also above, Ch. 3 n. 139.

[70] *CPR* Edward VI, I. 280–4; II. 60–1, 282–6.

[71] *Letters and Papers* XII. ii. 205.

[72] *The House of Commons, 1509–1558.*

manor of Ankerwicke near Eton, which was formed from the lands of a dissolved priory.[73] But the fact that many others in parliament also possessed former ecclesiastical property does not in itself rule out the possibility that the Bodley list may be one of men who opposed the crown's policy because it made them anxious about their landholdings.

The comment against John Throckmorton's name on the Bodley list—'*with* the laste act & agaynst the furste'—remains difficult to explain. It certainly suggests that more than one bill was discussed, but if this were so it is surprising that no record exists in the Journal—the original act repealing Henry and Edward's treason legislation is clearly marked to show that it was sent from the Lords to the Commons,[74] which precludes the possibility that the Lords' original bill had been dropped by the Commons and another substituted. It is not, therefore, possible to explain the comment, for Throckmorton's own career and character are too ambiguous to shed light. He came from a family famous later for both recusancy and puritanism. Two of his brothers, Clement and Nicholas, are marked on the Bodley list but another, Robert, who sat for Warwickshire, is not. Nicholas was to be a persistent critic of Mary's policies; Clement, the friend of the 'gospeller', Edward Underhill,[75] was described in 1564 as a 'favourer' of the protestant religion,[76] as might be expected in the father of Job Throckmorton. John was himself thought to have been responsible for Underhill's release from prison,[77] however, in 1564 his bishop said that he was 'not favorable to this religion',[78] and his wife was an open recusant. John prospered under Mary, for although he surrendered his position as attorney-general,[79] he became a master of requests and, in 1558, justice of Chester.[80] Thus there is no clear indica-

---

[73] M. Dewar, *Sir Thomas Smith*, 31, 67. Smith's name was marked on the Bodley list and then apparently erased.

[74] HLRO, Original Acts, 1 Mary, sess. 1, 1.

[75] *Narratives of the Days of the Reformation*, ed. J. G. Nichols (Camden Society, os, LXXVII, 1859), 163.

[76] *Camden Miscellany IX*, 7.

[77] *Narratives*, 151. See also *APC* IV. 324.

[78] *Camden Miscellany IX*, 17.

[79] *CPR* Philip and Mary, I. 63.

[80] Ibid. IV. 676, 461-2.

tion in his background or career of what led to his being named on the Bodley list.

Indeed, a study of the men whose names are marked on the list reveals that they have little in common beyond a tendency towards protestantism and, as might be expected in men of the parliamentary class, the possession of former ecclesiastical land. Twelve of them were knights of the shire, some of those sitting for borough seats were influential 'outsiders', others were true townsmen: Nicholas Adams, for example, burgess for Dartmouth, had been counsel to the town from 1542,[81] William Hawkins, the father of a famous son, had twice been mayor of Plymouth and was an active exporter of cloth and tin,[82] and Robert Eyre was a merchant at Yarmouth.[83] John Nethermill was a wealthy draper in Coventry, which he represented.[84] Humphrey Coningsby seems to have had a foot in both camps. A gentleman pensioner in 1547,[85] he was given an annuity in 1554 'in consideration of his services to King Henry VIII and King Edward VI in the office of gentleman pensioner for twelve years and more and in the wars of the same kings, in France and Scotland for the same time';[86] more surprising is a licence granted to him in June 1557 to maintain, despite the restrictions of the 1555 act, forty looms, 'in consideration of the great losses and charges lately sustained ... in building two clothing mills ... whereby a great number of artificers may be better able to maintain themselves and their families in continual work':[87] Coningsby was thus a courtier turned business man who received considerable benefits from Mary.

It would, in short, be a mistake to believe that all the men whose names are marked on the Bodley list were amongst the 'outs' of Mary's reign. Several of them prospered at this time, as John Throckmorton and Sir Thomas Cornwallis did. Sir Edward Bray, for instance, became Master of the Ordnance in 1554—he was already joint Constable of the Tower, and after

---

[81] *The House of Commons, 1509–1558*.

[82] J. A. Williamson, *Hawkins of Plymouth* (London, 1949), 29, 36, 37.

[83] W. Edgar Stephens, 'Great Yarmouth under Queen Mary', *Norfolk Archaeology*, XXIX (1946), 145.

[84] *The House of Commons, 1509–1558*.

[85] PRO LC 2/2, fo. 41ᵛ.

[86] *CPR* Philip and Mary, I. 84.

[87] Ibid. III. 487.

the death of Sir John Brydges, Constable.[88] In 1554 Bray was given a chain worth 200 crowns by the Spaniards,[89] a sure sign that he was regarded as of political importance. William Fitzwilliam and his brother John were given offices at Fotheringay and a favourable lease in recognition of their services there;[90] by 1555 William Fitzwilliam was a temporary keeper of the great seal of Ireland, where he was later to become Lord Deputy.[91] John Lyttelton had become keeper of Dudley Castle in September 1553 'in consideration of his service',[92] and in 1557 he was pricked as sheriff of Worcestershire. Francis Goldsmith preserved his position as surveyor of the melting house at the Tower from 1552 to 1559.[93]

Others, however, were less fortunate. Francis Fleming, for instance, had in 1549 been appointed to Thomas Seymour's former office of Master of the Royal Hospital of St Katherine by the Tower. This, however, had formerly been a clerical post, and in July 1554 Mary therefore granted the office to her chaplain, Francis Mallet; Fleming nevertheless did not surrender his patent until 1558, and his nephew and executor was later to claim the revenue of the office between 1554 and 1558.[94] Fleming was also Lieutenant of Ordnance and Munitions at the Tower, a post that he surrendered in June 1557.[95] Thus, although he was compensated for thses losses with a 40-year lease of Romsey Manor,[96] he had not prospered under Mary as he had under Edward. Similarly, John Gosnold had lost his position as solicitor-general to William Cordell in September 1553.[97]

Some of the men on the Bodley list, then, prospered under a catholic queen: others did not. Some were relatives or neighbours, and others had served the same master—both Throckmortons, for instance, had been amongst Catherine Parr's

[88] *CPR* Edward VI, V. 300; Philip and Mary, V. 86–7; *APC* I. 4, 136, 244.
[89] *CSP Sp.* XII. 315.
[90] *CPR* Philip and Mary, I. 327; IV. 416–17.
[91] Ibid. II. 344; *APC* V. 117.
[92] *CPR* Philip and Mary, I. 114.
[93] BL Stowe MS 571, fo. 24.
[94] C. Jamison, *The History of the Royal Hospital of St. Katherine by the Tower of London* (Oxford, 1952), 62, 64, 66.
[95] BL Stowe MS 571, fo. 22; *CPR* Philip and Mary, IV. 302.
[96] *CPR* Philip and Mary, V. 395.
[97] *CPR* Mary, I. 71.

servants in 1547,[98] as had Francis Goldsmith and a man who can probably be identified as William Smethwick,[99] who represented Grampound in 1553. Goldsmith was a friend of Nicholas Throckmorton, and they were said to have helped the future bishop, John Jewel, to escape to the continent in 1554;[100] Goldsmith also, at a later date, acted as London agent for some of the other men on the list, such as William Fitzwilliam.[101] Another old Seymour servant was Matthew Colthurst, but he had prudently transferred his loyalties to the Herberts, for it was 'on the petition of the earl of Pembroke' that he received in 1554 a 21-year lease of the manor of Dunheved, which had belonged to the attainted Thomas Grey,[102] and it was no doubt also through Pembroke's favour that he sat for Wilton in April 1554. Such links were common amongst the small and closely-knit governing class of the mid-sixteenth century, and are of no particular significance in this instance. In the 1540s ambitious young men were likely to attach themselves to the Seymours: when the Seymours fell, they found new patrons. Many of them continued to thrive in the 1550s, despite the change of religious climate: many of them were also to do well in the 1560s.

All that may be said with certainty about the Bodley list, then, is that it refers to an incident in the House of Commons in which some aspect of the queen's religious policy was opposed by a substantial part of the House. This fact, and the list of names, is more important than the question of precisely which bill it was that provoked the opposition, although it seems probable that it was the bill for the repeal of the treason legisla-tion of the reigns of Henry VIII and Edward VI.

---

[98] PRO LC 2/2, fos. 44–46.
[99] Ibid.
[100] C. Garrett, *The Manan Exiles* (Cambridge, 1938), 198.
[101] Northampton RO, Fitzwilliam MSS Catalogue: 749; 50, 51.
[102] Richardson, *History of the Court of Augmentations*, 154 n. 118; *CPR*, Philip and Mary, I. 179.

5

The Parliament of April 1554

WYATT's rebellion left the privy council in a state of disarray. Mary had survived, and her decision to marry Philip was unchanged, but her government was, for a time, dangerously divided. Although her advisers chose to believe, probably with some justification, that religious disaffection had been an important element in the revolt, they recognized that the immediate cause was dislike of the Spanish marriage: those who had furthered the alliance could be accused, therefore, of having permitted the queen to take a path that would lead to inevitable disaster, whilst it could equally plausibly be argued that without the known opposition to the marriage of some members of the council the rebels would not have dared so far. During the early months of 1554 accusations and denunciations reverberated through the council chamber, and the tension was heightened by a general jockeying for position preparatory to the arrival of Philip.

Thus the privy council approached the meeting with fewer settled proposals than usual. Even the question of the venue of the meeting was uncertain. Originally, parliament was summoned to Oxford, according to the French ambassador because this would make it easier both for the queen to call together only those members who were known to favour the Spanish marriage and to coerce those who were opposed to it;[1] the real reason was, of course, that the capital was still unsettled at the time when the writs were sent out. The Londoners, however, expressed their resentment forcefully, and on 15 March a proclamation altered the place of meeting to the capital.[2] At much the same time agreement was finally reached about one or two of the proposals to be laid before the parliament. The first priority was generally recognized to be the ratification of the

[1] Vertot, III. 87.
[2] Hughes and Larkin, *Tudor Royal Proclamations*, II, no. 40.

marriage treaty, and it was also decided that the treason law
should be extended to protect Philip,[3] a move necessitated by
the fact that the 1352 statute had not contemplated the existence of a female ruler and therefore dealt only with a male regnant and a female consort. It was also agreed that the
parliament should pass some act declaring that the recent
rebels had incurred the penalties of forfeiture.[4] But agreement
did not extend to the problem of what should be done about the
Princess Elizabeth, whom many believed to have been at least
cognizant of the rebellion. In late March the council was
reported to be divided even about the question of whether or
not she should be imprisoned in the Tower; when, finally, the
earl of Sussex escorted her there, he turned 'with weeping eyes'
to his companions, Paulet and Hastings, asking them
accusingly, 'What will ye doe, my Lordes ... She was a kinges
daughter and is the queenes syster, and ye have no sufficient
commyssyon so to do.'[5] In addition to Sussex, the group
opposed to any harsh treatment of Elizabeth, and, in particular, to any attempt to exclude her from the throne, included the
earls of Arundel, Derby, and Shrewsbury, and Sir Thomas
Cornwallis.[6] The 'hard-liners', members of Mary's household
such as Rochester, Waldegrave, Southwell, and Englefield,
were, rather surprisingly, headed by Gardiner, whose betrayal
by Courtenay seems to have produced in him a conviction that
the most important consideration was the security of the queen.
No decision on this vital issue was taken before parliament
opened, perhaps because one important factor, the question of
how the courts would treat the charge of treason brought
against those who, like Sir Nicholas Throckmorton, had been
involved in plotting but had not actually resorted to arms, was
as yet unknown:[7] if Throckmorton were found guilty, the way
would be open for the trial of Courtenay and, possibly, even of
Elizabeth herself. Although observers generally believed that
parliament would be asked to disinherit the princess, no specific
decision to do this had in fact been taken.

[3] *CSP Sp.* XII. 201–2.
[4] Ibid.
[5] *Queen Jane and Queen Mary*, 71.
[6] *CSP Sp.* XII. 167, 220.
[7] See below, 98.

There was another major question on which no agreement could be reached in the council. This was religion. Mary herself wanted to renounce formally the title of supreme head of the church, a title which she had ceased to use (it was not, for example, employed in the writs of summons for this second parliament),[8] and proceed towards reunion with Rome. Some of the lay peers, however, led by Paget and Pembroke, believed that the question of reconciliation should be postponed until the political situation was more settled.[9] Gardiner himself did not wish to go ahead as rapidly as did the queen, for he recognized that no steps could be taken towards reunion until some confirmation had been secured for the holders of former ecclesiastical property; however, he did want to introduce measures that would restore the authority of the bishops and church hierarchy. By mid-March he had drafted 'seven or eight clauses' dealing with these matters.[10] Many of Gardiner's colleagues suspected, however, that he was planning to do more than he was prepared to reveal; Paget was later to say that the chancellor had been very secretive and when it had been agreed by the council that no religious measures should be introduced in parliament that would cause trouble, he 'merely read over the headings of some articles on religion, disclosing a few points contained in them'.[11] Just before the opening of parliament tempers were raised, although Renard's story of Paget and Pembroke absenting themselves from the council in order to avoid giving their consent to Gardiner's proposals is not confirmed by the council register.[12]

Despite all this some bills were drafted and some steps were taken to strengthen the government position in the House of Lords. On the day before the formal opening of parliament six new bishops were consecrated: although these appointments were not political ones, the timing of the consecration showed an awareness of temporal considerations. The level of attendance of the new bishops was to be high.[13]

[8] See below, 174.
[9] *CSP Sp.* XII. 168; XIII. 88.
[10] Ibid. XII. 151.
[11] Ibid. XIII. 88.
[12] Ibid. XII. 168.
[13] See above, 22–3.

Gardiner's opening speech on 2 April reflected the confusions within the government. He began by saying that the main object of the meeting was the ratification of the marriage treaty, and stressed the virtues of the Spanish alliance; Wyatt's rebellion, he argued, had been inspired by religious dissent rather than hostility to the alliance.[14] He said that the property of Wyatt and his fellow rebels should be confiscated, the queen's constitutional position better protected, and the treason laws extended to protect Philip.[15] Then, perhaps expressing his own view rather than that of the whole council, Gardiner suggested that since a doubtful succession was always perilous, it would be wise to empower Mary to leave the crown and the government of her realms to whomsoever she pleased, as Henry VIII had been authorized to do.[16] Finally he returned to his own concern, the church. Reports vary about what precisely he said, but the impact made on one of his listeners, Humphrey Moseley, the member for Marlborough, led him to predict that 'religion this Parliamente is lyke to be armed with penall lawes'.[17]

After the Commons had chosen Robert Broke, Recorder of London, as their speaker, business began—in the Lower House with discussion of the laws relating to usury and bullion and with a consideration of bills dealing with cloth-making in Worcester and Norwich, in the Upper House with the bill for the queen's marriage. Despite government fears, the latter was dispatched speedily and easily, passing both Houses by 12 April:[18] Renard wrote a triumphant letter, gloating at the discomfiture of 'the heretics and French, who hoped there would be violent dissent', and Mary herself informed Charles V on 13 April that the parliament was making good progress.[19]

This was correct. At the same time as it read the marriage bill, the Upper House had considered a bill for the restoration of the great bishopric of Durham, which Mary had recreated in

---

[14] *CSP Sp.* XII. 201.
[15] Arch. Étr., XII. fo. 200 (Vertot, III. 151).
[16] Arch. Étr., XIII. fo. 201 (Vertot, III. 153).
[17] Longleat, Thynne MSS, II. fo. 195.
[18] HLRO, Original Acts, 1 Mary, sess. 3, 2.
[19] *CSP Sp.* XII. 216–17.

January by letters patent.[20] On 10 April the bill was passed, with Lord Rich alone registering a formal protest. A similar measure had passed the Lords in the previous December, only to be rejected by the Commons: this time, the bishop of Durham himself appeared in the Lower House to plead his cause, and, although there was a division, the bill was passed on 19 April by 201 votes to 120.[21] The opposition to the bill was almost certainly entirely secular: as the preamble to the statute stated, the Edwardian dissolution had been the work of men anxious to enrich themselves and their friends, and they were not now going to hand back their gains without a struggle. The most successful defender of his spoils was the earl of Shrewsbury, whose tenure of the bishop's London House, Coldharbour in Thames Street, and of other property, was confirmed in the bill. (Coldharbour had been given to the bishop in 1536 in partial compensation for the loss of Durham Place.[22]) Others, despite valiant efforts, were less fortunate. Sir Francis Jobson, elected for Colchester, attempted to secure the large grant he had received through his wife, who was Northumberland's half-sister, by a protective clause similar to that which had been added to the earlier bill on behalf of the Princess Elizabeth. However, he had in the end to be content with a formal request to the bishop from the House of Commons asking for favourable treatment for him.[23] On 17 and 18 April counsel for Newcastle, which had in a statute subsidiary to the main Edwardian act annexed Gateshead and its profitable tolls,[24] were heard in the Commons: the bill itself gave little recognition to the city's claims, but it has been plausibly argued that the favourable lease of Salt Meadow that the corporation secured from the bishop the next year was the price exacted for the withdrawal of opposition to the bill.[25] Opposition almost

---

[20] The Edwardian dissolution was affected by 7 Edward VI, c. 12. The letters patent of 1554 are in *CPR*, Mary, I. 378. On this see F. Heal, *Of Prelates and Princes* (Cambridge, 1980), 153–4.

[21] HLRO, Original Acts, 1 Mary, sess. 3, 3.

[22] *CPR* Edward VI, V. 230; Sturge, *Cuthbert Tunstal*, 204.

[23] *CJ* 18, 19 Apr. 1554. For his grant from the lands of the bishopric see *CPR* Edward VI, V. 133.

[24] 7 Edward VI, c. 10.

[25] R. Welford, *History of Newcastle and Gateshead* (London, 1885), II. 312.

certainly also came from men like Bertram Anderson, one of the burgesses for Newcastle, who in May 1553 had been granted a 21-year lease of the Elswick coal mines, upon which he was to build a considerable fortune.[26] It may also have come from those, like Rich, who owned no Durham land but were anxious about the general principle of restitution.

It was probably this widely felt fear that led to the introduction into the Commons on 20 April, the day after the Durham bill had been passed, of a proposal that would have prevented 'the bishop of Rome' or any other bishop from taking legal action to recover abbey lands. The bill passed the Commons on 27 April and was read in the Lords on 28 and 30 April, after which it disappeared. Whether this was a move by those who were worried about secularized property to consolidate their position or whether it was a government bill meant to soothe their fears is not clear, although the fact that the bill was committed to the speaker during its passage through the Lower House and the existence of an earlier rumour that Gardiner wished to see the introduction of some such measure[27] suggest government initiative.

Meanwhile, a rather curious bill declaring that the queen's power was identical to that of her male predecessors was passed.[28] In the Lower House, where it began, it was the occasion for a long speech by Ralph Skinner, Member for Penryn and a Reformed scholar, drawing attention to the odd behaviour of the government in proposing a statute to deal with a doubt that had never yet been voiced.[29] If an account of the incident written by William Fleetwood twenty years later is to be believed, Skinner argued that this 'needless bill' could be a sub-

[26] 'Members of Parliament for Newcastle-upon-Tyne, 1529–58', *Archaeologica Aeliana*, XLV (1937).
[27] *CSP Sp.* XII. 170. See also a letter to del Monte of 7 May in Vatican Arch. Flandra, II, fo. 77, cited in D. R. Ancel, 'La Réconciliation de l'Angleterre avec le Saint-Siège', *Revue d'histoire ecclésiastique*, X (1909), 778.
[28] HLRO, Original Acts, 1 Mary, sess. 3, 1.
[29] BL Harley MS 6234. This is an account by Fleetwood of a presumably fictitious journey—'Itinerarium ad Windsor'—during which he, Lord Buckhurst, and the earl of Leicester whiled away the time discussing the regality of English kings. (See also W. H. Dunham, 'Regal Power and the Rule of Law', *Journal of British Studies*, III (1963–4), 45–6.) Fleetwood was not a member of this parliament, nor is there any other evidence that Skinner himself sat, but the returns for Penryn, which he represented in Oct. 1553, are missing. For Skinner, see below, 217–18.

terfuge, whereby Mary was released from the provisions of Magna Carta and the Charter of the Forest, the 'sacred Charters' that God had provided for his people of England. Skinner declared that the queen might come, in time, to resemble William the Conqueror, 'who seized the land*e*s of the Englishe people, and did giue the same vnto strangers', or Edward I, who 'conquered all Wales, and then disposed of all men's lands in Wales 'at his owne Pleasure'. Despite these fears, the bill was passed in the Commons on 10 April, and in the Lords two days later. The bill is certainly a somewhat odd one, which might have been looked for in the first parliament of the reign, if at all. Fleetwood says that the bill was drawn up by Gardiner in an attempt to thwart some of the queen's advisers who had informed her that since no extant statute mentioned the name of a queen she was not bound by them, but Gardiner's comments in his opening speech about the uncertainties of the queen's constitutional position make it more probable that the bill arose out of a genuine desire to forestall difficulties.

None the less, the rift between Gardiner and some of the other councillors was widening. On 9 April a bill had been read in the Lower House 'to revive certain statutes repealed, touching heresies and Lollardies', to renew, that is, the medieval heresy laws. This was Gardiner's doing. On 12 April the Imperial ambassador reported that discord in the council had increased as a result of the chancellor's desire to introduce a bill 'concerning religion and the Pope's authority, establishing a form of Inquisition against the heretics, setting up again the power of the bishops and dealing with the Pope's authority': Paget, he wrote, considered that the bill should be delayed to a later parliament in order not to alienate the people and nobility.[30] The next day the bill had a second reading and was committed to a privy councillor, Sir Edward Hastings. Convocation meanwhile adjourned to Oxford to hear the disputation between the catholics and three of the 'heretics' against whom the bill was directed, Latimer, Ridley, and Cranmer.[31] On 17 April two new bills were read in the Commons. One, for the revival of Henry VIII's act of six articles, disappeared, but the

[30] *CSP Sp.* XII. 216.
[31] Foxe, VI. 439–520.

other, for the 'avoiding of erroneous opinions and books containing heresies', which was probably a redrafting of the original heresy bill, was engrossed on 20 April and passed by the Lower House on 25 April. This seems to have done little to appease Paget, who had written to the Imperial ambassador about 19 April, begging him to intervene with the queen and persuade her to dissolve parliament.[32]

Things were, indeed, beginning to look bleak. On 17 April a London jury unexpectedly acquitted Sir Nicholas Throckmorton, and his release was greeted by scenes of public rejoicing.[33] The queen was furious, and the jury, summoned before Star Chamber on 25 April, spent the remainder of the year in prison.[34] On the same day the bill extending to Philip the protection of the treason laws received its first reading in the Lords. The next day, 18 April, it was committed to Arundel, Shrewsbury, Rich, Paget, and the bishops of London and Worcester. It was passed on 24 April. However, it was passed in a much attenuated form, for instead of making it a treasonable offence even to plot to bring about the death of the queen's husband, the bill declared only that the physical act of taking up arms against him was to be considered treason.[35] The bill was never read in the Commons. The opposition to the original draft seems to have been led by Paget, the man who had most favoured the Spanish alliance and was later to be one of Philip's closest advisers.[36] What had caused this bizarre behaviour?

During the committe stage of the bill Paget was in a ferment of anxiety and anger. He was furious with Gardiner for introducing the heresy bill, and seems to have feared that the chancellor might commit the supreme folly of bringing in a bill to disinherit Elizabeth.[37] He perhaps simply lashed out, unthinkingly. Perhaps he felt that by exposing the fact that many peers still harboured anxieties about Philip he could warn Gardiner off the minefield of the Princess's position. Per-

[32] *CSP Sp.* XII. 219–20.
[33] Ibid. 221.
[34] T. B. Howell, *A Complete Collection of State Trials* (London, 1816), I. 900–1.
[35] *CSP Sp.* XII. 221.
[36] Ibid. 230, 251.
[37] Ibid. 220.

haps, and this may be the most likely explanation, he was simply demonstrating that he had a substantial following in the Upper House, a fact that was to be revealed even more clearly on 26 April, when, despite this shot across the bows, the bill for the revival of the heresy bills was introduced into the Lords.

It was not received sympathetically. On 27 April Renard reported that many peers disliked the capital penalty stipulated by the bill.[38] On 1 May, by a majority, the House rejected the bill. Paget subsequently admitted that he had led the opposition to the proposal, explaining that he had been persuaded by Lord Rich that the real purpose of the bill was to authorize the seizure of former church property.[39] Some of the other peers involved told Renard that they in their turn had been warned by Paget that the object of the measure was to take from them their secularized lands and to enable the bishops to behave towards them in a vindictive way.[40] They had not, they declared, meant to further heretics or heresy by their action. The bill has not been preserved, and there is nothing in the—presumably—similar bill that was enacted in the next parliament[41] to explain why the proposal should have aroused fears about former ecclesiastical property. Perhaps the revival of an act declaring forfeit the goods of an unrepentant heretic was mildly disturbing, but a general anxiety about taking any step towards reconciliation with Rome before the pope had given a definite undertaking about the security of secularized property seems to have been more important: on 23 April Noailles had predicted that Mary's plans for restoring England to the Roman obedience and returning to the bishops their former property and powers would founder on the unwillingness of the English nobility to be parted from their church land.[42] Gardiner had himself recognized how central the issue was when he had urged Pole to write to parliament reassuring the property-owners,[43] but he was, obviously, unprepared for the peers' tendency to see a threat where none existed.

[38] Ibid. 228, 230.
[39] Ibid. 251.
[40] Ibid. 240.
[41] 1 & 2 Philip and Mary, c. 6.
[42] Arch. Étr., XII. fo. 208ᵛ (Vertot, III. 174).
[43] *The Letters of Stephen Gardiner*, 464–6.

There is no need to doubt the peers' disavowal of any desire to protect heresy: it was, after all, a House almost unchanged in composition that six months later passed the heresy legislation under which nearly three hundred men and women were to suffer death. The Lords' treatment of other religious measures introduced in this parliament reveals no protestant bias. For instance, the House speedily dispatched a bill 'for the calling in of certain pensions granted out to religious persons who since the time of their dereignment [i.e., discharge from religious orders] have chanced to marry'.[44] This vindictive measure was read in the Commons on 20 and 24 April, and a new bill to the same purpose was read on 28 April, after which no further mention of it is made. The Lords did not reveal, in this instance, any sympathy for the very small number of ex-religious in receipt of a pension who had married under the permissive legislation of the previous reign. It is true that another, and rather mysterious, bill 'for Lollardy, against eating of flesh on divers days forbidden', having passed the Commons, was lost in the Lords, but the reason for this seems to have been no more than the pressure of time: the bill was read on 2 and 4 May, and parliament was dissolved on 5 May. If the peers had shown themselves inherently sympathetic to Lollardy or protestantism on 1 May, when the heresy bill was rejected, it is inconceivable that this bill would have received two formal readings within such a short time.

An analysis of the religious alignments of those present in the House of Lords undertaken by Graves in 1973 further indicates that the conservatives were in the ascendant.[45] All but one of the twelve bishops attending the meeting were stout catholics, and they were backed by a number of devout laymen who had opposed the religious changes of the previous reign, men like Derby, Morley, and Windsor. The 'politiques' such as Paget and Pembroke were in the minority, although it was a politi-

---

[44] Passed on 16 Apr., after readings on 11 and 12. On the problems presented by such pensions, see A. G. Dickens, 'The Edwardian Arrears in Augmentation payments and the Problem of the ex-Religious', *EHR* LV (1940).

[45] M. A. R. Graves, 'The House of Lords and the Politics of Opposition, April–May 1554', in *W. P. Morrell: A Tribute* ed. G. A. Wood and P. S. O'Connor (Dunedin, 1973), 8–15.

cally experienced and articulate minority. The reason why they were able to swing some, at least, of the conservatives behind them over the heresy bill must have been, as they told Mary, because their anxiety about the future of secularized property was acute. Lord Rich is an important figure here. His personal religious tendencies appear to have been conservative, although he was prepared to conform under Edward. However, he had accumulated a great deal of church land through the court of augmentations in Henry VIII's reign and he continued to acquire property under Edward VI, notably from the bishopric of London. His protest against the Durham bill and the part he played in the rejection of the heresy bill suggests that he was at this time in a state of great uneasiness about the future of his lands. These anxieties were undoubtedly common to most peers—as the Imperial ambassador once pointed out, the catholics had bought even more church land than had the protestants.[46]

All this explains how it was possible for Paget to wreck two important pieces of legislation, but it does not fully explain why he chose to do so. Although he later admitted that 'one of the English bishops had formerly led him into error on the question of Transsubstantiation',[47] and was to come under suspicion shortly after parliament ended because he was an associate of the undoubtedly protestant Hoby,[48] Paget was not, in fact, at all interested in the minutiae of theology. Religion, to Paget, was a social cement: in 1549 he had told Somerset:

societe in a realme dothe consiste and is maynteyned by fearefull love to god and the prince whïch procedeth by meane of religion and lawe / and these two or one wantinge farewell all juste societie, farewell kinge, gouernement, Justice and all other Vertue / and in cometh communalitie, sensualitie, iniquytie, ravyn and all other kinde of vice and myscheif.[49]

He accepted that the restoration of the old faith might, in time,

---

[46] *CSP Sp.* XIII. 46.
[47] Ibid. XII. 200.
[48] Ibid. 231.
[49] Northampton RO, Fitzwilliam (Molton) MSS, Paget Letter Book, July 1549.

actually improve the stability of the realm, but he believed that the restoration should be undertaken gradually and not by the policy of 'blood and fire' that he attributed to Gardiner. In late April and early May Paget, always prone to panic, believed that Gardiner's policies would lead to political disaster and that they must therefore be stopped at almost any price.

Of course, ambition played a part too. Paget had backed the winner in the marriage negotiations but he realized that Mary did not trust him as she did the councillors who had earlier been members of her household, such as Hastings or Rochester, or even as she did the Henrician catholics like Gardiner. Paget was never to be secure in her favour—in 1556, for example, he was in deep disgrace and reduced to approaching the queen through one of her gentlemen, James Bassett.[50] He later depended for his position on the support of Philip, who seems to have found in Paget one of the few of Mary's advisers with any understanding of and interest in European affairs. In the spring of 1554 he was perhaps trying to show the queen not only that his advice was better than that of his rivals such as Gardiner— something which she did, however reluctantly, come to admit—but that he had a powerful following and could be a great nuisance if his advice was disregarded.

Whatever the justification, the loss of the heresy bill left the government in a quandary. The scene had been set for the trial and, if necessary, the death of the heretic bishops, but the crown now found itself, despite Gardiner's brave words to the Imperial ambassador,[51] without the authority to act against them. It would be ten months before the burnings began.

Moreover, further troubles were to come, although Paget was not, this time, to be the agent of Mary's humiliation. The bill for the attainder of Suffolk, Wyatt, and their associates, one of the few measures upon which the whole council was in agreement, was not introduced, surprisingly, until 23 April: more surprisingly still, it was introduced in the Commons. There it passed speedily enough, although there was sufficient debate to merit two third readings. Because of the pressure of time the Lords then had to fit all three readings into one day, 4 May.

[50] Plas Newydd, Anglesey, Paget Papers, Box 2 nos. 25, 26.
[51] *CSP Sp*. XII. 240.

They passed the bill, but asked that the last seventeen lines, beginning 'forasmuch as divers of the same traitors', should be discarded. When the bill was next day returned to the Commons the clerk reported that 'upon the articles touching any high treason hereafter to be committed, the Lords required, that that clause might be put out: whereupon it came to the question, and the more part agreed, that that clause should not be put out of the bill ... which clause was to forfeit entailed lands.' The deadlock was not resolved before the session was ended that same afternoon.

The whole episode is mysterious. Although the clerk's words imply that the purpose of the clause to which the Lords objected was to secure the forfeiture of entailed lands, such land was in fact already covered by existing law.[52] It seems probable that Renard's report that Paget and those who opposed the bill were doing so because they wished to prevent the confiscation of land left by will is nearer to the truth.[53] There is little to be learnt from the attainder bill that was passed in the next parliament, which simply states that all estates, goods, and chattels were forfeit.[54] Even so, Lords Bath, Montagu, Stourton, Lumley, Evers, Wharton and Paget still registered a formal objection.[55]

At the end of the parliament Mary was clearly angry with the peers despite their evident contrition:[56] the master of the horse, Hastings, warned one suppliant that the time was not ripe for his petition, the queen 'being displeased with proceedings in parliament'.[57] Although the marriage treaty had been confirmed, Mary had been forced to abandon any plan she may have had for disinheriting Elizabeth and the protection of the treason law was not yet available for Philip. She had not been able to rid herself formally of the hated supreme head-

---

[52] Briefly, the Marian act of 1553 restoring the treason law to its 1352 basis should have prevented land in fee tail being seized. However, the judges continued to argue that entailed land was seizable. See J. Bellamy, *The Tudor Law of Treason* (London & Toronto, 1979), 59–60, 210–11, and below, 119.

[53] *CSP Sp.* XII. 220–1.

[54] HLRO, Original Acts, 1 & 2 Philip and Mary, 21.

[55] *LJ* 8 Jan. 1555.

[56] *CSP Sp.* XIII. 242.

[57] *The Papers of George Wyatt Esquire*, ed. D. M. Loades (Camden Fourth Series, 5 1968), 194.

ship.[58] But fourteen statutes had been passed, most of them dealing with specific economic problems. The most important of these, promulgated by the members for Worcester, amended a statute of 1552 which had enforced a seven-year apprenticeship on those involved in the making of broadcloth.[59] A number of statutes also dealt with private matters. One of them repealed an act of 1549 by which the parishes of Ongar and Greensted in Essex had been united;[60] somewhat in the style of the Durham bishopric act, the preamble to this measure declares that the unification had been the work of William Morice, who had been a burgess for Downton in the first Edwardian parliament, 'inordinately seeking his own private lucre and profit therein'. William Morice was the brother of Cranmer's secretary, Ralph, and there may have been religious undertones to the dispute; on the other hand, the fact that the privy council was forced a few weeks later to order the inhabitants of Ongar and Morice's widow to desist from their attempts to pull down the church walls suggests a bitter local rivalry.[61]

The interest of this parliament for the historian lies in the spilling over of court rivalries into the parliament chamber. However, although Paget was in disgrace with the queen for some time afterwards, what happened in parliament did not seriously imperil the stability of the regime. Yet, although Paget's activities had little long-term effect, two aspects of the incidents in which he was involved are worthy of note. One is the desperate anxiety of laymen about the future of their former church property, anxiety that made it possible for Paget and his associates to secure the rejection of the heresy bill on grounds that were almost certainly spurious. The second is that it was in the House of Lords, and not in the Commons, that these stirring events took place.

[58] The Venetian ambassador later reported that 'when she wished Parliament to pass an act rescinding it (the supreme headship), the bill was rejected, it being merely carried that she was at liberty to assume the title or not, in order not to utterly deprive her successors of it'. (*CSP Ven.* V. 534). However, no formal proposal appears to have been made.

[59] HLRO, Original Acts, 1 Mary, sess. 3, 6, amending 5 and 6 Edward VI, c. 8.

[60] HLRO, Original Acts, 1 Mary, sess. 3, 8, repealing 5 and 6 Edward VI, c. 15.

[61] *APC* V. 54. For William Morice see *DNB sub* Morice, Ralph.

6

The Parliament of November 1554

THE marriage between Mary Tudor and Philip of Spain took place at Winchester on 25 July 1554. Philip and his train did their best to appease the English, drinking beer and putting on a demonstration of cane-fighting, and the first few months of the alliance passed off well. Reassured, Charles V was now willing to lend his assistance to the negotiations that would lead to England's reconciliation with Rome: Pole's complaints now met with some response other than procrastination. There were, however, still substantial problems to be overcome. In July 1554 the pope had given Pole a brief empowering him 'to treat, discuss, agree, compound and dispense and do in a permanent way all that may be necessary and opportune so that those in possession of ecclesiastical property, moveables and immoveables, may without scruple retain that property hereafter',[1] but the English privy council, after carefully examining a copy of the brief sent by Renard from Brussels, decided that these instructions were not precise enough.[2] Renard talked to Pole in Brussels, Philip consulted the privy council, theologians and members of the council learned were brought in, and finally a letter was sent to the pope asking for an amplification of the original brief.[3] It was not, therefore, until 3 November that the council formally invited Pole to England.[4] None the less, it was widely recognized that the reconciliation would be the main task of parliament when it met, and a prayer for the pope was actually included in the opening ceremonies on 12 November; the chancellor explained in his address that parliament had been summoned for the confirmation of true religion, and the first piece of business was a bill to reverse Pole's

---

[1] Printed in P. Hughes, *The Reformation in England* (London, 1963), II. 223.
[2] *CSP Sp.* XIII. 93.
[3] Ibid.; *CSP Ven.* V. 581, 585.
[4] *CSP Sp.* XIII. 78.

attainder.[5] This passed both Houses rapidly, and the king and queen attended parliament on 22 November to give the bill their assent.[6] Two days later Pole took up residence at Lambeth.[7]

On 28 November parliament was summoned to court to hear Pole explain his mission. Earlier that day a Te Deum had been sung at St Paul's in thanksgiving for the queen's pregnancy,[8] and Pole referred to the conception in his speech.[9] He sat with the king and queen and paid both fulsome compliments, describing the preservation of Mary, 'a virgin, helpless, naked and unarmed', as miraculous, and Philip as a king 'of great might, armour and force' who had yet come to England 'by the way of love and amity'. He went on to compare Charles V, Philip's father, to David; despite his endeavours David had not been able to rebuild the temple at Jerusalem, but had been forced to leave the task to his son, Solomon, and the emperor, with all his travail for the church, had been forced to leave to his son the task of restoring England to the Roman obedience. But, the Cardinal went on, although great, the power of Philip and Mary was merely secular: he himself had come with the authority of the keys. 'My commission is not of prejudice to anye persone', he said: 'I cum not to destroy but to build. I cum to reconcyle, not to condemne. I cum not to compel, but to call againe'. He declared that 'all matters that be past' were as things 'cast into the sea of forgetfulnes'. Nevertheless, there were certain necessary formalities: just as he personally could not enter the realm until his attainder had been reversed, so England could not be reconciled until parliament had repealed the statutes by which she had been divorced from the Holy See.

Encouraged, no doubt, by Pole's assertion that 'this iland first of all ilandes received the light of Christes religion', the two Houses returned to Westminster. The next day the Lords asked for a Commons committee to join the chancellor, four other bishops, four earls, and four barons in drawing up a supplica-

[5] Machyn, 74; *A Chronicle of the Grey Friars of London*, II. 254; *CJ* 12 Nov.
[6] HLRO, Original Act, 1 & 2 Philip and Mary, 18.
[7] Machyn, 75–6; Wriothesley, II. 123.
[8] Machyn, 76; Wriothesley, II. 123–4.
[9] Reported in *John Elder's Letter*, reprinted as an appendix to *Queen Jane and Queen Mary*, 153–9.

tion to the king and queen asking that the realm should again seek union with Rome.[10] This supplication was drafted and agreed upon in one day. On 30 November it was presented to Philip and Mary. Then, with all those present 'sitting as on their knees', it was offered to Pole.[11] After he had 'in a few words given thanks to God', the Cardinal pronounced his blessing. Whilst he spoke there was 'a marvellous silence', and then those present 'cried with one voice, Amen'.[12]

As Pole had pointed out on 28 November, however, there were certain formalities still needed. On 4 December the Upper House again asked the Commons to join in a committee, and the privy councillors in the House together with twenty-one other members[13] were dispatched to assist Paulet, Arundel, Pembroke, Wharton, Paget, North, and the bishops of Durham, Worcester, and Lincoln in the preliminary drafting of the great bill that was to reunite England with Rome.[14] (The presence amongst Paget's papers of a list of 'certain acts and articles of acts and statutes to be repealed' suggests that he played a particularly important part in the formulation of the bill,[15] whilst Petre, one of the privy councillors sitting in the Commons, seems to have acted as an intermediary with Pole.[16]) The bill thus drafted had its first reading, in the Lords, on 20 December, was engrossed on 24 and finally passed on 26.[17]

This delay in what had previously been a swift and easy process was significant. Between the opening of parliament on 12 November and the first reading of the bill of repeal extraordinary unanimity seemed to prevail. Only once, when the presentation of the supplication was being discussed, had any hint of opposition appeared: Sir Ralph Bagnall, who represented Newcastle under Lyme, supported only, according to a

[10] *CJ* 29 Nov.
[11] Elder, op. cit. 160.
[12] 'Descriptio reductionis Angliae ad Catholicam unitatem', in *Epistolae Reginaldi Poli*, V. 313.
[13] *CJ* 4 Dec.
[14] *LJ* 6 Dec.
[15] Plas Newydd, Anglesey, Paget Papers, Box I Miscellaneous, no. 7.
[16] Emmison, *Tudor Secretary: Sir William Petre at Court and Home*, 184.
[17] 1 & 2 Philip and Mary, c. 8. Something has gone wrong with the clerk's dating in Christmas week.

contemporary Italian account,[18] by one silent associate, declared that he had scruples about agreeing to the supplication, since he had at an earlier date taken an oath 'to the opposite effect'.[19] He had, he said, 'sworne *the* contrary to king henry the eight, w*hich* was a worthy prince, *and* labourid xxv yeres before he could abolysh him [the pope]':[20] Bagnall's life shows no evidence of devoted protestantism, and the reason for his objection may simply have been, as his words suggest, loyalty to the memory of a man whom he had grown to admire when he had been one of a circle of dashing young courtiers.[21] His speech was greeted with laughter, and seeing that general opinion was against him, Bagnall gave in the next day.

Yet, beneath the surface, the issue of lay ownership of former ecclesiastical property still lurked. When, on 25 November, the dean of St Paul's, Feckenham, preached a sermon on the subject in which he declared that the owners of such property were under a moral obligation to return it the council was embarrassed and outraged: Feckenham was summoned and asked to explain himself.[22] The council's embarrassment was the greater because it was widely—and correctly—believed that Feckenham was expressing the views of the legate himself; Pole remained adamant that England should return to the Roman obedience before seeking to obtain concessions, even though Philip himself had visited the Cardinal shortly after his arrival in the country and had attempted to make him understand that without some firm agreement on this issue no reconciliation would be possible.[23]

Pole's views added to the problem of drafting this section of the bill. According to the Imperial ambassador, three separate schools of thought existed about whether the papal dispensation should be included in the bill or not: that of Pole himself, who believed that to include the dispensation would make it appear that the realm's return to the Roman obedience had been purchased by this concession, that of the holders of former

---

[18] *Copia d'una Lettera d'Inghilterra nella quale narra l'entrata del Rever [endissimo] Cardinale Polo . . . in Inghilterra* (Milan, 1554), sig. A 4.
[19] 'Descriptio reductionis', 314.
[20] BL Harley MS 419, fo. 132.
[21] See below, 221–2.
[22] *CSP Sp.* XIII. 108; Machyn, 76.
[23] *CSP Sp.* XIII. 119–20.

ecclesiastical property who thought that their title would be more secure if the dispensation were embodied in an act of parliament, and that of the lawyers, who argued that it was unnecessary to include the dispensation since English kings enjoyed complete sovereignty and jurisdiction over church lands within their kingdom.[24]

Whilst these uncertainties prevailed the bill hung fire. Finally, in an attempt to resolve the problems, a meeting was arranged for 21 December between Pole and the queen, Gardiner and other privy councillors, and various members of the council learned. Pole's secretary, Priuli, wrote a long—and hitherto largely ignored[25]—account of this meeting, which reveals very clearly how close the Cardinal's stubbornness came to wrecking the whole business. The lawyers began by arguing that since the realm of England was 'a perfect political body', it was unthinkable that any foreigner, even the pope, could intervene over the disposal of property; to support their argument they produced a number of historical illustrations, such as the case of Edward III, who had frequently quarrelled with the pope over this very question. They pointed out that parliament had, in fact, dictated what was to be done with the property of the church during the previous two reigns, a comment that infuriated Mary into declaring that if her subjects intended to be guided by what had been done in Edward's reign then she would abdicate. At this, Gardiner intervened and in a long discourse, full of examples and references to the statutes of the realm—Priuli unfortunately does not give the details—tried to prove that what the lawyers had said was mistaken. Gardiner's efforts were vitiated by a somewhat malicious speech by Pole, in which he declared that at last he could understand the difficulties with which princes were confronted, and could even feel some compassion for Henry VIII himself, since it seemed that spiritual advisers were prepared to leave all questions to be decided by temporal councillors: the result, inevitably, was something like the spoliation of the monasteries.

---

[24] Ibid. 125. See also p. 130.
[25] BL Additional MS 41577, fos. 161–166. There is a short summary of the document in J. H. Crehan, 'The Return to Obedience: New Judgement on Cardinal Pole', *The Month*, NS, XIV (1955), 221–9.

Of course, he said, lawyers found it hard to understand matters higher than those of the craft in which they had been trained, but it was not impossible for them: they could not be forgiven the sins of the past simply on grounds of ignorance. Yes, he went on, England was a perfect political body, but he hoped that it was also a Christian one, and therefore subject to the pope, to whom belonged jurisdiction not only in matters of faith but also over temporal goods that had been freely dedicated to the service of God. Even in the Roman republic, he said, it had been recognized that once goods had been dedicated to the worship of the gods they could not afterwards be applied to profane use: when Cicero was in exile, for instance, his house had been dedicated to the gods and it had proved extremely difficult for him to recover it on his return and was, indeed, only possible at all because the rites of consecration were not complete.

Having dealt with the lawyers, Pole then turned to laymen. He spoke of the sacrilege that had recently taken place, and the evidence of God's wrath that had been displayed towards Cromwell, Somerset, and Northumberland. (However, he declared, the preservation from sin of Fisher and More, the accession of Mary, and the willingness of the pope to forgive England proved that all was not lost.) He told the nobles who were present that they should show true penitence and a sincere desire for the restoration of religion, reminding them that in the time of Innocent III the Lateran Council, at which English envoys were present, had stated that no temporal power could interfere with ecclesiastical property. He quoted other precedents including incidents from the reign of Edward III which seemed to him to prove the contrary to what the lawyers had suggested, and cited the example of Wolsey, who had received a papal dispensation when he wanted to dissolve some monastic houses for the foundation of his college in Oxford. Above all, he said, his audience should beware of adopting an attitude to the pope that was one of mocking homage, like that of those who cried 'Hail, king of the Jews', as they crucified Christ. It was a terrible thing to put supplications, intercession, and papal bulls into statutes, and it would make the title of the holders of former church property less, not more, secure, for their claim would rest only on the authority of parliament rather than on that of the Holy See; indeed, parliament, by trying to prove that it had authority over this kind of property, was doing the opposite of returning to obedience. After he finished Mary spoke again, declaring that no position other than Pole's was tenable. This intervention appears to have dismayed her councillors, and the meeting was adjourned until the next day.

Things were calmer on 22 December. The bill was examined clause by clause. Pole won a small triumph when it was agreed that the period during which property might be given to the church without incurring the penalties of mortmain should be extended from seven to twenty years, and he also obtained an assurance that property that had once belonged to the church might be restored even after that date without penalty, although there was considerable argument about this. Some questions were still unresolved at the end of the meeting, but Priuli added a postscript on 24 December saying that it had finally been agreed that the supplication about former church property should be included in the bill.[26] Pole had lost, but the lawyers who had argued that there was no need for the dispensation had also been forced to concede to the anxieties of the property-owners.

Having passed the Lords the bill was read in the Commons for the first time on 27 December, the feast of St John the Evangelist, when it was committed, very surprisingly, to Henry Carey (Elizabeth's cousin, later Baron Hunsdon). It was read again on 29 December, discussed on 31 and on 2 January and finally passed on 3 January 1555.[27] In its final form it consisted of a preamble declaring that the realm of England 'after sundry long and grievous plagues and calamities' was to be restored to the bosom of the church; the petition presented by parliament on 30 November; a list of nineteen acts to be repealed,[28] and the two supplications about which there had been so much controversy, one from parliament and one from convocation. In the first of the supplications parliament asked the pope for a

---

[26] The postscript is published as an anonymous fragment in *CSP Ven.* V. 588.
[27] 1 & 2 Philip and Mary, c. 8.
[28] 21 Henry VIII, c. 13; 23 Henry VIII, c. 9; 24 Henry VIII, c. 12; 23 Henry VIII, c. 20; 25 Henry VIII, c. 19; 25 Henry VIII, c. 20; 25 Henry VIII, c. 21; 26 Henry VIII, c. 1; 26 Henry VIII, c. 14; 27 Henry VIII, c. 15; 28 Henry VIII, c. 10; 28 Henry VIII, c. 16; 28 Henry VIII, c. 7; 31 Henry VIII, c. 9; 32 Henry VIII, c. 38; 35 Henry VIII, c. 3; 35 Henry VIII, c. 1; 37 Henry VIII, c. 17; 1 Edward VI, c. 12.

dispensation to cover religious foundations instituted after the schism, marriages that had been solemnized between persons whom Rome would consider to have been related by forbidden degrees of consanguinity, appointments made and judicial decisions taken during the same period. This supplication also asked that church property that had passed into lay hands might be allowed to remain there, 'clear from all dangers of censures of the church'. Convocation's supplication, which follows, declares that since any attempt to recover this property would disturb 'the peace and tranquillity' of the realm and 'the unity' of the church, it supported the lay petition. (It also requested the restoration of ecclesiastical jurisdiction.) Following the two supplications is Pole's dispensation, which is dated 24 December, that is, the day after the final discussions described by Priuli, and the day on which the whole bill received its second reading in the House of Lords: the dispensation is in a different hand from the remainder of the document and has clearly been inserted into the text.[29] It grants the requests made in the two supplications, with the proviso that the new bishoprics should be confirmed by the pope. But Pole had not given way entirely over the issue of former church property. The dispensation required those in possession of church goods such as plate to return them, and the consciences of the owners of former church lands were not absolved although they were, of course, freed from the risk of ecclesiastical censure.[30] This limitation undoubtedly contributed to the continuing uncertainty felt by many holders of such land.

The dispensation is followed by a statement declaring that it should be regarded as part of the law of the land—a defeat for Pole, who had so vehemently protested on 21 December that it would be a wicked thing if a papal dispensation were to be reduced to the status of a parliamentary statute. Worse, after describing the statutes of Henry and Edward's reigns by which the lands had come into lay ownership, the bill goes on to declare that because title to land in England is always based

[29] HLRO, Original Acts, 1 & 2 Philip and Mary, 8.
[30] *CSP Ven.* VI. i. 10; W. Schenk, *Reginald Pole, Cardinal of England* (London, 1950), 132; Crehan, *Return to Obedience*, 228.

on 'the laws, statutes and customs' of the realm and on the authority of the 'crown imperial', questions of title could be tried only in crown courts—not, that is, in church courts. The bill then states that the English ruler may never again have attributed to him the title of supreme head of the church, although legal writings in which he had been given such a title were to be considered valid as, also, were those in which Mary had omitted the title. (Under Elizabeth, Foxe and others were to argue that most Marian statutes were invalid, since after her first parliament Mary did not use the title of supreme head of the church even in the writs of summons.[31]) This is followed by a clause dealing with gifts of land to spiritual bodies, the clause where, according to Priuli, Pole had won a concession over mortmain. Finally, there is a clause saving the liberties of the crown and another general statement that the Holy See should have that authority in the kingdom that it had enjoyed until the twentieth year of Henry VIII's reign.

During its passage through the House of Commons the bill had two provisos added. The first referred back to the clause about mortmain and permitted the donor of lands to spiritual bodies to reserve a tenure in frankalmoigne or a tenure by divine service. The second proviso laid down that persons or institutions in receipt of tithe or holding ecclesiastical possessions such as glebe land might have the same legal remedies available to them if they needed to recover their rights as they had done before the statute was passed: this was a measure presumably intended to reduce the possibility of conflict over whether such cases should be heard in crown or church courts. However, when the entire bill was sent back to the Upper House the peers disliked the wording of the proviso and drew up their own.[32] Even after this, the bishops of London and Coventry as well as Lord Montagu registered formal protests when the proviso was formally agreed:[33] the feelings of the bishop of London, Bonner, are clear enough, for he also protested against the bill as a whole, but the action of the other two is more difficult to explain. Ralph Baines, bishop of Coventry,

---

[31] See below, 174.
[32] *LJ* 4 Jan. 1555. The clerk again confuses the date.
[33] Ibid.

may have been moved by circumstances peculiar to his own see;[34] Montagu, a devoted catholic, may simply have followed Bonner.

The Commons had also demanded that 'the two clauses containing xix lines and concerning the bishop of London . . . and the Lords Wentworth, etc., should be clearly put out'.[35] The Lords agreed to this, and Gardiner, who as chancellor was speaker of the House of Lords, cut through the offending passage, saying as he did so, 'I now do rightly the office of a chancellor'—a pun on the Latin word *cancelli* meaning a lattice or railings, and later the bar in a court of justice: Gardiner cut the document through several times so that it resembled a lattice. Because he did this, instead of erasing the offending passage entirely, it is still possible to read the clauses to which the Commons took exception.[36] They provide that the bishops of London, Winchester, Worcester, and Chichester 'shall enjoy and possess in the right of their churches . . . all such manors, lands, rents and hereditaments as they now possess . . . without molestation, disquiet or trouble by pretence of any act or acts done' during the period in which the bishoprics had fallen into the hands of what were described as 'usurpers'—that is, the Edwardian bishops. However, certain peers to whom grants had been made from the possessions of the bishop of London were protected: Lord Wentworth and his heirs were to continue to hold the manors of Stepney and Hackney, Lord Rich would retain Braintree in Essex, and Lord Darcy was to keep Southminster. The instigator of the passage was probably Bonner, the restored bishop of London, who was to seek for the remainder of his life to overturn the leases made by Ridley during his occupation of the see.[37] But if Bonner was more energetic than most in his attempts to recover the revenues of his see, he was not without support from his colleagues, and on 31 December, whilst the House of Commons was still considering the great

---

[34] 4 & 5 Philip and Mary, c. 10, regulated the payment of tithes in Coventry.
[35] *LJ* 4 Jan. 1555.
[36] HLRO, Original Acts, 1 & 2 Philip and Mary, 8.
[37] Gina Alexander, 'Victim or Spendthrift? The Bishop of London and his Income in the Sixteenth Century', in *Wealth and Power in Tudor England: Essays presented to S. T. Bindoff*, ed. E. W. Ives, R. J. Knecht, and J. J. Scarisbrick (London, 1978), 130, 143.

bill but after this particular clause had been rejected, there is a note in the Lords' Journal of a bill 'touching the wrongful and undue letting out of the lands and hereditaments belonging to the bishoprics of Chester, Coventry and Lichfield, by the late bishops there'; the bill was committed, and then disappeared. As the Imperial ambassador noted, the bishops were trying very hard to persuade parliament to repudiate the legal transactions of their Edwardian predecessors.[38]

Finally, after many delays and difficulties, the bill was passed. England was once more united with Rome: as Gardiner declared, in the words of David, 'mercy and truth are met together; righteousness and peace have kissed each other'.[39] Just in case righteousness and peace did not prove strong enough, the medieval heresy laws were also revived.[40] The bill went swiftly through the Commons on 12, 13, and 14 December and through the Lords on 15, 17, and 18 December. Not one peer registered a protest against the measure. Since there had been no marked change in the composition of the House of Lords between the second Marian parliament and the third it would appear that the reason why a bill rejected in May was passed without difficulty in December was that the anxieties of lay peers had to some extent been allayed by the agreement reached with the pope. Doctrinal purity was now more acceptable.

Indeed, it appears as if some members of the Commons were prepared to go a long way in pursuit of doctrinal purity. An act was passed which removed the protection offered to the lessees of ecclesiastical benefices by a clause in the 1536 first fruits act;[41] this had given the lessee security of tenure for up to six years if the lessor resigned the benefice during the period for which the lease had run. The preamble in the 1554 act declared that the purpose of the measure was to enable 'parsons and vicars and other having the cure of souls' to 'the better attend and be the more vigilant in their mystery and function'—in

---

[38] *CSP Sp.* XIII. 134.
[39] Quoted in J. A. Muller, *Stephen Gardiner and the Tudor Reaction* (London, 1926), 267.
[40] 1 & 2 Philip and Mary, c. 6.
[41] 28 Henry VIII, c. 11, clause 5.

other words, it was intended to deal with the recurrent six-teenth-century problem of leasing of benefices and absentee clergy.[42] The measure may well also have been intended to prevent simoniacal agreements between patron and incumbent.[43] Initially, the scope of the measure had been even wider. On 23 November a bill was introduced in the Commons 'to avoid leases made by married priests'. This ominous-sounding proposal was committed to the former speaker, Pollard, and discussed on five occasions[44] before being transformed into a bill 'for leases made by spiritual persons not to be good after resignation'.[45] This was in its turn changed into a bill 'touching repeal of the act for leases upon resignation and non-residence' passed in the Commons on 7 January and by the Lords three days later.[46] The original proposal, then, was to invalidate all leases made by married priests. In the circumstances of 1554 and 1555, when numerous married priests were resigning or being deprived, the impact would have been enormous: in the end, caution or good sense seem to have prevailed.

Important statutes were also enacted extending the law of treason, which had been much diminished by the act of repeal passed in Mary's first parliament. One of these was intended to punish those who openly wished that the queen might change her religious views or die:[47] this was introduced at the end of the session after the discovery of a protestant congregation in Bow Church Yard allegedly praying that Mary's life might be shortened.[48] A more traditional measure was also implemented, making it treasonable to bring into the country counterfeit foreign coins.[49] A third proposal, probably coming from the government, was read in the Commons on 17 November, the first working day of the meeting. It was aimed at the punish-

---

[42] See C. Hill, *Economic Problems of the Church* (London, pb. edn., 1971), 114.

[43] For such arrangements see R. Houlbrooke, *Church Courts and the People during the English Reformation, 1520–1570* (Oxford, 1979), 191–5.

[44] 27, 29 Nov., 5 Dec. (when 'Mr Recorder' is mentioned), 8 and 10 Dec. (when Bourne's name is mentioned).

[45] 19 Dec.

[46] 1 & 2 Philip and Mary, c. 17.

[47] 1 & 2 Philip and Mary, c. 9. Introduced into the Commons on 14 Jan., it was read there on 15 and 16 Jan. The Lords read it, exceptionally, three times in the afternoon of 16 Jan.

[48] Machyn, 79; Foxe, VIII. 584.

[49] 1 & 2 Philip and Mary, c. 11.

ment of those who spoke seditiously against the king, queen or privy council: the need for further restrictions on what was said or written about the monarch and her husband had been highlighted by the discovery just before parliament opened of a quantity of books disparaging the queen and the catholic church,[50] as well as by the earl of Derby's story of picking up a paper in the street that warned of the evil intentions of the Spaniards.[51] However, the bill was dropped after a second reading in favour of a redrafted version first read on 22 November. The passage of the bill was none the less slow; the Commons modified it further by adding a proviso offering financial penalties as an alternative to the harsh physical punishment that had been laid down, whilst the Lords put in a second proviso drafted on 10 December by one of the judges, William Stanford, protecting the privileges of their rank.[52]

But the most significant addition to the treason law came in a statute dealing with Philip's position.[53] The measure was primarily intended to provide for a male consort the protection offered to the king's wife by sections of the 1352 act, but the question of what Philip's role should be were the queen to die in childbirth was also defined in the statute: this combination, plus the lengthy and tortuous progress of the bill in parliament, makes the history of the bill and of opposition to it almost incomprehensible.

On 17 November a bill 'for the limitation of treasons' was read in the Lords; it was committed the following day but did not receive a third reading until 6 December. It was read in the Commons on 7 and 17 December but seems to have been considered rather cloudy and obscure,[54] and was dropped in favour of a new bill read for the first time on 20 December. This bill was probably then submitted to the king and queen for their approval. At the queen's command, Petre and Inglefield also discussed the measure with Renard although, to his irritation, they did not carry this constitutional impropriety to the point

---

[50] Arch. Étr. XII, fo. 270ᵛ.

[51] *CSP Sp.* XIII. 102.

[52] HLRO, Original Acts, 1 & 2 Philip and Mary, 3. (Note that Bellamy, *The Tudor Law of Treason*, 59, cites this statute as 1 & 2 Philip and Mary, c. 9.)

[53] 1 & 2 Philip and Mary, c. 10.

[54] *CSP Sp.* XIII. 125.

of actually showing him the bill.[55] Renard raised various objections, all of which turned on the question of Philip's position
in relation to his child. He argued, for example, that the bill
diminished Philip's rights, since at common law a father was
entitled not only to sole charge of the person of his child but
also of the child's property—in this instance, the realm of
England. The draft also set up a council of six earls, six bishops,
and six barons to assist Philip during the child's minority, a
provision that Renard believed would lead to rivalries about
who was chosen. He was overall highly suspicious of the draft
and worried lest it should in reality limit Philip's power whilst
appearing to extend it: he later learnt that the bill did indeed
impose restrictions on Philip's right as guardian to choose
marriage partners for his children.

Whether as a result of Renard's criticisms or not, the substance of the bill was much changed before it was passed by the
Commons on 14 January. There was further consultation with
the queen; one version of the measure showed to Mary allowed
her to decide what the age of majority should be for her children provided it did not exceed eighteen years.[56] This draft, in
Petre's hand, also requested that, notwithstanding 'the mani-
fold vertues of his Maj*es*te his godly dispositions and greatt
fau*or*s to vs all', as well as the assurances given at the opening of
parliament, the king should promise that no foreigner would
hold office in the realm. When it was finally passed by the
Lords on 16 January—after a swift and easy passage in marked
contrast to the difficulties that had been encountered in
April—the bill gave Philip the guardianship of a female child
until she reached her majority at fifteen and the guardianship
of a male child until eighteen.[57] The council to which Renard
had objected had vanished and, more important, Philip was to
control the realm, and not just the person of the heir, during
the minority. This was a considerable triumph for the Imperialists, although Philip was annoyed by another clause of the
statute which insisted that during a minority the provisions of

---

[55] Ibid. 128–9.
[56] SP 11/5/2.
[57] 1 & 2 Philip and Mary, c. 10.

the marriage treaty should remain in force. Other sections extended to Philip protection similar to that enjoyed by the queen herself: it would in future be treasonable to declare that the king ought not to enjoy his title, or to compass his death by word or deed. The statute did something to resolve the problem of whether two witnesses were necessary to prove a treasonable deed or whether one would do, a question which had been raised by Sir Nicholas Throckmorton at his trial.[58] It also permitted judges to argue subsequently that, despite the 1553 repeal of the 1552 treason act, entails and uses were forfeit in treason convictions.[59]

It is impossible to reconstruct the whole history of this statute. The drafts were attacked both by those who were suspicious of Philip and believed that the bill gave him too much power, and by those who wanted, or wished it to be thought that they wanted, to extend Philip's power.[60] The latter apparently included Sir John Pollard, speaker of the 1553 parliament and knight of the shire for Oxfordshire, the privy councillor Sir John Baker, and a lawyer who can probably be identified as Anthony Browne, later chief justice of common pleas. Sir Richard Southwell, another privy councillor, was also anxious, according to Foxe, to push the bill forward.[61] It is possible that Philip's supporters went so far as to suggest that the prince himself should have some claim to the throne, a suggestion that the Lower House roundly rejected.[62] It is less easy to identify the opponents of the bill, or even to decide how reasonable criticism of it was, since only a sketchy description of the earlier draft exists, in the report sent by Renard to Charles V. However, Mr Graves, noting the drift of members away from the Lower House about which Mary became so angry, and observing that some peers were also at this time not very assiduous in

---

[58] Howell, *A Complete Collection of State Trials* I. 876–81. On this see L. M. Hill, 'The Two Witness Rule in English Treason Trials', *American Journal of Legal History*, XII (1968), 96–7; Bellamy, *The Tudor Law of Treason*, 152–8.

[59] Loach, 'Opposition to the Crown in Parliament, 1553–1558' (Oxford Univ. D. Phil. thesis, 1974), 333–8; Bellamy, op. cit., 59–60. In 1571 the judges in Dowtie's case appear to have decided that entailed land was normally forfeit (Coke, *Reports* (London, 1776), II. iii. fo. 10b).

[60] *CSP Sp.* XIII. 125.

[61] Foxe, VI. 580.

[62] Bodley MS Tanner 391, fo. 37. See Appendix C.

their attendance in the House, has argued that the parliamentary exodus was due to dissatisfaction with this bill.[63] The case
of the Commons has already been considered: there is no reason
to assume that members of the Commons left parliament early
for any reason other than their desire to celebrate Christmas
with their families.[64] The absentee peers are a more complicated matter, since we have Renard's explanation of the absence of Arundel, Pembroke, Westmorland, and Cumberland
as due to their desire 'not to give their consent to a measure
infringing upon the right hitherto exercised by the nobility to
appoint a protector when need has arisen',[65] and because a bill
similar to that under discussion had been watered down by the
House of Lords only six months before.[66]

An examination of the attendance record of the peers in
question, in so far as the manuscript of the Lords' Journal
allows, is the only means available by which Mr Graves's claim
can be judged. Arundel, according to Mr Graves's own figures,
was present in the parliament on only 48 per cent of the days on
which the Lords sat.[67] Pembroke was present only 30 per cent
of the time, Westmorland 63 per cent, and Cumberland 37 per
cent. Graves also mentions as defaulters Sussex, Grey de Wilton, Fitzwalter, and St John:[68] Sussex was present on only 37
per cent of the days on which the House sat, Grey 13 per cent of
the time, and Fitzwalter 46 per cent. St John was present 65 per
cent of the time. Given an average attendance amongst the
forty-two lay peers who were present at this parliament of 60
per cent,[69] it becomes clear that most of those named by
Graves had attendance records below average, and their absence on particular days in January therefore loses some of its
significance. What of the earl of Bedford, of whose absence Mr

[63] Graves, *The House of Lords*, 196–8.
[64] See above, 47–50.
[65] *CSP Sp.* XIII. 134. Renard did not, in fact, claim that this was the case, merely
that it was what 'several persons have said'.
[66] See above, 98.
[67] Graves, *The House of Lords*, 223–7.
[68] Ibid. 86.
[69] It is interesting that the attendance average of members of the council who sat in
the Lords—eleven, excluding Wentworth–was 58 per cent.

Graves makes a good deal?[70] Bedford was a better attender than the remainder of the peers mentioned, being in the House on 70 per cent of the occasions on which it sat, but he none the less absented himself from a number of meetings; he did not appear on 19, 20, and 21 November, for instance, and he did not attend the morning session on 29 November, in which the bill for letters patent received a second reading,[71] although he did attend in the afternoon, when no business was reported by the clerk. He was present in the House on 17 and 19 November, when the first bill for the guardianship of the heir was discussed, and he was present on 6 December, when it was passed. On 17 December he was issued with a licence for absence, but he was still appearing intermittently in the House a month later, although he was not present on 14 and 15 January, when the regency bill was discussed, nor on the morning of 16 January, when it was passed. He was present in the afternoon of 16 January, but there is no need to regard this, as does Mr Graves, as 'a consummate exercise in the politics of discretion', since he might well have felt that the closing ceremonies of the session merited his attendance. (The earl was, in any case, by now seriously ill; he died on 14 March.[72])

It is obviously important not to make too much of the fact that many of the nine men mentioned by Mr Graves had low attendance figures in this session, since their total is necessarily reduced by the very fact that some of them were not present during the discussions on the regency bill—neither Bedford nor Arundel nor Westmorland nor Sussex nor Pembroke was present on 15 January, for instance. The significant point is that all of them save Bedford had been low attenders long before that day, and even Bedford had been away on a number of other occasions. It is possible that Renard's sources were correct in seeing the absence of Arundel, Pembroke, Westmorland, Cumberland, and Dacre—mentioned by the ambassador but not by Mr Graves—as politically motivated: the case is unproven. But it is curious that Bedford was not picked out by Renard as a dissident if he were. It is as reasonable to argue

[70] Graves, *The House of Lords*, 86–7.
[71] See below, 193.
[72] D. Willen, *John Russell, First Earl of Bedford* (London, 1981), 98–100.

that he disliked the bill for the lands of the duchess of Suffolk,[73] discussed in his absence on 5 and 7 January, as it is to argue that he did not care for the regency bill, also read in his absence.

The cautious historian must conclude that the evidence of these peers' attendance records is not, in itself, sufficient proof of Renard's claim that they so much disliked the regency bill that they stayed away in order to avoid giving their consent to it. They may have done, just as they may have encouraged members of the Lower House to oppose the measure: both notions rest solely on the testimony of Renard. The episode is interesting, but the evidence does not justify the emphasis placed upon it by Mr Graves.

None the less, there was undoubtedly anxiety about Philip's constitutional position at this time, anxiety that was heightened by continuing rumours that the queen intended to introduce a proposal for the prince's coronation. Mary was under considerable pressure to do so from the Imperial court and from Philip himself. On 6 November Renard declared that he had spoken to the queen about the coronation, and on 14 November he wrote that he was now slyly mentioning the matter to her and to Gardiner as if it were a thing agreed.[74] Indeed, although only he reported that the coronation had been mentioned in the chancellor's opening speech to parliament,[75] and the journals record no formal proposal during the session, it is even possible that members of the Lower House themselves raised the matter: on 14 January Noailles said that 'depuis six jours' a plan to crown Philip had been 'particulierement fait rechercher ceulx de la basse chambre ... qui iuy ont tous d'une voix rejetté'.[76]

Noailles was extremely worried about these discussions because of their international implications. He believed that parliament had been summoned specifically 'pour faire des impostz et subsides sur le peuple, pour commencer la guerre'[77] and war was, according to his reports, several times mentioned in the course of the parliament; in a dispatch written in the

[73] See below, 123-4.
[74] *CSP Sp.* XIII. 78, 84.
[75] For the French ambassador's report, see Arch. Étr., XII. fo. 280 (Vertot, IV. 20).
[76] Arch. Étr., XII. fo. 317 (Vertot, IV 136-7).
[77] Arch. Étr., XII. fo. 292 (Vertot, IV. 62).

middle of December he said that a specific demand had been made and refused, and added that in order to change parliament's mood the queen and council had encouraged a number of people who had been 'pillés et robbés par mer par les Francoys de tous leur biens' to complain to the assembly.[78] (There is nothing in the Journals to support this story.) He reported on 26 December that 'ung personnaige de la haulte chambre', when taking a bill to the Lower House, had there proposed that it was proper for the son to assist the father, and thus for Philip to assist Charles V, but the Commons had pointed out that by the marriage treaty, passed in the previous parliament, England was protected against such claims.[79] Later, towards the end of parliament, Noailles claimed that Sir John Bourne had asked for 'l'ouverture de la guerre', arguing that England should aid the Netherlands, 'en ensuyvant les ancyens traictez qu'ilz ont reciprocquement avecques eulx'.[80] Parliament had evidently, therefore, shown no enthusiasm for continental warfare, and the government subsequently concentrated on acting as an intermediary between the two powers.

Whilst Philip's powers and position were under consideration a bill was passed confirming the attainder under existing treason law of the duke of Suffolk, Wyatt, and fifty-two others.[81] Although the passage of the bill through the Lords was swift—it was read three times in the course of 7 and 8 January—a number of peers registered protests: Bath, Montagu, Stourton, Lumley, Evers, Wharton, and Paget. Taken in conjunction with the failure of a similar bill in the previous parliament, these protests imply that the Lords were deeply unhappy about the property aspects of the measure.[82]

Indeed, the history of another bill discussed at this time suggests that a great deal of concern was felt about the rights of property owners. This bill, introduced in the Lords on 4

[78] Arch. Étr., IX. fo. 327ᵛ. The dispatch is headed 16 Dec. but dated the 17th at the end. There is a translation of the passage in Harbison, *Rival Ambassadors at the Court of Queen Mary*, 220.

[79] Arch. Étr., XII. fo. 297 (Vertot, IV. 76).

[80] PRO Transcripts 31/3/22: 8 Feb. 1554/5. See also Vertot, IV. 144.

[81] HLRO, Original Acts, 1 & 2 Philip and Mary, 21.

[82] See above, 102–3.

January by, presumably, Lord Willoughby of Parham,[83] was for 'the limitation of the estates of certain lands descended to the duchess of Suffolk from the late Lord Willoughby, her father'. Catherine Bertie, as she was by this time, was the widow of Charles Brandon, duke of Suffolk, and had succeeded her father in 1526 as Lord Willoughby d'Eresby in her own right; she was a devout protestant and at the period when the bill was under consideration was proceeding in a stately way towards Gravesend, whence she embarked on 5 February for exile in Germany. The bill swiftly passed the Lords and was read in the Commons on 7 January, when it was described as a bill for the assurance of the lands to Willoughby after the deaths of Catherine and Richard Bertie and of her heirs. The following day the duchess's legal advisers asked for copies of the bill, which were given to them. On 9 January they appeared before the Commons, as did Willoughby; he argued that 'the duchess's counsel, having no warrant, should not be heard' and that the Commons should remember 'his estate of barony, which was given him for possibility of that reversion'—implying that he would not be able to support the title given him in 1547 in a fitting manner without these lands. Willoughby added that one of the duchess's counsel, Erenden, actually possessed '£50 of these lands in fee simple' and was, therefore, an interested party. A committee was set up under a privy councillor, Sir Francis Englefield, to look into the matter. On 10 January the committee reported that 'divers manors, named in the bill' were not in fact included in 'the indenture touching the entail mentioned by Lord Willoughby'. The bill was read once more on 15 January before being rejected in a division on 16 January by 120 votes to 73. Whether it was sympathy for the duchess that led to this rejection, whether the House felt that Willoughby had been trying to deceive or whether the Commons was simply being scrupulous over property rights is not clear, but the rejection of Willoughby's bill for a woman so out of favour with the queen is a vindication of the independence of parliament at this time.

A great deal of the legislation of this parliament was, of course, not at all controversial politically. Proposals that had

---

[83] He was present on both the relevant days.

failed in earlier parliaments now came to fruition; such were the bill for the restraint of excess in apparel,[84] a bill concerned with the manufacture of certain types of cloth in Norwich,[85] and a bill to prevent those who lived in rural areas from selling cloth and various other commodities except at fairs or in corporate towns.[86] Other proposals to do with the cloth industry, with the hat-making and leather trades, and with herring fishing, failed. A bill that sought to prevent the decay of houses of husbandry was abandoned, although a similar measure was to be successful a year later.[87] However, a statute was enacted that increased the restrictions on the export of corn, timber, and various other products[88]—a rather puzzling measure, since it was not until the following summer that prices rose sharply. Another important measure to be passed in this parliament dealt with the collusive bailing of suspected felons by corrupt justices of the peace.[89] A bill to this end passed the Lords without apparent difficulty,[90] but after it had been committed to Secretary Petre in the Commons it disappeared and a new bill was read on 19 December. This new bill was committed on 22 December to the lawyer, Sir John Pollard; on 24 December it was apparently committed again, this time to a Mr Cholmeley, probably Sir Roger Cholmeley, who sat for Middlesex and was the former chief justice of king's bench—before being read on 31 December, 10 January, and—for the sixth time—on 12 January. It was passed two days later, although it still remained for the Lords to agree to the words added to the bill by the Lower House. It has sometimes been suggested that this statute, together with one passed in the next parliament dealing with the right of justices to examine in cases of

[84] 1 & 2 Philip and Mary, c. 2; *LJ* 12 Jan. 1555 (2 readings) and 14 Jan.; *CJ* 14 Jan. (2 readings) and 16 Jan. A bill had been read in the Commons on 10, 12, and 14 Apr. 1554, and in the Lords on 16, 19, and 21 Apr.; a new bill was read on 25 and 28 Apr. and on 1 May, when the Lords passed it. This bill was read in the Commons on 2, 4, and 5 May, when it was passed, but a proviso that had been added and a request that 'certain words might be amended', coming to the Lords on the last afternoon of the session, seem to have led to the loss of the entire measure.

[85] 1 & 2 Philip and Mary, c. 14. See above, 37. A bill had been read in the Commons on 9, 10, and 13 Apr., when it was 're-delivered'.

[86] 1 & 2 Philip and Mary, c. 7. A bill had been read in the Commons on 10 Apr.

[87] See below, 145.

[88] 1 & 2 Philip and Mary, c. 5.

[89] 1 & 2 Philip and Mary, c. 13.

[90] *LJ* 21 Nov., 4, 5, and 6 Dec. (with a proviso).

manslaughter and felony,[91] sought to introduce to England 'a variety of Roman canon Inquisitionsprozess'.[92] If this is so, then the difficulties encountered in the Lower House by the bail bill might be seen as 'the valiant Commons straining against the importation of the secular inquisition'.[93] However, the 1555 bill passed both Houses without undue delay, suggesting that those in parliament were far less aware than legal historians of the possibly sinister implications of the proposal, and it seems probable that the delays in the passing of the 1554 bail statute were rather, as Mr Langbein argues, the reaction of an assembly packed with interested parties to a proposal that limited the discretion of the magistrates and 'required the JPs to create a written record by which the central authorities could review their actions regularly in an important class of business'.[94]

Parliament was dissolved on 16 January 1555. Gardiner made a speech in which he compared the dissension and disunity that there had been in parliament at the time of the break with Rome with the harmony and concord that had marked the reunion.[95] Indeed, he had cause to feel satisfied. The Marian compromise had emerged: the queen had her spiritual satisfaction and her subjects their secularized property. Politically, it is true, the meeting had been less successful, and some commentators reported that the king and queen dissolved the meeting rather unceremoniously—Noailles declared that they were thus 'monstrans et faisans congnoistre à ung chascun, avoir quelque grand mescontement contre l'assemblé d'icceluy, encores que l'effect de la religion y eust succedé, comme ils desiroient, que estoit assez d'occasion à eulx pour y aller avecques plaisir'.[96] Although Philip had won control of the realm

---

[91] 2 & 3 Philip and Mary, c. 10. .

[92] See, for example, W. S. Holdsworth, *A History of English Law* (London, 1922–66), IV. 528.

[93] J. H. Langbein, *Prosecuting Crime in the Renaissance* (Cambridge, Mass., 1974), 59. Langbein also notes (p. 58) that in terms of readings in the House of Commons the proposal appears the most controversial considered in the course of this parliament.

[94] Ibid. 60–1.

[95] BL Additional MS 15,388, fo. 336.

[96] Arch. Étr., XII. fo. 322ᵛ (Vertot, IV. 153). See also *Original Letters Relative to the English Reformation*, I. 159.

as well as of the person of his child should Mary die, he was still to be confined within the limits of the marriage treaty. This, together with Mary's inability to win her subjects' approval for his coronation, was a matter of significance for Europe as well as for England.

7

The Parliament of 1555

THE political situation in England changed profoundly
between the end of Mary's third parliament and the opening of
the fourth on 21 October 1555. One factor, and perhaps the
most important, was Mary's failure to produce the heir whose
conception had been announced before the third parliament,
but other factors contributing to change were the burning of
heretics and the queen's manifest determination to give back to
the church the former ecclesiastical property in her hands.

Initially, the heir to the throne was expected in April; then,
when the dates were thought to have been mistaken, in June.
At the beginning of August, however, all hope was abandoned
and the preparations that had been made for the birth were
slowly dismantled. On 29 August Philip left the country.
England was from now on to be secondary to his other concerns; these were immense, for Charles V resigned the lordship
of the Netherlands to him in October, and in January 1556 the
crowns of Aragon and Castile. Philip now wanted power in
England in his own right, not simply as a regent for the heir,
and he put great pressure on Mary to allow him to be
crowned.[1]

As a result of the heresy laws that had been revived in the
third parliament proceedings could now be taken against recal-
citrant protestants, and on 4 February 1555 the first Marian
martyr, John Rogers, was burned at Smithfield; Lawrence
Sanders was burned at Coventry on 8 February and Hooper at
Gloucester the following day. Only five days before the opening
of parliament Latimer and Ridley suffered at Oxford.
Although many of those who witnessed their often heroic struggles expressed sympathy for the martyrs—both Renard and
Noailles reported that onlookers had urged Rogers to have

---

[1] *CSP Ven.* VI. i. 212, 227, 281. See below, 194–7.

courage[2]—it would be a mistake to assume that the policy of persecution was widely disliked, especially amongst the governing classes. As Mrs Alexander pointed out in her study of Bonner, no heretics could have been convicted without the participation of lay magistrates and lay jurors.[3] With a few conspicuous exceptions those burnt came from the lower classes, and they may well have been regarded by men higher up the social scale simply as trouble-makers. As far as relations between crown and parliament were concerned, the policy of persecution was probably of less importance than the continuing unease about former church property. One of Paul IV's first actions after his election in 1555 was to issue a bull denouncing the alienation of ecclesiastical property. Partly through the efforts of the protestants in exile news of the bull soon reached England;[4] the privy council was alarmed and Pole was forced to ask the pope for another bull dealing specifically with the English situation.[5] When this second bull arrived it was read publicly at Paul's Cross[6] and, at the council's insistence, it was published in Latin and English.[7] Most significant of all, it was read in the House of Commons on 23 October, the first day of business.

The reason why the council was so anxious about the bull was that the queen was in the process of restoring to the church much of the property that remained in her control, and it was widely believed that this was but the first step towards a more general, and perhaps even a forcible, restoration. Pole had made it clear to Mary that he could not sanction her possession of former ecclesiastical property, and on 17 January 1555 Renard noted that the Legate had already succeeded in persuading the queen to give up revenues worth 60,000 crowns, although she had not finally decided what to do about the remainder of her church property.[8] A committee of councillors

---

[2] *CSP Sp.* XIII. 138; Vertot, IV. 173.

[3] G. Alexander, 'Bonner and the Marian Persecutions', *History*, LX (1975), 38.

[4] *CSP Ven.* VI. i. 189. On this subject, see R. H. Pogson, 'Cardinal Pole—Papal Legate to England in Mary Tudor's Reign' (Cambridge Univ. Ph.D thesis 1972), 147–9.

[5] Ibid. 154.

[6] Wriothesley, II. 130.

[7] SP 11/6/18.

[8] *CSP Sp.* XIII. 134. See also *CSP Ven.* VI. i. 10 (wrongly dated Jan. 1555).

was set up to oversee the restoration, consisting of Gardiner, Paulet, Rochester, Petre, and probably Englefield.[9] Mary was persuaded that parliamentary approval was needed if the restoration were to be legally secure, but she was clearly and openly committed to a policy of restoration long before parliament was summoned,[10] monasteries at Greenwich and Richmond being set up by the Franciscans in the late spring of 1555.[11]

It was against the background of these problems that the council considered its plans for a fourth parliament. The economic outlook was bleak: as a result of what Machyn described as 'the greatest rayn and fludes that ever was sene in England'[12] the price of grain and arable crops had risen sharply.[13] It was not a propitious moment to seek a grant of taxation, but the government was short of money and it was decided that parliament should be asked for the subsidy that had been remitted at the beginning of the reign, and for three fifteenths.[14] The other major piece of legislation, according to a memorandum sent to Philip, was to be for 'de abrogatione statutorum de primis fructibus et *petris* petius dicimis, et confirmatione cessionis beneficiorum ecclesiasticorum, *qua* premissa sine Parlamento experiri non possint'.[15] The council also considered that there should be some measure to deal with gaol delivery and a bill for the licensing of taverns. In none of these memoranda was the great question of Philip's coronation mentioned, although informed observers believed that the matter would be raised in parliament, the French ambassador, for instance, reporting that 'l'on dict que l'occasion pour laquelle ledict parlement a esté assemblé, ne tend à aultre fin que pour faire, s'il est possible, tumber le gouvernement absolu de ce royaulme entre les mains de ce roy, et pourvoir par ce moyen

---

[9] *CSP Ven.* VI. i. 27, lists Gardiner, Paulet, Rochester, Petre, and two other unnamed councillors. Foxe (VII. 34) lists the first four and Englefield.

[10] *CSP Ven.* VI. i. 27.

[11] Wriothesley, II. 8.

[12] Machyn, 94.

[13] *The Agrarian History of England and Wales*, IV, ed. J. Thirsk (Cambridge, 1967), 842–3.

[14] SP 11/6/19.

[15] SP 11/6/18.

disposer des forces et estats d'icelluy à sa volunté'.[16] The French were, of course, extremely worried in case Philip's position in England should be strong enough for him to drag the country into the Habsburg–Valois conflict. Whether the lord chancellor touched on this delicate matter in his speech at the opening of parliament on 21 October is not clear; the Venetian ambassador reported that he had said, rather disingenuously perhaps, that nothing would be proposed in the forthcoming session relating to the authority or position of the king.[17]

Most of Gardiner's speech was in fact taken up with the problem of royal finance.[18] He explained that Mary had found the revenues of the crown exhausted at her accession, and that she had been further burdened by the debts of her father and brother; nevertheless, he pointed out, she had neither collected the subsidy that had been granted to Edward before his death nor confiscated much land from rebellious subjects. Dwelling on 'les bienfaicts que les subjectz avoient par elle et son mary recues', he begged parliament to find a means of relieving the queen's difficulties.[19]

On 23 October the queen was present for the reading in parliament of a letter from Philip that explained why he was absent from the opening of the session and urged members to obey the queen and honour God.[20] Gardiner, although mortally sick, was reported as having made another speech, presumably after the reading of the papal bull, reassuring his audience that no measure was planned that would affect the tenure by private individuals of former church land.[21] However, the first bill read in the Commons dealt with a quite different although equally perennial problem; it was intended to prevent members of the House from leaving during the parliamentary session without a licence from the speaker[22]—it was, therefore, an attempt to continue the drive against absenteeism upon which

[16] Arch. Étr. XII. fo. 444 (Vertot, V. 171). See also *CSP Ven.* VI. i. 188.
[17] *CSP Ven.* VI. i. 229.
[18] Ibid. 217.
[19] Arch. Étr. XII. fo. 449 (Vertot, V. 184).
[20] SP 11/6/28.
[21] *CSP Ven.* VI. i. 225.
[22] *CJ* 23 Oct.

the crown had embarked at the end of the previous meeting.[23] The bill was read three times[24] and then dropped in favour of another, read for the first time on 30 October. Yet a third bill was read once only, on 8 November. The matter would seem of little interest were it not for a remark made by the Venetian ambassador. In the course of his account on 18 November of the difficulties encountered by the exiles bill he wrote that the House of Commons

is quite full of gentry and nobility . . . and therefore more daring and licentious than former houses, which consisted of burgesses and plebians . . . In order, therefore, for the future to prevent admission into the Lower House of so many noblemen, from whom this licentiousness is supposed to proceed, a proposal was made lately . . . [for burgesses to be resident in the towns they represent] which proposal seems to have been rejected, because to return entirely to the ancient order of things, the opposition insisted on simultaneously prohibiting the election of any stipendiary, pensioner, or official, or of any person deriving profit in any other way from the King and the royal Council, and being dependent on them.[25]

This passage, with its description of a complicated 'tacking' device, led Professor Neale to write of 'the opposition group' displaying 'a tactical precocity more in line with the maturer days of Elizabeth';[26] it has, in fact, become a highly important part of the evidence for the existence of an 'opposition' in this parliament. However, Neale, whilst acknowledging that the passage cannot be squared with entries in the Commons' Journal, did not apparently consult the Italian from which the entry in the *Venetian Calendar* was made. Had he done so, he would have realized that historians have been ill-served by the

---

[23] See above, 45–6.
[24] *CJ* 24 and 26 Oct., when it was committed to Mr Rastell, the lawyer and member of the More circle, who represented Canterbury in this parliament.
[25] *CSP Ven.* VI. i. 251–2.
[26] J. E. Neale, *Elizabeth I and her Parliaments, 1559–1581* (London, 1953), 26.

translation of this key passage.[27] First of all, Michieli's information is more vague than the *Calendar* allows, for the printed
version omits the Venetian's phrase, 'I have been told', and by
translating 'ultimamente' as 'lately' rather than 'recently'
implies that the proposal has been made since the debate of 8
November, to which it would be reasonable to assume that the
comment actually applies. More important, there is no mention at all in the original Italian of 'the opposition': indeed, the
general drift of the passage suggests that the original proposal
contained both the clauses about the need for burgesses to be
resident and the place-clauses, and that there was therefore no
first draft to which the place-clause was 'tacked'. Thus, it seems
that this whole celebrated episode tells us nothing about 'the
opposition' and its 'tactical precocity', but only about the concern of some at least of those in the House for legal niceties:
Michieli's account of the debate should be set against the report
in the anonymous journal of a discussion in April 1571 about
the desirability of the fifteenth-century residence qualifica-
tions.[28]

The chancellor's exposition of financial needs of the crown
resulted in the setting up on 24 October of a committee consisting of Sir Robert Rochester, Sir William Petre, and eighteen

[27] PRO Transcripts 31/14/4, fo. 24 'per provedere che non siano più nella Casa
admessi tanti nobili dalli quali è riputato nasci questa licentia; mi è ditto esser, ultimamente stata fatta una proposta per ridurre le cose alli ordini et uso antiquo, che non
possino più nell'avenire entrar in quel loco alcuni che non siano nativi et che effettual-
mente non habitino nelli contadi, terre, et borghi per li quali intervengono et sono
deputati; la qual proposta pare sia stata ributtata perché per ritornar intieramente
all'uso antiquo volevano si proibisse et si rimovesse insieme che alcuno che fusse salari-
ato, o provisionato, o officiale ... (fo. 25) non potesse esservi admesso ... Dicasi non
essendosi proposta la regolatione di questa ultima parte per il preguiditio che ne rice-
verebbe il principe escludendosi li ministri et dependenti sui che sogliono sempre esser li
primi admessi et nominati non è stata secondo intendo approbata anco l'altra.' [To
prevent the admission into the Commons of so many nobles, from whom, it is thought,
this licentiousness proceeds, a proposal was recently made, I have been told, that the
ancient usage and order should be restored whereby no one should in future be elected
who is not a native or inhabitant of the county, lands or town which he represents. This
proposal, it seems, was rejected, because, in order to restore the ancient usage in its
entirety, they wished at the same time to prohibit and remove anyone who was salaried
or an official or in any way received benefits [from the crown] ... Since this second
suggestion would hinder the monarch by depriving him of his ministers and depen-
dents, who are always the first to be admitted and elected, the other suggestion has not,
according to what I understand, been approved either.]

[28] *Proceedings in the Parliaments of Elizabeth I* I, ed. T. E. Hartley (Leicester, 1981),
226–31.

other members to draw up 'articles for aid to the Queen's majesty'.[29] Although the privy council had decided that one subsidy and three fifteenths were what was required, the bill read on 28 October was for one subsidy and only two fifteenths. It may be that it was the House, and not the committee, that insisted on the lower sum, for a letter written by James Bassett, knight of the shire for Devon, although very damaged, suggests that changes were made to the bill after the committee reported on 26 October,[30] whilst a dispatch from the French ambassador, written the following day, declared that although the queen would eventually secure a grant of taxation, 'ce ne sera pas pour telle somme que ladicte Dame prétend'.[31] However, even the smaller grant ran into difficulties. Noailles, busy stirring things up, at one point reported that the grant would be made only on condition that the queen spent the money on paying off her debts[32]—and not, presumably, on expensive wars—whilst the Venetian envoy believed that there was opposition to the grant of fifteenths on the grounds that the tax fell on the poor and needy; he reported that some members had said that the queen should recover the money owed to her by her greater subjects before seeking assistance from the humble.[33] They had also, and more ominously, argued that the queen should not give back her former church property, thus reducing her revenues, if she were short of money. Whether as a result of Noailles's encouragement of what he described as 'quatres bonnes testes', who had assured him that they would prevent the bill from passing or not,[34] discussion of the bill appears to have been heated. On 31 October, therefore, Petre brought a message from Mary announcing that she remitted, with thanks, the offer of the two fifteenths. The subsidy bill subsequently passed the Commons on 2 November.[35] Thus the crown finished up with a smaller grant than that for which it had hoped: although the queen had saved

---

[29] *CJ* 24 oct.
[30] *CSP Ven.* VI. i. 233.
[31] Arch. Étr., XII. fo. 449 (Vertot, V. 184).
[32] Ibid. V. 187.
[33] *CSP Ven.* VI. i. 229.
[34] Vertot, V. 190.
[35] HLRO, Original Acts, 2 & 3 Philip and Mary, 25. The subsidy was to be paid in two instalments, and based on a new assessment.

face by giving up any attempt to obtain fifteenths, it was un-
deniably a bad start to the session.

The next important bill to be discussed in the Lower House
did little to reduce tension: this was a bill permitting the fourth
duke of Norfolk, a minor, to alienate part of his estate. It took
up a large part of six days and involved the hearing of outside
petitioners.[36] The final result left dissatisfied many of those to
whom Howard property had earlier been granted, including
several members of the Lower House; since it had been Mary's
restoration of the old duke of Norfolk at the beginning of her
reign which had created the problem, some of this resentment
may have been directed towards the crown.[37]

But it was Mary's wish to restore to the church revenues and
property that had been confiscated during the reigns of her
father and brother that infuriated a large number of those sitting in parliament. A bill was first read in the Lords on 11
November. It obviously ran into immediate difficulties, for it
was not read again before the queen, on 19 November, summoned fifty members of the Lower House[38] and 'a great part of
the lords and barons' to explain that to ease her conscience she
intended to rid herself of first fruits and tenths, and of the cure
of souls. Pole spoke after her, declaring that as the annuities
paid from these revenues to ex-religious amounted to £25,000
per annum, the crown would not in fact lose financially by
restoring its property to the church, a somewhat specious argument since the pensions of course ceased on the death of the
recipient. According to the Venetian ambassador, who was
usually well informed about matters in which Pole was
involved, the legate went on to say that the country as a whole,
and members of parliament in particular, would gain by the return to the church of some eight hundred rectories, which
would then be distributed amongst the relatives of his audience,
without the incumbrance of tenths or first fruits.[39]

This meeting was obviously intended to pave the way for a

---

[36] *CJ* 7 Nov.; the bill had speedily passed the Lords after three readings on 6 and 7
Nov. For a general discussion of the importance of this matter, see above, 64–71.

[37] Noailles reported that Mary had suffered a setback over the bill 'qu'elle preten-
doit conduire en la fabveur du duc de Nortfort' (Vertot, V. 252).

[38] Fifty members according to *CJ*, sixty according to the Venetian ambassador (*CSP
Ven.* VI. i. 259).

[39] *CSP Ven.* VI. i. 259–61.

new bill which was read in the Lords the following day. This second bill was passed on 23 November, with protests being recorded by Hereford and Cobham. There was one significant difference between this bill and the earlier version. The first bill was described in the Journal on 11 November as a measure whereby 'the King and Queen's Majesties surrender and give into the hands of the Pope's Holiness the first fruits and tenths, etc.'.[40] That the proposal was to restore these monies to Rome is confirmed by Michieli's dispatch of 18 November in which he records objections to the crown's renouncing of its revenues for the benefit of someone who was an alien and a foreigner, a clear reference to the pope.[41] However, the second and successful bill was for 'the extinguishment of the first fruits and touching order and disposition of rectories and parsonages impropriate and also of the tenths of spiritual and ecclesiastical promotions remaining in the Queen's Majesty's hands':[42] the idea of restoring the revenues to the pope had been dropped. This change explains the emphasis that Pole laid in his speech of 19 November on the advantages that the laity would receive by the queen's renunciation, and also the purpose of his visit to the Commons on 20 November when he explained why tithes and impropriated benefices should not be in lay hands—all the benefits to the realm of England were being stressed, and the pope forgotten.

But even after this change the bill was not popular when it reached the Commons. Some members were reported to be worried about the alienation of royal revenues, arguing that a permanent reduction in the income of the crown might be much resented by the succeeding monarch.[43] More important seems to have been a fear that the queen's surrender of her property was but the first step towards a general restoration: the Venetian envoy said that some men believed that they

[40] *LJ* 11 Nov.
[41] *CSP Ven.* VI. i. 251. On its first reading in the Lords the second bill was, misleadingly, described as one whereby 'the King and Queen's Majesty surrender and give into the Hands of the Laity, the first-fruits and tenths'. This erroneous description was probably the result of Pole's speech of 19 Nov.
[42] *LJ*, 23 Nov.
[43] *CSP Ven.* VI. i. 251.

might be forced by virtue of the statute to make a similar cession of their own former church property at a later point.[44]
The bill therefore progressed only slowly. After its first reading
on 23 November it was committed to, amongst others, William
Cecil, who sat in this parliament as one of the knights for
Lincolnshire. It was read again on 26 November, and discussed
without a formal reading on the following day. The Venetian
ambassador records that a committee of two earls, two barons,
two bishops, and ten members of the Commons, together with
some of the law officers, was set up to consider and revise the
bill.[45] There is no other evidence for the existence of this committee, but its composition as described by the ambassador is so
like that of other committees for which there is abundant evidence that the story may be correct. However, the committee,
if it existed, did not change the bill much, since it returned to
the Lords with only one alteration, which was the addition of a
schedule giving asignees of chantry lands the same remedies at
law as those enjoyed by lessees—this clause had originally been
a separate bill, passed on 3 December, but the Lower House
appears to have then decided that it would more appropriately
form a part of the first fruits bill. Although the first fruits bill
was not much changed in the course of its passage through the
Commons, its progress was marked by great disputes and contention. On 3 December, in a division, 193 members of the
Commons voted for the bill and 126 against. Moreover, the
number opposed to the bill might have been even greater had
the doors of the Chamber not been locked, preventing anyone
from entering.[46]

By the statute, first fruits, which had been payable to the
crown since 1534, were declared to have come to an end on 8
August 1555.[47] Impropriated benefices which had come into
the possession of the crown since 1529 were restored to the
church, and the crown abandoned its own claim to tithes. The
revenue from the restored benefices and the tithe income were
to be used to supplement poor livings, to assist needy scholars,
and to pay certain pensions: however, when the pensions came

[44] Ibid. 268.
[45] Ibid.
[46] *CSP Ven.* VI. i. 270.
[47] 2 & 3 Philip and Mary, c. 4.

to an end on the death of the recipient the tithes that had been
allocated for their payment would also cease to be exacted.
Eventually, therefore, the church would receive very considerable benefits by the statute: £15,000 from the release of first
fruits and tenths, £10,000 from the restoration of impropriated
benefices and tithes.[48]

Relations between crown and Commons, strained by the first
fruits bill, were brought to breaking point by a bill which had
been introduced into the Lords on 31 October. It was described
as 'for punishment of those such as being gone into parts beyond the sea shall contemptuously remain there, notwithstanding the King's and Queen's letters to them sent, or
proclamation openly made for their calling home', but was also
known as 'the duchess of Suffolk's bill', after the most prestigious of the exiles against whom it was aimed. The bill was
committed on 7 November, after its third reading in the Upper
House, to the earl of Derby, the bishops of Durham and Ely,
Lords Montagu, Fitzwalter, and Rich; it was engrossed five
days later. But all was not well. The bill was recommitted the
following day, this time to the earl of Rutland, the bishop of
Chester, and, again, to Lord Rich. On 18 November Michieli
reported that the bill was being hotly debated: it was not
passed until 26 November. In the Lower House, where the bill
was read on 28 November, 5 December, and 6 December, a
quarrel broke out between Sir George Howard, who opposed
the bill, and Sir Edward Hastings, who supported it, and blows
were only narrowly avoided.[49] Howard, the brother of the former queen, was a courtier of long standing. Although he had
supported Jane Grey,[50] he soon recovered favour by service
against Wyatt,[51] and received both a position in Philip's
household and a Spanish pension.[52] In July 1554 he annoyed
the queen by leaving court without her permission,[53] but he

---

[48] SP 12/1/64. See also R. Pogson, 'Revival and Reform in Mary Tudor's Church: a
Question of Money', *Journal of Ecclesiastical History*, XXVI (1975).
[49] *CSP Ven.* VI. i. 283.
[50] *APC* IV. 302.
[51] Machyn, 52. He was rewarded with an annuity (*APC* IV. 407).
[52] *CSP Sp.* XII. 297, 315.
[53] Ibid. 290.

was forgiven, and in March 1555 featured in a great joust at Westminster, where 'the chalyngers was a Spaneard and ser Gorge Haward; and all ther men and ther horsses trymmyd in whyt'.[54] There is no obvious reason why Howard should have felt so strongly about this bill. The earl of Pembroke was also reported by the French ambassador as having quarrelled about the bill over dinner with some of his followers. One of them, Sir John Perrot, became so angry that he drew his dagger, for which he was dismissed, taking with him, it was said, forty other of the earl's clients who felt the same way about the exiles bill.[55]

The opponents of the bill feared that the government would repeat its successful manœuvre of 3 December when the doors of the Chamber had been locked and a division forced on the first fruits bill: when, therefore, on 6 December they noticed after the third reading of the exiles bill that there was present in the House a majority against the bill, Sir Anthony Kingston, knight of the shire for Gloucestershire, and his associates seized the key of the Chamber from the serjeant-at-arms, blockaded the door, presumably to prevent anyone from leaving to fetch government reinforcements, and insisted that the speaker should put the question.[56] The bill was defeated.[57]

The government reacted sharply, committing Kingston to the Tower on 10 December, the day after parliament ended, 'upon a contemptuouse behaviour and great disorder by him lately committed in the Parliament House'.[58] Kingston remained in the Tower, being questioned by crown lawyers Stanford and Browne, until 24 December, when he was released 'uppon his humble submission and knowledge of his offence'.[59] The serjeant-at-arms was also committed for having allowed his keys to be taken from him, and he remained in custody from 11 until 18 December.[60]

So dramatic had the whole scene been that it could be

[54] Machyn, 84.
[55] Arch. Étr., XII. fo. 470 (Vertot, V. 252). For Perrot, see below, 211–13.
[56] *CSP Ven.* VI. i. 283.
[57] *CJ.* 6 Dec. No division figures were recorded.
[58] *APC* 1554–6, 202.
[59] Ibid. 208.
[60] Ibid. 202, 204.

recalled vividly thirty years later by one of those present, Sir Nicholas Bagnall, burgess for Newcastle under Lyme.[61] Bagnall used precisely the same tactics to defeat a subsidy bill introduced into the Irish parliament in 1586. 'Finding the negative voice able to prevail the day the bill should come in question', Bagnall would 'suffer no ear to be given' to a motion of the speaker's that the committees should consult with the Lord Deputy. Instead, he persuaded his colleagues that 'the door should be kept locked and no man suffered to leave the House until it were divided, alleging therein a precedent of the like done in England in Queen Mary's time'.[62]

Why did the exiles bill arouse so much hostility? The bill itself has disappeared, but the Venetian ambassador reported that it threatened all exiles, including those who had received permission from the queen to depart, with the confiscation of their property if they did not return to England within a given time after being ordered to do so.[63] To forestall criticism about harming future generations, Michieli noted, the exiles' property was not to be lost for ever, but simply confiscated for the period of their absence.[64] The bill seems, then, to have resembled a measure passed in 1571 declaring that those who had departed the realm without a licence and did not return within six months of a proclamation ordering them to do so should lose their chattels and forfeit the profits from their lands for the remainder of their own lifetimes.[65] (The same applied to those who had originally secured a licence if they did not return within six months of the expiry of the licence.) The Elizabethan statute further stated that conveyances made to avoid the provisions of the act would be held void, whilst another statute of

[61] For Bagnall, see below, 221–2.
[62] Letter of Sir John Perrot to Lord Burghley, 24 May 1586, amongst the Perrot Papers calendared by C. McNeill, in *Analecta Hibernica*, XII (1943), 54. I owe this reference to Mr Victor Treadwell.
[63] *CSP Ven.* VI. i. 243.
[64] It is possible that the bill was subsequently restricted to those who had gone abroad without a licence, for in a letter to his father of 3 Nov. 1555 Lord Talbot reported that there was a bill under discussion concerning the duchess of Suffolk and others who have gone beyond the sea 'wit*h*oute a lyssanse, that if they come nott home by a daye apoynted', the Queen's Majesty shall have the benefit of their livings during their abode forth of the realm. (Lodge, *Illustrations of English History*, I. 207.)
[65] 13 Elizabeth, c. 3.

the following year permitted the queen to make grants 'pour terme dauter vie' from land thus confiscated.[66]

The interpretation of the law concerning Englishmen who went abroad was unclear. For instance, some lawyers believed that it was not necessary for a subject to secure a royal licence before he went overseas: in 1570 it was decided in the case of a merchant who had fled the realm to escape an impending law-suit that an unlicensed departure was not 'any offence or contempt, for it is a thing indifferent to depart the kingdom, and the purpose and cause, which is secret in the heart, is not examinable'.[67] Some members of the Lower House in 1555 were critical of the exiles bill because it seemed to imply restrictions on the liberty of the Englishman to go wherever he wished, and the bill may indeed have involved a principle new to the six-teenth century.[68] Moreover, it seemed to some improper to res-cind a licence once it had been obtained,[69] and many of the exiles had in fact secured royal permission to depart; indeed, in 1560 the judges were to decide in the case of Mr Bertie, the husband of the duchess of Suffolk, that 'the licence which was granted for a time certain was not countermandable or revocable by the prince'.[70]

The main object of the bill was probably to permit the confiscation of the exiles' land rather than to secure their return. Whilst some exiles were undoubtedly a great nuisance to the government—at the very time when parliament was debating the exiles bill, books attacking 'the King individually and his mode of government', mentioning in particular the examples of Naples and Milan, were distributed clandestinely throughout England, many of them the work of the exiles[71]—the crown never altered its policy of turning a blind eye to the flight of dissidents, provided that no charges relating to rebellion were

[66] 14 Elizabeth, c. 6.
[67] Dyer, *Reports of Cases*, 296.
[68] *CSP Ven.* VI. i. 251.
[69] Ibid.
[70] Dyer, *Reports of Cases*, 176b. However, a letter from the queen of 28 Sept. 1555 commissioning St Pol to collect the revenues of their estates states that Bertie and the Duchess 'hath lately withdrawn them selfes out of our Realms and be fledd and departed in to the partes of beyonde the seas with out our spicall Licence' (Lincolnshire Archives Office 3 Anc 8/1/3; I owe this reference to Mr G. Hill). The duchess apparently had no licence, although Bertie did.
[71] *CSP Ven.* VI. i. 269–70.

involved. The government needed money, as the chancellor had pointed out at the opening of parliament, and some of the exiles were of considerable wealth: only a few weeks before the introduction of the bill the privy council had ordered that a list should be drawn up of the possessions of the duchess of Suffolk.[72] But, again, there was uncertainty about what the scope of confiscation was in such cases. In Hilary Term 1556, after the failure of the exiles bill, the crown asked the judges whether lands and chattels might be seized for contempt if those who had departed without a licence chose to ignore a summons sent under the privy seal requiring their return by a certain date:[73] it would appear that the crown did not receive the answer for which it hoped. Probably chattels were seizable under a statute of 1381, but even this was not certain.[74] It was presumably lack of certainty that the exiles bill had been meant to quell.

Whatever the main purpose of the bill was, the significant question concerns the motives of the men who opposed it. Did they dislike the bill because it increased the power of the crown to confiscate landed property, or did they dislike it because it would harm the exiles, many of whom had close family connections with men sitting in the 1555 parliament? And if members did dislike the bill because it harmed the exiles, were they concerned about exiles in general, or only about those who were exiles for religion? It must be remembered that Miss Garrett, in her valuable work *The Marian Exiles*, gives the somewhat misleading impression that almost all the English who went abroad in Mary's reign did so because they disliked her religious policy: this view ignores the fact that some went abroad to seek employment or to escape their creditors, or, like the majority of those who travelled to Italy, to complete their education.[75] Potentially, the bill affected them all. One major obstacle in the way of any interpretation of the motives impelling members of the House of Commons to oppose the bill is the fact that the clerk was too excited at the time of the division to note

[72] *APC* 1554–1556, 180.
[73] Dyer, *Reports of Cases*, 128b.
[74] 5 Richard II, 1, c. 2.
[75] On this see K. R. Bartlett, 'The Role of the Marian Exiles', in *The House of Commons, 1558–1603*, 102–10.

the size of the vote for and against the bill: we do not, therefore, know whether Kingston's friends made up the larger part of the whole House, or whether they were simply a vociferous and aggressive, but nonetheless tiny, minority who just happened to find themselves in a position of strength. Moreover, we do not know which individuals opposed the measure—only Kingston, Howard, and Perrot can be positively identified as hostile to this particular proposal. None of the three was especially closely associated with the exiles, or with *émigré* politics. Although a number of other members can be linked with opposition to government policies in this parliament[76] there is no positive evidence that permits identification with Kingston's group. To explain the opposition to the bill one must, therefore, go back to the comments of the Venetian ambassador, and those comments certainly imply that a concern for property and for what might be called the freedom of the individual were as important in creating an atmosphere of hostility for the proposal as protestant inclinations and family connections with those in exile.

Relations between crown and parliament were sour for the few days that remained of the session. When the queen came to end the meeting on 9 December Noailles reported that she was so angry and frustrated that she hardly bothered to conceal the fact.[77] From a personal point of view it is true that the meeting had not been a success. Mary had wanted a parliament because she wished to strengthen Philip's constitutional position. In the event, neither Philip's coronation nor the closely related question of the succession had been sanctioned or settled by statute[78]—as Peter Martyr wrote triumphantly to Bullinger, 'the English have dissolved their parliament without having installed Philip in possession of the kingdom'.[79] This failure was to be a source of much misery to the queen.[80]

But in fact most government objectives had been attained. The crown had rid itself of first fruits and of its former church property, it had been given financial aid, albeit on a smaller

[76] See below, 152–7.
[77] Arch. Étr., XII. fo. 468ᵛ (Vertot, V, 246).
[78] But see below, Appendix C.
[79] *Original Letters Relative to the English Reformation*, ed. H. Robinson (Parker Society, 1846–7), II. 518.
[80] e.g., *CSP Ven.* VI. i. 281.

scale than had been hoped, and it had implemented most of the proposals discussed by the privy council before the parliament opened, such as the licensing of alehouses[81] and a further measure to deal with gaol delivery.[82] The North had been made more secure by a statute for the rebuilding of fortifications[83] and by the restoration of the Nevilles.[84] A statute that restored to the Duchy of Lancaster all lands that had been alienated since the death of Henry VIII did something to improve royal finances.[85] Thus, although the queen and her advisers had been surprised by the vehement opposition that met some of their proposals, finding members 'plus rudes et obstinez qu'ilz n'avoient esté de tout son regne',[86] the meeting was far from unsuccessful.

Indeed, those who sat in parliament could go home with a real sense of achievement: this session is remarkable in particular for the amount of social and economic legislation that was passed. Most of this legislation, a response to the worsening economic situation, was conservative in tone. For instance, a bill was passed reviving Henrician and Edwardian legislation on poverty and vagrancy which also permitted local authorities to issue licences to beg.[87] A whole group of bills dealing with the cloth industry was successful, the most important of them being a measure restricting the number of looms that might be operated by any individual, and confining all weaving to corporate towns.[88] This statute appears to have grown out of a bill read for the first time on 4 November for 'weavers in Gloucestershire to have greater wages'. On its second reading this bill was committed to one of the knights for that county, Kingston, but it was then abandoned in favour of a new measure 'touching weavers, and keeping of looms', a bill again committed to

---

[81] 2 & 3 Philip and Mary, c. 9.
[82] 2 & 3 Philip and Mary, c. 10. See above, 125–6, and Langbein, *Prosecuting Crime in the Renaissance*, 15–45, 61–2.
[83] 2 & 3 Philip and Mary, c. 1.
[84] HLRO, Original Acts, 2 & 3 Philip and Mary, 22.
[85] 2 & 3 Philip and Mary, c. 20. On this see Loades, *The Reign of Mary Tudor*, 275–6.
[86] Vertot, V. 239.
[87] 2 & 3 Philip and Mary, c. 5. Lords Rich, Willoughby, and Chandos registered protests when this bill passed the Lords on 26 Nov.
[88] 2 & 3 Philip and Mary, c. 11.

Kingston on its second reading.[89] On 25 November yet another new bill was read and this was finally passed on 27 November.[90] Concern about the cloth industry was considerable, for the Lords had passed a bill reviving 5 & 6 Edward VI, c. 6, a statute that had tightened up standards of cloth production, although this bill was rejected on its third reading in the Commons on 4 December. Other successful bills dealt with the making of cloths in Somerset[91] and with the exemption of the town of Halifax from the Edwardian statute regulating the purchase of wool, 5 & 6 Edward VI, c. 7.[92] However, bills to encourage the making of coloured cloth in England, for Norfolk and Norwich cloths, and for Devon weavers were all rejected or lost.[93]

Another indication of concern about the economic situation is the number of bills that were introduced relating to the decay of tillage. On 4 November, under the aegis of Cecil, two bills were read, one for the increase of tillage and one for the rebuilding of decayed houses of husbandry. A new bill on tillage was read on 11 November, when it was described as a measure intended to amend some part of 5 & 6 Edward VI c. 6. This bill was passed the following day without a formal second reading being recorded. It received its first reading in the Lords on 16 November, when it was committed, and subsequently disappeared. Meanwhile, in the Commons on 13 November, a bill was read for the re-edifying of houses and the conversion of pasture into tillage. Yet another bill on the same subject was read on 16 November, when Cecil's name was again mentioned. This bill, read for a second time on 25 November and passed on 28, subsequently became a statute whereby the 1489 act for the maintenance of houses of husbandry was confirmed: it also authorized the establishment of four commissions to investigate infringements of relevant statutes passed since 1536.[94] (The statute for the rebuilding of castles and fortifications in the North of course also contained a clause about the mainten-

---

[89] *CJ* 6 Nov., 14 and 19 Nov.
[90] No second reading is recorded in the Journal.
[91] 2 & 3 Philip and Mary, c. 12.
[92] 2 & 3 Philip and Mary, c. 13.
[93] *CJ* 9 Nov.; 9 and 12 Nov.; 22 Nov.
[94] 2 & 3 Philip and Mary, c. 2. The commissions do not appear to have operated.

ance of tillage.[95]) As with the cloth bills, there is no evidence of government initiative in the discussions about tillage; there was no one on the council in Mary's reign who had the same informed interest in economic matters as, for instance, Cecil himself. However, another measure requiring farmers with more than 120 sheep to maintain one milk cow per sixty sheep and farmers with more than twenty oxen to maintain one milk cow per ten beasts, which bears some resemblance to Hales's abortive proposal of 1549,[96] seems to have been sponsored by Sir John Bourne, secretary of state, whose name is recorded on 25 October in connection with a bill 'to avoid killing of calves to sale'; this bill was abandoned in favour of another which was first read on 4 November. In the Lords the bill produced formal protests from Williams, Willoughby, Paget, and Chandos: it is not clear why they objected to a measure intended to reduce the price of dairy produce, an essential part of the diet of the poor.[97] It is perhaps significant that Willoughby and Chandos, with Rich, had also protested against the poor relief bill.[98]

The House of Lords was, overall, more unwilling than usual to pass bills from the House of Commons. On 18 November the House rejected a bill that would have prevented anyone's servant 'Wearing their Cloths', except those of the king and queen, from becoming a justice of the peace.[99] The next day two bills, one about silk workers and another about Teignmouth, were rejected.[100] More seriously, the House on 28 November rejected the bill giving protection to some of those who had received grants from the duke of Norfolk's lands at the time of his attainder.[101]

This parliament also witnessed a resurgence in the kind of anticlericalism so common in Henrician parliaments. It arose out of a particularly nasty murder case in which the prime mover, one Benet Smith, put in a plea of benefit of clergy. This seems to have caused general outrage, and on 25 October the

---

[95] 2 & 3 Philip and Mary, c. 1.
[96] *A Discourse of the Common Weal*, ed. E. Lamond (Cambridge, 1893; 1929), lxiii.
[97] *LJ* 20 Nov.
[98] *LJ* 26 Nov.
[99] Introduced into the Commons on 30 Oct.
[100] Introduced into the Commons on 4 Nov. and 28 Oct.
[101] See above, 67–8.

Commons read a bill preventing accessories in murder cases from pleading their clergy. After a second reading this bill was replaced by another, which was lost in the Lords. On 6 November a more restricted bill, dealing only with Smith himself, was read in the Commons. On 18 November the House ordered that the widow of the murdered man and two of the council should petition the queen asking that Smith might be allowed out of the Tower to appear before the Commons. This was permitted, and on 22 November the House interviewed Smith and his associates. The bill stripping him of benefit of clergy was subsequently passed,[102] although even in this very restricted form the bill provoked protests from nine members of the Upper House, including five bishops.[103] A third bill, to punish procurers of murder, was rejected by the Commons on 3 December. This was not the end of the matter, however, for another general bill came before the next parliament.[104]

Parliamentary historians have tended to regard the events of the parliament of 1555, and in particular what went on in the House of Commons, as of more than transitory significance. 'There was, indeed, a degree of organisation about the parliamentary opposition in 1555', Sir John Neale wrote in the first of his volumes on *Elizabeth I and her Parliaments*, 'which though in some ways a flash in the pan, marks a significant stage in the evolution of the House of Commons'.[105] Neale's verdict was widely accepted, and has become a commonplace of history textbooks.[106] Does Neale's judgement remain valid? Was the opposition in the House of Commons to certain government measures in any sense 'organized'? Was it, indeed, successful— after all, there was widespread hostility in the House to the first fruits bill, yet the government's coup of 3 December was carried through triumphantly.

Evidence for the existence of an organized opposition in 1555

---

[102] HLRO, Original Acts, 2 & 3 Philip and Mary, 16. Smith was hanged four months later. (Machyn, 102.)

[103] *LJ* 3 Dec.

[104] See below, 166.

[105] Neale, *Elizabeth I and her Parliaments, 1559–1581*, 23.

[106] For example, R. G. Gilkes, *The Tudor Parliament* (London, 1969), 127–8.

is, in fact, slight. Eight members of the Commons grumbled to the French ambassador, but we do not know which they were nor whether their words were transformed into action.[107] As well as the Noailles residence, another centre for the disaffected of this parliament was Arundel's tavern in Fleet Street. Several months after the dissolution of parliament when a rather amateur conspiracy was discovered, involving some of the *émigrés* in France and a plan to seize the Treasury and depose Mary,[108] one of those questioned, John Danyell, revealed that

in the parlement tyme: these men, whos names do folow, did moche Assemble together At one harandayles house, that is to say, Mr courtney, Mr pollard, Mr chamberne, Mr chechester,[109] Mr perret, Mr yong,[110] Mr pekkam: with such other yong heads . . . And I have perceyved by there talke *and* behayveyoure that with gret wilfullnesse thei intended to resiste such matters as shuld be spoken off in the parleyment other then lyked them, And that thei did very sore myslyke such catholik procedynges as thei perceyved the quene and all catholike men went Aboute, As in dede thei Did euery way declayr them selfes to be right protestantes. And if I had bene A parleyment man my selfe, as I was not: I thynk I shuld have knowne of them some further matter in some certeyn *and* more synglar poyntes than I do.[111]

(The last point refers to the convention that parliamentary

---

[107] Arch. Étr. IX. fo. 565 (Vertot, V. 223). One of those involved may, however, have been Courtenay, as Noailles wrote '. . . douze gentilizhommes de ceste nation, qui vindrent hier fort privement disner avecques moy, m'ont faict entendre desquelz les huict sont dudict parlement et les aultres personnages de bonne part, mesmes l'ung est fort proche et du mesme nom de Courtenay'.

[108] Loades, *Two Tudor Conspiracies*, ch. 8.

[109] This is the only evidence for Chichester's return for this parliament:
Danyell may well have been mistaken, since Chichester cannot have sat for Devon as he did in 1547 and Apr. 1554 because the knights in 1555 are known to have been James Basset and Robert Dennys. It is a pity that his election cannot be confirmed, since he spent some time in Venice in 1555 and there may have become involved with the earl of Devon's circle (Garrett, *Manan Exiles*, 118; K. Bartlett, '"The misfortune that is wished for him": The Exile and Death of Edward Courtenay, eighth Earl of Devon', *Canadian Journal of History*, XIV (1979), 1–28)—this link would obviously be of great interest in the context of the defeat of the exiles bill.

[110] John Young, who sat for Plymouth. He is probably the man who accompanied Northampton, with Perrot, Henry Carey, and the Verney brothers to France in 1551 (*CSP For. 1547–53*, 122–3).

[111] SP 11/8/35.

matters should not be discussed outside the Chamber.) As a result of Danyell's statement, Sir William Courtenay, Sir John Pollard, and Sir John Perrot were sent to the Tower.[112] (Henry Peckham was already in custody.) Sir Arthur Champernon, who sat with Courtenay for Plympton, was probably also arrested.[113] However, the evidence for actively treasonable activity was more or less non-existent in the cases of Pollard, Chichester, Perrot, and Champernon, slight for Courtenay and conclusive only for Peckham, who was executed. Interestingly, the knights of the shire for Buckinghamshire, Edmund and Francis Verney, who had been deeply involved in the plotting, were not amongst those mentioned by Danyell, and it therefore seems likely that the meetings at Arundel's were occasions for grumbling and for indiscreet complaints rather than for plotting.

None the less, the fact remains that several members of the 1555 House of Commons had been involved in the conspiracy. Against Sir Nicholas Arnold, one of the knights for Gloucestershire, and Sir John St Loe, whose constituency is unknown, there was little hard evidence, but Edmund Verney came under grave suspicion and his brother Francis was, like Peckham, condemned to death, although he was subsequently reprieved.[114] Sir Anthony Kingston died before he could be brought to trial; he would surely otherwise have shared Peckham's fate. By the middle of November[115] Kingston had become involved in plotting with the French and before the end of the parliament other critics of royal policy had allowed themselves to drift into conspiracy: these facts surely argue against the theory that the session of 1555 witnessed any startling evolution in the conception and planning of constitutional opposition. Great 'parliamentarians' do not plot with the enemies of their country: their interest is in tactics, not treason.

It is in any case difficult to see Kingston's activities in this parliament as evidence for 'tactical precocity': locking the door of the Chamber was hardly a sophisticated manœuvre. It was, however, an action typical of Kingston, a man confident in his

[112] Machyn, 104.
[113] *APC* V. 304, 373.
[114] Loades, *Two Tudor Conspiracies*, 211–12, 228, 234.
[115] Ibid. 186–7.

wealth and position, but of hasty and violent temper. The son of a royal official, Sir William Kingston, who had fought at Flodden before becoming constable of the Tower and comptroller of the royal household,[116] Sir Anthony Kingston had assisted the crown in the insurrection of 1536, for which he was knighted.[117] He gradually amassed a number of minor offices, many of them from Augmentations: in May 1556, when Sir Henry Jerningham was granted many of the posts formerly held by Kingston, these included the chief stewardship of Tewkesbury, the stewardship of lordships in Gloucestershire and Worcestershire, and the chief mastership of the hunt within the chase of Corstlawnd, Gloucestershire.[118] (When Kingston was asked to settle his Augmentations debt it totalled £2,182— he was permitted, after transferring land in Herefordshire to the crown, to pay off the remainder by annual sums of £50.[119]) In Edward's reign Kingston received further substantial grants for his services to the crown, including a reward for his part in the suppression of the Western Rising, in which he served as provost-marshal for Cornwall under Russell.[120] He was high steward of the lordship of Berkeley and held an office on the Buckingham estates.[121] It is not surprising, therefore, to find him described to the Constable of France in 1555 as a man who could 'assuredly raise more than six thousand men in his district and more than sixty of the most important knights of the district';[122] Michieli said of him at the same period that he was 'a gentleman of renown, who has followers, both on account of his wealth' and because of the favours he had received from Henry VIII.[123] He was, then, 'a man of great influence'.[124]

However, he was a man of action and not a man of

---

[116] *DNB sub* William Kingston.

[117] *DNB sub* Sir Anthony Kingston.

[118] *CPR* Philip and Mary, III. 222, 229. See also *Letters and Papers*, XXI. i. 643.

[119] Richardson, *History of the Court of Augmentations, 1536–1554*, 242. The demand that he should pay his debt came, I think, in 1546, when he was summoned before the Council 'to answer his debt' (*Letters and Papers*, XXI. i. 925).

[120] SP 10/19.

[121] G. Baskerville, 'The Dispossessed Religious of Gloucestershire', *Trans. Bristol and Gloucestershire Arch. Soc.* XLIX (1927), 108, 109.

[122] Harbison, *Rival Ambassadors*, 280, citing Arch. Étr. IX. fo. 660.

[123] *CSP Ven.* VI. i. 283, 300.

[124] *Original Letters Relative to the English Reformation*, 441–2: John ab Ulmis to Bullinger, 1551.

manœuvre, as the story of his relationship with Bishop Hooper illustrates. At an early age Kingston tried to have his first marriage dissolved, but the archbishop of Canterbury, Cranmer, refused to grant a decree of nullity 'that he may live in adultery with another woman and she with another man'.[125] None the less in 1536 Kingston married the widow of Sir William Courtenay of Powderham—his stepson, William, was also to be involved in Dudley's conspiracy.[126] For this, Kingston was cited before Hooper when the bishop visited his diocese in 1551. Kingston 'at first refused to make his appearance', but finally came, and was rebuked, whereupon he struck Hooper 'a blow on the cheek before all the people, and loaded him with abuse': he was summoned to London, fined £500, and forced to do penance.[127] However, according to Foxe, the tale has a happy ending. When Hooper was taken to Gloucester for his execution in 1555, Kingston came to him in prison and wept for his fate; he declared that he had been 'an adulterer and a fornicator' but that Hooper had redeemed him.[128] There are other examples of Kingston's violent behaviour. He was reputed to have put down the Western Rising with extreme and unnecessary brutality.[129] After Kingston's imprisonment for his behaviour in the parliament of 1555 Sir Nicholas Arnold had to warn him about his rash talk 'towching hys late imprysonmentt mysslyking the same'.[130] He was said to have told the conspirator Dudley, 'If you go into the service of the King [of France], and land in my county, I will go to meet you with all my forces to chase these tyrants from our country':[131] harsh words to a fellow conspirator.

To see in Kingston, therefore, the beginning of a process by which the opposition to the crown in the House of Commons developed techniques and tactics as sophisticated as those of the crown itself is to misunderstand Kingston's character and to

---

[125] Ibid. See also J. Ridley, *Thomas Cranmer* (Oxford, 1962), 134–5, Cranmer to Sir William Kingston, July 1533.

[126] See above, 149.

[127] *Original Letters Relative to the English Reformation*, 441–2.

[128] Foxe, VI. 653–4.

[129] T. Fuller, *The Worthies of England* (London, 1662), I. 397; F. Rose-Troup, *The Western Rebellion of 1549* (London, 1913), 306–17.

[130] SP 11/8/49.

[131] Harbison, *Rival Ambassadors*, 281, citing Arch. Étr. IX. fo. 660.

gloss over his actual conduct. It was not by delicate and tortuous manipulations of procedure, by lobbying or persuasion, that Kingston succeeded in defeating the exiles bill, but by force. Indeed, it would have been surprising to find any great ability to manage the House of Commons in Kingston, as he had not sat in the Chamber since the first of Edward's parliaments: if opposition had evolved during Mary's reign Kingston had not witnessed it. Nor was he able, of course, to carry forward any skills into the next meeting. In fact, the parliament of 1558 was remarkably quiescent; the critics of crown policy in 1559 were men who had been out of the country during Mary's reign.

Both the degree of organization and the subtlety of tactics of crown critics in 1555 have probably, therefore, been overestimated, as has their part in any 'evolution' of opposition practice. None the less, there does appear to have been a little more coherence in the opposition group of that parliament, a little more consistency of personnel and principle than can be found in any other Marian assembly. The crown could recognize its opponents over the first fruits bill and permit a division only when they had been forced by pressure of other business, hunger or fatigue, to leave the Chamber. Similarly, Kingston, according to the Venetian envoy, could tell by a glance round the Chamber that a majority in favour of rejecting the exiles bill was present.[132] Perhaps these two groups were the same, and those who were hostile to the crown over the first fruits bill also disliked the exiles bill? We cannot be sure.

There does, however, exist amongst the More-Molyneux papers a document that might be a list of such hostile members, drawn up for the crown or some other interested party. This is a list of those who 'in quene marys tyme were in *t*he *p*arliament fyrst holden ageynst the general repele of al treasens etc whereby the statute of *t*he supremisy was repelyd'.[133] Although the title implies that the document refers to the parliament of November 1554 and to the bill reuniting England with Rome,

---

[132] *CSP Ven.* VI. i. 283.
[133] Guildford Museum, Loseley MS 1331/1: See Appendix D. The History of Parliament Trust drew my attention to this list, and I benefited from a number of discussions about the interpretation of the list with Professor Bindoff and others, although our views were not the same.

there is ample evidence that it in fact refers to 1555.[134] Obviously the title at least was written in Elizabeth's reign, and it may be that the list, like another in the same collection of the sheriffs of Surrey and Sussex 'that did burn the innocents, with the names of such whom they burnt'[135] is a record of who did what in the 1550s.

What were the men in the list 'ageynst', and when? The most obvious explanation of the Loseley list is that it provides a record of one side in a division in the Commons. However, it is difficult to identify the list with any known division in this parliament: in the division on the first fruits bill, for instance, 126 members opposed the motion, but there are only 106 men on the Loseley list, whilst the clerk was so flustered on 6 December that he did not record the figures in the division on the exiles bill. A link with the exiles debate might be found in the fact that the Loseley list begins with Kingston's name: on the other hand, this may simply be a reflection of his high social standing—the list, a neat and formal document, places all the knights first. However, it is of interest that two other members who are known to have been opposed to the exiles bill, Sir George Howard and Sir John Perrot, are also on the list. It is possible, therefore, that the Loseley document records those who were expected to be opposed to the exiles bill, or those who on the day showed themselves hostile to it.

The list includes a number of men who were later to be questioned in connection with the Treasury plot,[136] as well as the names of two other members who are known from different sources to have displeased the queen in the course of this parliament, Thomas Gargrave and Gabriel Pleydell. Sir Thomas Gargrave, knight of the shire for Yorkshire, was a client of the

---

[134] Only 10 of the names on the list are not known from other sources to have members of the 1555 House of Commons. Two Mr Jones sat in Apr. 1554, as well as in 1555, but only in 1555 did a Mr Porter of Gray's Inn (William) and a Mr Porter of Gloucester (Arthur) appear together in the House. Only in 1555 did both Edmund and Francis Verney sit in the Commons. A Mr Thomas Phillips and another Mr Phillips sat in the same House only in Nov. 1554 and in 1555. The evidence that the list refers to the parliament of 1555 seems, therefore, conclusive.

[135] Printed in *HMC More-Molyneux MSS* VII. 6. The document is either from the papers of William More of Loseley (for whom, see below, 213–15) who, as one of the burgesses for Guildford, appears on the list, or from the papers of his friend Sir Thomas Cawarden.

[136] See above, 148–9.

earl of Shrewsbury to whom he wrote in January 1556 regretting that he had offended the queen 'by only sitting still in the passing of a bill in the parliament without any obstinacy or other doing or speaking'; he also complained that he 'should be so reported in religion'.[137] There is no means of ascertaining to which bill Gargrave was here referring. Pleydell, who sat for Marlborough, was a quite different character from the usually conformist Gargrave. An extremely quarrelsome and litigious man,[138] he was at this time under suspicion of having harboured a burglar,[139] and on 10 December, that is, as soon as the parliament ended, he was sent to the Fleet. He was later to claim that this was not 'for any matter depending in the Court of Star Chamber'—that is, the burglar—'but for speaking his conscience in the parliament in a bill concerning the commonwealth'.[140] Whatever the true explanation for his detention was, it is clear that Pleydell believed that he had done something during the course of the session to offend the crown; this same action may account for his inclusion on the Loseley list.

There is, however, one surprising omission from the list, another member who is known to have been involved in an attack on royal policy in the course of this parliament but who is not named here. This is William Cecil. According to Cecil's anonymous biographer

there was a matter in question for something the Queen would have pass, wherein Sir Anthony Kingston, Sir William Courtenay, Sir John Pollard, and many others of value, especially western men, were opposite. Sir William Cecil, being their speaker, and having that day told a good tale for them, when the House rose they came to him and said they would dine with him that day. He answered, they should be welcome, so they did not speak of any matters of parliament, which they promised.[141] Yet some began to break promise, for which he challenged them.[142]

---

[137] *HMC Shrewsbury MSS in Lambeth Palace Library*, 704. (The unsuccessful bill for justices of the peace was given to him for articling on 31 Oct. but it seems unlikely that this is relevant to his comments.)

[138] e.g., PRO Star Chamber 4/8/49, 4/9/6.

[139] Star Chamber 4/3/72. The issuing of a recognizance for Pleydell to appear in Star Chamber led to debate in the Commons on 6 Dec. as to whether the privilege of a member had thus been breached. It was decided that it had not.

[140] BL Harley MS 2143, fo. 3ʳ.

[141] Because of the convention of secrecy about parliamentary affairs.

[142] F. Peck, *Desiderata Curiosa* (London, 1732) I. 9.

The account relates that all those mentioned were subsequently examined by the privy council and committed:[143] Cecil himself recorded in his diary that he had been questioned by Paget and Petre because he had incurred 'some ill will' by speaking freely in parliament. (He added, with a little complacency, that it was, after all still 'better to obey God than man'.[144])

What was the 'matter in question' over which Cecil challenged the crown? His main involvement in this parliament appears to have been with the tillage bills, but these were not politically controversial.[145] On 10 November a subsequently unsuccessful bill 'for the execution of divers statutes and laws' had been committed to him: again, this seems unlikely to have been the cause of the trouble. More relevant, perhaps, is the fact that the first fruits bill was committed to him for articling on 23 November. Perhaps it was Cecil's speeches on this bill that worried the council and led to the approach from Kingston and the other 'western men'; this would explain his absence from the Loseley list, if that is in fact a list of men who opposed the exiles bill. None the less, it would be surprising if Cecil had not in fact opposed the exiles bill, since not only his brother-in-law, Cheke, but several more of his relatives and friends had gone abroad: moreover, at the end of the session Cheke wrote to Cecil congratulating him on his 'well-doing' in the Parliament.[146]

Can anything be learned from a consideration of the names on the list? Twenty-two knights of the shire are mentioned; this is a large number, and fits in with what is already known of the crown's critics in this parliament, who were substantial and powerful men. Kingston, Howard, and Gargrave have already been noted. Perrot, who will be discussed later, was a wealthy Pembrokeshire gentleman.[147] Sir Nicholas Arnold, afterwards to be lord justice of Ireland, was a rich landowner who had played a prominent part at court and in military affairs in the reigns of Henry and Edward.[148] Sir John St Loe had large

---

[143] There is no record of this in the council register.
[144] C. Read, *Mr Secretary Cecil and Queen Elizabeth* (London, 1955), 109, translating BL Lansdowne MS 118.
[145] See above, 145.
[146] BL Lansdowne MS 94, no. 63.
[147] See below, 211–13.
[148] *DNB Supplement, sub* Arnold, Sir Nicholas.

estates in Gloucestershire and in Somerset, the county for which he may have sat in 1555: the recipient of royal favours for three decades, he seems none the less to have confined his activities largely to his own locality.[149] Sir William Courtenay was one of the most important landowners in Devon.[150] Although it is possible that he held reformed religious ideas— he can almost certainly be identified with the 'sir . . . Courtenay knight' who assaulted a priest in December 1553[151]—his involvement in opposition probably stemmed from his relationship with his stepfather, Kingston. Another Devon landowner was Sir John Pollard, whose election for Exeter in 1555 involved the reversal of a decision the city had taken only a year before, that no one save citizens and freemen should serve as its representatives in parliament.[152]

Besides the high social status of many of the men listed, the other interesting fact about the list as a whole is its geographical spread. Of the ninety-three men whose constituencies can be identified with any certainty, twenty come from Dorset and Wiltshire and another twelve from the three counties of Gloucestershire, Devon, and Cornwall. Most of the remainder come from the east and south, rather than the midlands or north: one of the knights for Cheshire, Sir Laurence Smith, is listed, and so, as we have noted, is Gargrave, but the general pattern is striking, and cannot be explained simply in terms of the over-representation of the southern counties.[153] Is this a list, then, of the 'western men' of whom Cecil spoke?[154]

The religious views of the men on the list, whatever they may have been in 1555, developed differently thereafter. Some subsequently embraced protestantism wholeheartedly; St Loe, who died in 1559, was buried 'nodur crosse nor prest, nor

---

[149] *The House of Commons, 1509–1558.*

[150] *CSP Ven.* VI. i. 439: Loades, *Two Tudor Conspiracies*, 211.

[151] *Queen Jane and Queen Mary*, 33. Courtenay had certainly been in London a few weeks earlier, since he was knighted on 2 Oct.

[152] Exeter City RO, Act Book II, fos. 135ᵛ, 143. He was immediately admitted as a freeman. He must be distinguished from the speaker, for whom see, Ch. 2 n. 103.

[153] Several members are also listed with their colleagues: both members for Rochester, for instance, both of those representing Bletchingley, both of those for Gloucester, Hythe, Wycombe, Wareham, Huntingdonshire, and so on.

[154] See above, 154.

clarkes, but a sermon and after a salme of Davyd'[155] and Robert Bowyer, who died about 1567, left a firmly protestant will—'I may wholely refer my evil will to His good will' and so on.[156] William Porter of Gray's Inn was described by his bishop in 1564 as 'earnest' in religion,[157] as was Sir Andrew Corbet, one of the knights of the shire for Shropshire in 1555.[158] Sir Nicholas Lestrange, who sat for King's Lynn in 1555, was in 1564 described as one of the 'metest men to help' with the establishment of the 1559 settlement.[159] William Devenish, a burgess for Lewes in 1555, was, however, said in 1564 to be a 'misliker of godly orders'[160] and Richard Cornwall, the 'baron of Burford', described by his bishop as a 'neuter', was subsequently removed from the bench.[161] Sir George Blount, who sat for Much Wenlock in 1555, was said by the bishop of Coventry and Lichfield to be 'an adversary to religion' in 1564, and in 1577 he was returned as a recusant.[162] Although the general drift of the men listed on the Loseley document was, then, towards protestantism, it seems probable, given the number of conservatives also noted, that the issue at stake was not a purely doctrinal one.

The evidence for the organization of opposition in the House of Commons in 1555 thus amounts to a list of which the purpose is unknown and to the statement about meetings in a public house of a man who, by his own admission, was excluded from the most intimate discussions.[163] The only real success of the opposition, the defeat of the exiles bill, was brought about by force on Kingston's part and not by subtle manœuvrings. It seems likely that what occurred in this parliament was not an evolution of opposition organization but rather a failure of management by the crown. There were many fewer privy

---

[155] Machyn, 191.
[156] *The House of Commons, 1509–1558*, citing PCC 24 Babington.
[157] *Camden Miscellany IX*, 27.
[158] Ibid. 44. In the 1570s Corbet delegated to his parishioners the choice of clergyman at Moreton Corbet, of which he was patron (P. Collinson, *The Elizabethan Puritan Movement* (London, 1967), 139, 337). See also A. E. C(orbet), *The Family of Corbet* (n.p., n.d.), 287.
[159] *Camden Miscellany IX*, 58.
[160] Ibid. 10.
[161] Ibid. 15: *House of Commons, 1509–1558*.
[162] *Camden Miscellany IX*, 42; *House of Commons, 1558–1603*.
[163] See above, 148–9.

councillors in this House of Commons than in any of the other parliaments of the reign, a bad error.[164] The death of the chancellor in 12 November removed a master of the arts of political management, someone who was, in Paget's words, a good man at stopping up a dangerous hole'.[165] Michieli commented on the increased boldness of members of the House of Commons after Gardiner's death,[166] whilst Noailles reported that afterwards the nobility and 'jusqu'aux plus petitz parlent plus licentieusement ... contre ladicte religion qu'ilz n'ont faict devant'.[167] Perhaps with firmer management the Commons might not have reached the boiling point of 6 December.

[164] See above, Table 1.
[165] *CSP Sp.* XIII. 89.
[166] *CSP Ven.* VI. i. 251.
[167] Vertot, V. 205.

8

The Parliament of 1558

THE only parliament that Mary found sympathetic and satisfactory enough to prorogue rather than dissolve was that of
1558. Count Feria told Philip that this was 'because the Queen
considers that the persons sent to it have transacted business
very well and served with so much good will that these same
persons had better be summoned when Parliament assembles
again'.[1] Perhaps the circular letters sent out by the crown had
met with a particularly good response,[2] perhaps there was a
sense of unity in the face of foreign war, perhaps members were
anxious to finish business quickly so that they could leave the
perils of a disease-ridden capital.

The overwhelming concern of the government at this time
was with the cost and conduct of the war with France. The
attempt of Thomas Stafford to seize Scarborough Castle with
French assistance had been, for Mary and her advisers, the last
straw, and war was declared on 7 June 1557. At first things
went well, and an army under the command of the earl of
Pembroke defeated the Constable of France, Anne de Mont-
morency, at St-Quentin, but English hopes and English pride
were shattered by the loss of Calais in the first week of 1558.[3]
The gloom felt by many members of the privy council can be
seen in a reply of February 1558 to Charles V's offer of assistance with the recovery of Calais: the council believed that it
would be impossible to raise an army at home because of other
defence commitments and because of the cost which 'neither,
we doubt, wilbe granted of the people, nor, if it were, can be
conveniently levyed in tyme', for the money could not be raised

---

[1] *CSP Sp.* XIII. 357.
[2] See above, 30.
[3] See C. S. L. Davies, 'England and the French War, 1557-9', in Loach and Tittler,
The Mid-Tudor Polity, 159-85.

by 'straunge imposic*i*ons' which 'we thinke, they could not beare'.[4] The council went on to explain that:

The Qwenis Ma*je*sties owne revenue is scarse hable to mainteine her Estate/ The noblemen and gentlemen for the most parte (receiving no more than they were wont to receive, and paying thrise asmoche for every thing they provyd, by reason of the basenes of the money) are not hable to do, as they have done, in tymes paste/ The marchaunt*e*s haue had great losses of late, wherby the clothiers be never the richer/ The fermors, grasiers, and other people, how well willing soever they be taken to be, will not be . . . of their wealthe, and by the miscontentement of this losse, be growne stubbone, and liberall of talk.

Even at the time when the war was first discussed the council believed that there was little hope of raising money by taxation since most of the common people were 'pinched w*i*th famine and want of payment due to them', whilst others were 'miscontented for matters of Religion and generally all yet talking of the smarte of the last warres':[5] the prospect looked even bleaker after the ill-success of English arms. Probably, then, the council approached the parliamentary session with some anxiety.

Parliament opened on 20 January. On 24 January the Lords asked the Commons to send the speaker and a group of ten or twelve members to talk to them; the speaker reported to the Commons afterwards that 'to seek for the sure defence of the Realm, and a Relief for the same', a committee had been set up consisting of three earls, three bishops, and three barons, and the Commons chose twenty-one of their number to join them.[6] Subsequently, 'to the intent that no way or polliecyis should be vndeuysed or not thought vpon' the committee was divided into three groups, each including one earl, one baron, and one bishop, together with ten members of the Commons.[7] These groups consulted for three days before meeting on the fourth to compare their ideas; they then decided that to make an offer of

[4] There are several copies of this letter in the British Library. I have here used Cotton MS Titus B. II, fo. 59.
[5] There are also several copies of this memorandum. This is Cotton MS Titus C. VII. fo. 148.
[6] *CJ* 24 Jan.
[7] SP 11/13/31, fo. 66. The discrepancy was presumably made up by members of the privy council.

two fifteenths and a subsidy of eight shillings in the pound on land and five shillings and fourpence on goods, one half to be paid in 1558 and the other in 1559. On 4 February a bill to this effect was read in the Commons. It received a second reading on 7 February, but on that same day Thomas Mason wrote to Sir John Thynne telling him that 'theare hathe byn hard hold in the nether howse for the payment of the subsydye'.[8] On 9 February the speaker sought an audience with the queen. He told her that the Commons were not ready to make a grant for 1559 because she had already received considerable assistance from her subjects in the shape of loans; moreover, if there were to be an invasion in the course of 1558 private individuals would have to buy armour and weapons, which they could not afford as well as taxes. However, the Commons would agree to one subsidy, to be paid before 10 June 1558, and one fifteenth, to be paid in October of that same year.[9] The queen had little choice but to accept, and a bill granting this smaller sum was quickly passed.[10] Even so, according to the Venetian ambassador on 12 February, various members were reluctant to make a grant for the recovery of Calais, arguing that 'if the French have taken Calais they thus took nothing from the English, but recovered what was their own'.[11]

Despite such grumbles, most of those in parliament were clearly hostile to the French. The speaker had told the queen that the Commons would like to pass a law 'to bannysshie them all aswell denyzens as not denyzens out of this Realme', and a bill 'to make void letters patents made to Frenchmen to be denizens' was in fact read that same day. It ran into difficulties and was rejected in a division on 18 February, but a new bill was read the next day. That, too, appeared unsatisfactory and a third bill was read on 24 February, being passed two days later. There were no difficulties in the Upper House. All Frenchmen not denizens were ordered to leave the country, and denizens might in future have their letters patent repealed

---

[8] Longleat, Thynne Papers, III, fo. 5.
[9] SP 11/12/31, fo. 67ᵛ.
[10] HLRO, Original Acts, 4 & 5 Philip and Mary, 16. The bill was read in the Lords on 17, 18, and 19 Feb. The clergy granted a subsidy of eight shillings in the pound, to be paid over four years. (HLRO, Original Acts, 4 & 5 Philip and Mary, 15.)
[11] *CSP Ven.* VI. iii. 1449.

by proclamation, the queen then enjoying the profits of the Frenchmen's land.[12] Other punitive—and ingenious—bills against the French failed, however. A bill read in the Commons on 3 February for the fortification of Melcombe Regis 'by Frenchmen dwelling in Dorset or Wiltshire'[13] seems to have been abandoned in favour of a more general bill read on 10 February 'for an imposition to be gathered yearly of Frenchmen, inhabiting in this realm'. On 15 February the bill, now described as 'for Frenchmen to pay a yearly contribution to Melcombe Regis, and divers other places', was read again, and the Commons passed it on 26 February. The Lords, unanimously, rejected it on 2 March. Curiously enough, a bill passed by the Lords to prohibit the import of French wines was lost in the Commons.

Meanwhile, the problem still remained of how best to defend the country against possible invasion. On 25 January the Commons' Journal rather cryptically recorded a 'Communication for an Act to be made' against soldiers who sold their armour. The next day Secretary Bourne and eleven others were instructed to draw up a bill about 'soldiers and captains': a bill 'touching captains, and soldiers, and armour' was introduced by Bourne on 3 February. In his audience with the queen on 9 February the speaker mentioned the need for some law about the provision of weapons and armour, and that same day a bill was read in the Commons 'for the having of armour and weapons for the wars by the subjects'. But the Lords were also concerned with the problem of how to raise an army and how to equip it. On 10 February a bill was read in the Upper House about weapons and armour. This was passed on 21 February, was committed in the Commons to Mr Heigham and others on 24, discussed the next day without a formal reading, and 'delivered' to Heigham again on 28 February, together with another bill that had come from the Lords dealing with the problem of musters. Both bills were passed on 3 March, although complications then arose about amendments made by the Commons. The Lords removed one of the provisos that the

---

[12] 4 & 5 Philip and Mary, c. 6.

[13] A bill simply 'for the fortification of Melcombe Regis' had been read on 28 and 29 Jan.

Lower House had added to the bill on weapons and armour.[14] They also substituted a proviso of their own for two added to the musters bill by the Commons, sending 'a billet' asking that 'the two provisos annexed to the bill' by the Commons 'might be taken away; and a new proviso, devised by the Lords, might be put in that place, and the indorsement reformed'. The Commons agreed to this, although only after an intervention by Sir Edward Rogers, George St Poll, and Richard Grafton, who probably proposed that the raising of aids to pay soldiers be limited to the present emergency.[15]

In its final form the musters act set out penalties for non-appearance, penalized corrupt muster masters, and revived an Edwardian statute making desertion a felony.[16] The weapons and horses act specified what quantity of horses, armour, and weapons each person was bound to provide according to his position in the social hierarchy.[17] Although both measures went some way to improve the deplorable state of English defences, neither could be enforced with total success.[18] Probably the depression and general apathy explain this, although, in the light of the drafting difficulties encountered by the bills, it is interesting to find one bitterly anti-Spanish commentator asking in 1559 what the true purpose of the weapons act had been:

... what ment they may we gesse by the forcyng of the late statute of armour? but only bycaus having colour to haue armour themselues, vnder name of a quantitee they might take to them as mooche as they lyst. So that if nede wear when they sawe tyme they might strengthen theyr matters hereafter aswell wyth polles bloody Sworde as they haue doon already with peters counterfit key of theyrs.[19]

A related bill to permit the import of armour and bowstaves

---

[14] HLRO, Original Acts, 4 & 5 Philip and Mary, 2.
[15] HLRO, MS Commons Journal, 7 Mar. 1557/8; C. G. Ericson, 'Parliament as a Representative Institution in the Reigns of Edward VI and Mary' (University of London Ph.D thesis, 1974), 274.
[16] 4 & 5 Philip and Mary, c. 3.
[17] 4 & 5 Philip and Mary, c. 2.
[18] See, for example, *APC* VI. 259. On both acts see L. Boynton, *The Elizabethan Militia, 1558–1638* (London, 1967), 9–11.
[19] BL Royal MS 17 C. 3, fo. 10ᵛ.

without customs charges had been read in the Commons on 10 February. It passed the Commons without, apparently, causing any controversy, but the Lords seem to have been anxious about its implications for the royal prerogative and asked the attorney-general 'to moue the quenes highnes therein':[20] that is, they decided to proceed by petition rather than bill. Nothing more, certainly, was heard of the bill.

The war, of course, stretched even further the crown's meagre resources. In an attempt to recover money that it was owed—something that had been recommended by certain members of the Lower House in 1555[21]—the government introduced a bill into the Lords on 31 January 'touching treasurers, receivers, collectors, customers, and other accomptants of the Queen's Majesty's money, rents, revenues and profits'. In a letter to Sir John Thynne, Thomas Mason explained the purpose of the measure thus: 'that any tresere or officer dying in the queenes debt, his landes by any way conveied ether to the wife in ionture ether to the children or to any other solde or convaied to be leyable to the payment of the queen debtes and this act to take force sence the first year of the queenes raigne'.[22] (The bill resembled one that the government had intended to introduce in the parliament of 1546, 'that treasurers and receivers of the King's money be bound under a great penalty to account yearly, and if any die within the year, the King to have his remedy against their heirs and executors':[23] this plan had come to nothing because of Henry's illness.) The bill was passed by the Lords on 8 February after a period of discussion long enough to suggest that it had encountered difficulties. It was read in the Commons the next day, and then disappeared until, on 5 March, the queen sent a message declaring that since the bill 'extended to divers accomptants, that already have accompted, they should not further proceed'.[24] Not until 1570 did the crown secure an act 'to make the lands,

---

[20] *LJ* 22 Feb.
[21] See above, 134.
[22] Longleat, Thynne Papers, III, fo. 5ᵛ.
[23] *Letters and Papers* XXI. ii. 344.
[24] *CJ* 5 Mar.

tenements, goods and chattels of tellers, receivers, etc., liable to the payment of their debts'.[25]

The interest of this bill lies in the fact that it is possible to see how private interests worked to change the course of government action. The leader of the opposition to the bill was Lady Elizabeth Cavendish, widow of Sir William Cavendish and perhaps best known as Bess of Hardwick. On 12 October 1557 Sir William had written, in response to a request from the council, an account of the sums of money that had passed through his hands as treasurer of the chamber and of the court of surveyors.[26] In this account he admitted debts to the crown of £5,237. Soon afterwards he died, and it was the subsequent difficulty of recovering the money from his estate that seems to have moved the government to introduce this bill. Lady Cavendish rallied her friends. She wrote to Thynne asking him to come to London, for if he could she would 'haue many more [friends] by your meanes then by a great sorte of hothers'.[27] The matter was pressing, for the bill had at that point received two readings in the Upper House.[28] On 25 February, when, as we have seen, the bill was hanging fire in the Commons, Lady Cavendish wrote to Thynne again saying, 'hetherto I haue taken no hurte by the parlamente yet do I stylle stande yn great fear and shall do untyll such tyme as the parlamente · ende whych I wysshe dayly for'.[29] She went on, 'the byll hath as yet been but once redde and ys so euyll lyked of the howse that [I] trust through [the] helpe [of such as] you and other trewe mene my frendes yt shall take [small effect to do me any] hurt'. As Lady Cavendish had noted, 'yt ys aganarall byll and dothe towche many and yf yt passe yt wyll not only ondo me and my poore Chylders but agreat nombre of hotheres', and 'the mater of yt selfe makyth me mo frendes then I loked for, for ther be fewe yn the howse but they or there frendes shulde smart yf the acte sholde passe'. Indeed, Sir John Mason declared in a letter to Thynne also dated 25 February that 'if the act passe touch-

[25] 13 Elizabeth, c. 15.
[26] PRO E 101/424/10.
[27] Longleat, Thynne Papers, III, fo. 9.
[28] Ibid.
[29] Ibid., fo. 11.

ing my lady cavendisshe itt shall be agay*n*st my will'.[30] The crown seems to have given way beneath this overwhelming opposition.[31]

Legislation dealing with ecclesiastical matters of a non-sectarian kind took up a surprising amount of time in this parliament. The problems that arose from benefit of clergy were considered again, the Lords reading on the first day of the meeting a bill to reduce the privilege in cases of murder: the memory of Benet Smith obviously still provoked resentment.[32] However, this bill ran into difficulties and a new bill was drafted, which was passed by a majority of the House on 31 January. After two readings, the Commons decided to produce a fresh bill, which was read for the first time on 8 February, alongside a bill to restrict sanctuary. This bill passed on 10 February, and was quickly dealt with by the Lords, although, again, only a majority of the House would agree to it.[33]

The sanctuary bill, committed after its second reading on 9 February to the former speaker, Clement Heigham, was less successful. This was the result of an intervention by the head of one of the institutions that would have been affected by it, John Feckenham, head of the reconstituted Abbey of Westminster. On 12 February, after the bill had been twice discussed, Feckenham came, by invitation, to the Lower House, bringing with him the original grant of sanctuary allegedly made by Edward the Confessor and the new charter of Philip and Mary.[34] His argument was that since the House did not wish to destroy sanctuary entirely the Members should acknowledge that Westminster was especially deserving of the privilege.[35] Of course, he told the House of Commons, if all princes were like Philip and Mary, there would be no need of sanctuary, 'such a

[30] Ibid., fo. 14.

[31] The crown attempted to recover money from Cavendish's widow again in the next reign (*CPR*, Elizabeth, II, 495–6).

[32] See above, 146–7.

[33] 4 & 5 Philip & Mary, c. 4.

[34] For the Edwardian charter, see P. Chaplais, 'The Original Charters of Herbert and Gervase Abbots of Westminster (1121–1157)', in *A Mediaeval Miscellany for Doris Mary Stenton*, ed. P. M. Barnes and C. F. Slade (Pipe Roll Society, NS, XXXVI, 1960), 89–110.

[35] Bodley MS Rawlinson D. 68 (formerly Miscellaneous 68). The speech is printed with some alterations in A. P. Stanley's *Historical Memorials of Westminster Abbey* (London) in the 1876 edition and some others.

perpetuall sancuarie haue their reposed in therie own clemen-
cie', but, alas, they were not immortal and things might
change. He told the House of the miraculous preservation of
the supposed first grant, which had been saved by a servant of
Cardinal Pole, who had found a child playing with it in the
gutter. Feckenham returned to the House on 15 February with
his learned counsel, Mr Plowden and Dr Story. Since the Journal does not mention the bill again Feckenham's eloquence
clearly had some effect. An attempt in 1566 to deal with the
problem was equally unsuccessful: the dean of Westminster
appeared at the Bar of the House with his counsel, Mr Plowden
and Mr Ford, and made 'an oration in defence of sanctuary,
and alleged divers grants by King Lucius and other Christian
Kings, and Mr Plowden alleged the grant of sanctuary there by
King Edward five hundred years ago; viz., *Dat. in an.* 1066 with
great reason in law and chronicle; and Mr. Ford alleged divers
stories and laws for the same; and thereupon the bill was committed to the Master of the Rolls and others to peruse the
grants and to certify the force of the law now for sanctuaries.'[36]

Another bill that failed was one intended to 'confirm the
bishoprics of Winchester and Worcester' to their present
owners. This bill passed the Lords and was read in the Commons on 3 and 4 March but was lost at the prorogation. Perhaps only shortage of time prevented the bill becoming law,
perhaps the Commons were in no hurry to pass it.

In all, sixteen acts were passed in this session. They ranged
from a bill restoring the children of the late duke of Northumberland[37]—Sir Ambrose and Sir Robert Dudley, Lady Mary
Sidney, and Lady Catherine Hastings—to a bill 'touching the
making of woollen cloths' which forbade the making of cloth
outside corporate towns.[38] (Although this last was a measure of
some importance its passage appears to have been uneventful.)
A rather obscure measure concerning under-age heiresses took
up a considerable amount of time. A first bill was described by
Thomas Mason in a letter to his friend Sir John Thynne as a
proposal, 'vpon chetuind his case for steling of gentlwomen or

---

[36] D. S. D'Ewes, *The Journals of All the Parliaments during the Reign of Queen Elizabeth*
(London, 1682; Shannon reprint, 1973), 124.
[37] 4 & 5 Philip and Mary, c. 12. The bill passed both Houses speedily.
[38] 4 & 5 Philip and Mary, c. 5.

maidens not abowe the age of syxtene or pryvytye contracting
with owt theyr parens good will vppon pain of too yeares
emprysonment to them that steale them or couse them to be
stolne or pryvyly contract with them and the losse of suche
landes as shuld fall vnto herre'.[39] This bill was dropped in
favour of another which, when passed, dealt in general terms
with 'such as take away maidens Inheriting'.[40] Five peers
objected to the measure.[41] The Commons rejected bills dealing
with forged convent seals, the return of writs, and apprentices.
A number of other bills were lost, some of which were introduced again in the second session. The Lords rejected or neg-
lected a number of bills passed by the Lower House, and spent
some considerable time on the problem of the relative preced-
ence of Lords Clinton and Stafford: Arundel, Shrewsbury, and
Darcy being appointed 'to ensearche and trye owt aswell by
thanncyent Recorded and parlamente roolles . . . as also by the
Herawldes Bookes and other monumentes' the question of the
ancestry of the two peers.[42]

The session ended on a discordant note. A dispute arose out
of the bill confirming letters patent, which amongst other
things confirmed the queen's religious foundations.[43] In the
Lords the rather miscellaneous group of Oxford, Arundel,
Derby, Morley, Cobham, and Mountjoy objected to the bill,[44]
and in the Commons it was 'reformed',[45] after it had been discussed in an afternoon session, an unusual occurrence.[46] During the debate the young Thomas Copley, sitting for his

[39] Longleat, Thynne Papers, III, fo. 5ᵛ. Richard Chetwode, a gentleman of
Edward's privy chamber, had eloped in 1556 with a fourteen-year-old heiress, Agnes
Woodhull. The marriage was declared void by the ecclesiastical court, and Chetwode
appealed to Rome. His case was covered by a proviso to the 1559 Act of Supremacy.

[40] 4 & 5 Philip and Mary, c. 8.

[41] *LJ* 7 Mar. 1558. It is interesting that a member of this parliament, Thomas Key-
nell, had been before Star Chamber in 1555 (PRO Star Chamber 2/24/275) together
with John Buller, member for Weymouth in the parliament of that year, accused of kid-
napping and marrying an heiress.

[42] Ibid., 12 Feb.

[43] 4 & 5 Philip and Mary, c. 1.

[44] *LJ* 26 Feb.

[45] *CJ* 5 Mar. 'the bill to be reformed by Mr. Baker and others'.

[46] On 3 Mar. Hooker, over a decade later, said that the House met in the afternoon
only 'vpon some vrgent cause' (Exeter City Library, Book 6oh, fo. 17).

family's pocket borough of Gatton, spoke 'unreverent words of the Queen's Majesty ... saying, that he feared the Queen might thereby give away the crown from the right inheritours'.[47] The House considered what action it should take, and decided that Copley should be given into the custody of the serjeant-at-arms while the speaker consulted the queen.[48] Copley asked the House to remember his tender years, and the speaker was instructed to beg the queen for mercy. The matter was unresolved at the time of the prorogation, the queen having asked that Copley should be examined 'whereof such matter did spring' but that she 'would well consider the request of this House ... for him'. What lay behind the incident is not clear: Copley at this time was in a circle of protestants: the other burgess for Gatton, whom Copley had chosen, was Thomas Norton, described by Sir John Neale as a 'hammer of Catholics',[49] and Copley was also friendly with the protestant Thomas Cawarden.[50] Thus, although the meeting was more docile than any other Mary encountered, it was not entirely subservient.

The second session began on Saturday, 5 November. Hanging over the assembly was the shadow of the plague: the house was called on 8 November, and on the following day a bill was introduced for the attendance of knights and burgesses, a bill which once again indicates the government's desire to prevent absenteeism. On 10 November the House decided that members who were sick should not 'take damage by their absence during their sickness', and on the next day the House rejected a request that sick members should be removed and fresh writs issued to fill their places. The anxiety felt by some constituencies in the absence of their representatives can be seen in the case of York, which decided on 14 October that a letter should be sent to the speaker asking that the city's burgesses might be excused because of their illness, and begging that 'if any matter

[47] *CJ* 5 Mar.
[48] *CJ* 7 Mar.
[49] *Elizabeth I and her Parliaments, 1559–1581*, 91. See also, however, M. A. R. Graves, 'Thomas Norton the Parliament Man', *Historical Journal*, XXIII (1980).
[50] *HMC More-Molyneux* VII. 610. For Cawarden, see below, 214. Copley later became a catholic.

shall chanse to be putt in ageynst this Citie that he wilbe soo good to staye it'.[51] In addition, a letter was also sent to the Recorder of York instructing him 'to learne from tyme to tyme of Maister Speaker if ought be put in ageynst this Citie that he may forsee therfor as occasion serveth'.[52]

The queen herself was also gravely ill. Foreign observers reported that during the first days of this session the Commons sent a message to the Lords noting that Mary was near to death and Elizabeth the next heir 'by the laws of this kingdom'; they suggested that some formal acknowledgement of her claim should be made.[53] The Lords are said to have agreed, and asked the council to act: with Mary's blessing the council sent the comptroller of the household, Sir Thomas Cornwallis, and the master of the rolls, William Cordell, to speak to Elizabeth. There is no record of these discussions in the Journals, but on 7 November the speaker—who was, of course, William Cordell— was summoned to the queen 'about weighty affairs'.[54]

Despite the imminent threat of the queen's death, business went on in parliament. Indeed, on 14 November the attorney and solicitor, who had brought a bill from the Lords for the corporation of Trinity Hall, Cambridge, also conveyed a request for a joint conference.[55] The lord chancellor, the treasurer, Norfolk, Shrewsbury, Pembroke, the bishops of Winchester, London, Lincoln, and Carlisle, Mountagu, the Admiral and Lord William Howard came down to the Commons and sat 'where the Queen's Privy Council of this House use to sit'—the speaker and the privy council had to sit on the lowest benches. The lord chancellor explained that because of the threat from the French and the Scots, a fresh subsidy was needed. The Commons discussed this request on 15 November, whilst the Lords were debating a bill that would have prevented anyone from printing any 'books, ballads, etc. unless he be authorised thereunto by the King and Queen's Majesty's licence, under the Great Seal of England'.[56] But neither this bill nor the sub-

[51] *York Civic Records*, 157.
[52] Ibid.
[53] 'The Count of Feria's Despatch to Philip II of 14 November 1558', ed. M. J. Rodriguez-Salgado and S. Adams, *Camden Miscellany XXVIII* (1984), 335–6 and n. 45.
[54] *CJ* 7 Nov.
[55] *CJ* 14 Nov.
[56] *LJ* 12 Nov.

sidy bill were to come to anything, for on 17 November the two Houses were summoned together and informed that Mary had died early that morning, and that the Lady Elizabeth was now their queen.

9

Occasions for Opposition

THERE were, then, several occasions in Mary's reign when the queen's plans were thwarted by the behaviour of men in parliament. More important still, the queen did not introduce certain measures very dear to her because she recognized that they were unlikely to succeed: the crown did not usually put forward proposals unless they stood a good chance of being passed. What limits were thus imposed on royal policy, and why did parliament take a stand on the things it did?

Parliament intervened frequently, and usually successfully, in constitutional matters. Open and vociferous criticism in parliament did not, it is true, prevent Mary's marriage to Philip, but the attitude adopted by parliament probably served to ensure that the provisions of the marriage treaty imposed strict limits on Philip's power. Parliament's great triumph was to stop Mary from raising explicitly the question of Philip's coronation: the suspicions and hostility revealed in the course of debates such as that on the guardianship of Mary's child convinced Mary that she could alter the position of her husband only at the risk of her own. This was of immense significance. Moreover, Elizabeth was never specifically barred from the throne, again because Mary no doubt realized that any bill to disinherit her would run up against considerable opposition. Parliament was thus successful in preventing the queen from altering the constitutional powers and position of either her husband or her sister.

On religious matters parliament was less active. Few of those who sat in parliament in these years appear to have been fundamentally opposed to the restoration of, at least, Henrician catholicism. None the less, the reunion with Rome was delayed until satisfactory arrangements had been made about the future of secularized property. This was of importance, since it is clear that Mary and Pole, given a free hand, would have preferred to leave the matter unresolved until after the absolution of the realm: only the constant vigilance of parliament—and Philip's recognition of the force of its concern—prevented an unconditional return to Rome. Even with such constant vigilance more pressure than is sometimes realized was put on individuals to return their ecclesiastical property. However, parliament, despite strenuous endeavours, was not able to prevent Mary from returning to the church her own former ecclesiastical property, and this brought about a substantial diminution in royal revenues. The revival of the medieval heresy laws was held up by the House of Lords in the parliament of spring 1554, but they were sanctioned in the next meeting: opposition in parliament, however, protected from further harrassment those who had fled to avoid such laws. Parliament did not, therefore, act in the way in which devout protestants might have wished: its concern was primarily for material interests, not questions of theology. What went on in the parliaments of Mary's reign suggests that the governing classes were willing enough to allow the crown to make major decisions about matters of belief, provided that their own well-being was not thereby affected.

From the first days of her reign, Mary had made it clear that she wished to restore England to the Roman obedience. This she did, but the process took eighteen months. The reasons for the delay were not doctrinal: it was fear for the future of secularized land that produced suspicion and wariness, together with a vague attachment to the notion of the monarch as head of the English church. Mary's first parliament was, after all, willing to restore church services and religious ceremonies to the pattern of the early 1540s, with no more than one third of those present in the House of Commons voting against the measure, but it was not prepared to see the title of supreme head taken from the crown. Her second parliament was marked by the Lords' rejection of a bill renewing the medieval heresy laws, but the reasons for that rejection do not appear to have been religious: only six months later both Houses passed without difficulty an apparently similar measure. By that time parliament, having reassured itself by means of a papal bull that the future of former ecclesiastical lands was tolerably secure, welcomed the return of Roman jurisdiction. But this welcome was not entirely sincere, for less than a year later anti-papal feeling was acute enough to force the government into a remodelling of the first fruits bill whereby any benefit that might have accrued to the pope was removed. Thus, anxiety about church land and hostility to Rome, a hostility perhaps exacerbated by twenty years of antipapal propaganda, combined with a dislike of powerful church courts and of episcopal authority—a dislike which was particularly strong in the Upper House—delayed the return to Rome and even after the reunion caused Mary some difficulty.

The positive side of this latent hostility towards Rome was an attachment to the notion of the monarch as head of the English church. Mary longed to be rid of the title of supreme head: she stopped using it early in 1554, and the royal articles of March 1554 forbade the use of 'regia auctoritate fulcitus' in ecclesiastical writings.[1] However, Mary seems to have been doubtful whether she could simply abandon the title on her own authority, for about this time she asked the judges and serjeants whether the title could be jettisoned.[2] A majority decided that '*supreme head* is not parcel of the name of the queen, but addition'. In the writs for her second parliament, therefore, Mary did not use the title, although it was not formally discarded until after Pole had pronounced his absolution. In 1559 John Aylmer was to ask whether Mary had acted legally, for if she did not, 'of what force were the writtes, whereby the Parliament was called, that took awaye the Supremacie?'[3] Elizabeth in this respect followed the example of her sister, for the writs in 1559 did not mention the supreme headship but contained only an ambiguous 'etc.': a Commons committee led by John Caryll, knight of the shire for Sussex, decided that the Elizabethan writs were valid, although in 1554 Caryll had been one of the minority of legal experts who believed that the title was more than a mere addition to the queen's name.[4]

However, the real block in the path back to Rome was

---

[1] Wilkins, *Concilia* IV. 89. D. M. Loades, 'The Last Years of Cuthbert Tunstall, 1547–1559', *Durham University Journal*, XXXV (1973–4), 19.

[2] Dyer, *Reports of Cases*, 98a (Easter, 1 Mary).

[3] *An harborowe for faithfvll and trewe subiectes* (n.p., 1559), sig. O.

[4] *CJ* 3 Feb. 1559. See also Neale, *Elizabeth I and Her Parliaments 1559–1581*, 46–7; N. L. Jones, *Faith by Statute* (London, 1982), 85–6.

anxiety about secularized property. It was this that delayed matters until concessions had been obtained from the pope, and it was this fear that underlay much of the opposition to government proposals, even when these had in fact nothing to do with former church land—the delay in the revival of the heresy laws, for example, was due to Paget's manipulation of aristocratic anxiety about episcopal authority and the security of secularized property. Such fears were, in fact, justified by Pole's attitude. In rough drafts of the speech he made in parliament at the time of the absolution, for instance, he dwelt on the sacrilege that laymen were committing by retaining such land, although in the speech that he finally delivered he was apparently more tactful. The wrath of God, he wrote, was the more stern, 'yow retourneng to the obedyence of the churche, nott moved by yout dewtye to god, but for more suretye to kepe your spoyle'.[5] His views were not changed by his defeat over the terms of the great bill of repeal, and one commentator reported that he had 'condescended in such a way to the retention of this property that everybody might very easily perceive that his dispensation was a mere permission'.[6] Indeed, as soon as parliament ended in January 1555 Pole began to work on the conscience of the queen about her own secularized land,[7] and his urgency in the matter may have alarmed other lay owners. His ideas became widely known after the sermon he preached on the third anniversary of the ending of schism, in which he argued that although the church had allowed laymen to keep former ecclesiastical property, like an indulgent mother who allows her child to keep an apple even though it will make him ill to eat it, God the father would take a sterner line.[8]

In the atmosphere of uncertainty created by statements such as these, laymen in a position to do so covered themselves: Petre, for example, obtained a bull specifically permitting him to keep his church land,[9] and Sir Thomas Smith and others obtained papal bulls of indulgence.[10] Lay fears were exacerbated

[5] Bodley film 33: Vatican Library 5968, fo. 120. See also Schenk, *Reginald Pole, Cardinal of England*, 130.

[6] *CSP Ven*. VI. i. 10.

[7] Ibid. 16.

[8] Strype, *Ecclesiastical Memorials* III. ii. 482–3.

[9] Emmison, *Tudor Secretary: Sir William Petre at Court and Home*, 185.

[10] Dewar, *Sir Thomas Smith*, 78.

by the fact that some former church property was more or less forcibly restored. For instance, as early as 27 July 1553, Gardiner was reported as having told the marquess of Northampton's wife that she should leave the house that Edward had bestowed on her husband, and as having 'intimated to the earl of Pembroke that he is to give him back certain revenues that proceed from the cathedral church of Winchester':[11] on 11 August two chroniclers noted that 'the bushope of Winchester hathe his howse againe that the marques of Northampton had'.[12] (It was presumably to this that Aylmer was referring when he wrote in 1559 of 'some noble men and Gentlemen' who were 'depryued of those landes whiche the Kynge has geuen them withoute tarrying for any lawe lest my Lord of Winchester should haue lost his quarters rent'.[13]) The Henrician bishops who had been ejected in Edward's reign certainly made strenuous and sometimes successful attempts to recover lost lands and revenues. At Worcester, for example, a see that had been much depleted during Hooper's tenure, Heath was able to secure his rents, although he was not able to eject all new occupants.[14] However, if Sir Francis Jobson, that great Edwardian profiteer,[15] was able to retain Hartlebury Castle,[16] John Throckmorton, burgess for Old Sarum in 1553 and for Coventry in November 1554 and 1558, was less successful. Writing to his brother in 1565 about a proposal to buy the manor of Hanbury, Throckmorton declared that the purchase was a risky one because the property had once belonged to the bishopric of Worcester. He explained that 'not long before king Edward's death, my lord of Northumberland, in an exchange with the king, took divers manors of that bishopric, assured to the King by Bishop Hooper, and sold and assured them to divers of his friends and followers, as the lordship of Hartlebury to Jobson ... and Wellond to me'—a purchase for which Throckmorton had paid more than 200 marks. Heath was restored to the bishopric of Worcester, Throckmorton continued,

---

[11] *CSP Sp.* XI. 120.
[12] *Queen Jane and Queen Mary*, 15; Wriothesley, 97.
[13] *An harborowe for faithvll and trewe subiectes* sig. O 4.
[14] Heal, *Of Prelates and Princes*, 152–3.
[15] See above, 95.
[16] Heal, ibid.

'so I lost my land and money also, and had no recompence'; Throckmorton felt that the queen should have compensated him as 'by my Lord of Leicester's help' Jobson had been compensated.[17] Bonner was particularly assiduous in his attempts to recover the property of his see, and tried desperately to have the leases made by his successor, Ridley, declared invalid.[18] As late as 1558, he can be found writing to Pole asking for assistance with the recovery of 'Great Darcie Sudymyster and other thinges belonging to my churche'; he commented bitterly that if he had been 'an heretike and in the time of that noughty Duke and Dukes that were in the late tyme, I should not fayle to have my lyving increased'.[19]

Both in Pole's known opposition to their continued tenure of former church property and in the efforts made by certain bishops to rescind the land transactions of the 1540s and early 1550s, lay owners had cause for anxiety; only a few incidents of the kind described by Throckmorton could produce panic. So embedded did this anxiety become amongst the English landed classes that it could still be played upon by the Whig pamphleteers of the 1670s and 1680s. Robert Ferguson wrote in 1679, for example, that 'if any men who have estates in abbey lands desire to beg their bread and relinquish their habitation and fortunes to some old-greasy bald-pated Abbot, monk or friar, then let them vote for a popish successor and popery'.[20]

Much of the parliamentary debate on religious matters was thus overshadowed by anxiety about the future of former ecclesiastical property. It is easy to conclude from this that those who sat in Marian parliaments were profoundly secular men, concerned only with their material well-being. This was certainly the view of contemporary pamphleteers, who believed

[17] *Calendar of State Papers Domestic, 1601–3, with Addenda, 1547–1565*, ed. M. A. E. Green (London, 1870), 574–5. I owe this reference to Mr P. H. Williams.

[18] Strype, *Ecclesiastical Memorials*, III. 57: G. Alexander, 'Victim or Spendthrift? The Bishop of London and his Income in the Sixteenth Century', in *Wealth and Power in Tudor England*, ed. E. W. Ives, R. J. Knecht, J. J. Scarisbrick (London, 1978), 143.

[19] Inner Temple, Petyt MS 538, vol. XLVII, fo. 407. The letter is unfortunately very damaged.

[20] Quoted by O. W. Furley, 'The Whig Exclusionists: Pamphlet Literature 1679–81', *Cambridge Historical Journal*, XIII (1957). The second Earl of Nottingham also noted in 1688 that abbey land went at lower prices than comparable estates. (H. J. Habakkuk, 'Daniel Finch, 2nd Earl of Nottingham: His House and Estate', in *Studies in Social History: A Tribute to G. M. Trevelyan*, ed. J. H. Plumb (London, 1955), 144.)

that parliament would never have permitted the restoration of catholicism if it had not been corrupted: Cranmer himself, in *A Confutatio[n] of vnwritte[n] verities*, argued that it was the members of Henry VIII's council who had gone on to become Mary's advisers who had 'lured' Lords and Commons into restoring the oath *ex officio* and diminishing the scope of the statutes of mortmain and praemunire.[21] But these writers were disappointed men; initially hoping that Mary's religious proposals would be blocked by the powerful of the land, they were profoundly disillusioned when this did not happen.[22] Traditionally, it was no part of parliament's function to discuss the finer points of doctrine, but only to implement the conclusions reached by convocation. In the chaotic days of the reformation, parliament had occasionally been permitted to discuss doctrine, and this had led the lower house of convocation to ask, in 1547, if it might be represented in the Commons as the bishops were in the Lords, but such notions were anathema to many of the Marian bishops. Their views were clearly expressed by one of their number, Cuthbert Scot, in 1559:

as for the certainy of our faith . . . if it shall hang upon an act of Parliament, we shall have but a weak staff to lean unto . . . I shall desire you to take me here [not] as to speak in derogation of the authority of the Parliament, which I acknowledge to be of great strength in matters whereto it extendeth. But for matters of religion, I do not think it ought to meddle withal, . . . partly for that the Parliament consisteth for the most part of the noblemen of the realm, and certain of the commons, being lay and temporal men; which, although they be of good wisdom and learning, yet not so studied nor exercised in the scriptures, the holy doctors and practice of the church, as to be accounted judges in such matters.[23]

For the more vehement opponents of the royal supremacy the notion of laymen discussing doctrine, and, even worse, deciding what it should be, was a linked and horrible evil. Historians

---

[21] N.p., n.d. sig. C 5 v.

[22] See, for example, *An Exhortation to the carienge of Chrystes crosse* (n.p., n.d.), 44, and Knox, *A faythfull admonition* . . . (Kalykow, 1554), sig. E 4, and *The first blast of the trumpet* (n.p., 1558), 52.

[23] Scot's speech on the supremacy bill, from BL Cotton MS Vespasian D. XVIII, printed in C. Cross, *The Royal Supremacy in the Elizabethan Church* (London, 1969), 122–3.

who have examined the debate in the House of Lords of 1548 or the frequent discussions of doctrinal matters that took place in Elizabethan parliaments too easily forget that what they are examining is the decline of convocation: Marian parliaments were not more materialistic than those of Edward's reign, or those of Elizabeth's, but they were, perhaps, more limited in their scope. They were called to discuss matters relating to the commonwealth, not doctrine: they concerned themselves, therefore, with former ecclesiastical property rather than theories about the sacraments, with tithes and exiles' property rights rather than with definitions of heresy.

Given parliament's concern about property, its inheritance, tenure, and dispersal, it is not surprising that the queen's requests for aid were considered carefully. In 1555 her demand for taxation was tactlessly juxtaposed to a bill permitting her to divest herself of first fruits and tenths, and the sum finally granted was less than she had originally hoped.[24] The next request for taxation, in 1558, came at the end of a long series of demands for assistance from various groups of Mary's subjects, and was reduced on the grounds that she had already received considerable aid.[25] Certainly, the City of London had been asked for grants in 1554 and 1556, and the whole country for a Forced Loan in 1556–7.[26] The loan had not been paid with alacrity, and various gentlemen were summoned before the council to explain their failure to pay.[27] When Mary asked the City for another loan in 1558, the corporation was sufficiently moved to send the mayor and some of the aldermen to explain to the queen that the City was much impoverished; the loan was finally made only after the crown had provided some surety in the form of land.[28] However, although these loans were regarded as a justification for a reduction in the amount of taxation that the country should be asked to provide, there does not appear to have been any criticism in parliament of Mary's constant recourse to prests and forced loans: these were, clearly,

[24] See above, 134.
[25] See above, 161.
[26] City of London RO Repertory Book 13, i, fos. 130, 138ᵛ; Journal 16 fo. 284ᵛ; Repertory Book, i, fo. 420.
[27] *APC* VI. 20.
[28] Wriothesley, 140–1; City of London RO, Journal 17, fo. 63.

still regarded as something that the crown had every right to demand.

What is more surprising is that whereas Lancastrian parliaments had been so worried about the impoverishment of the crown that they passed acts of resumption, Mary's parliaments tacitly acquiesced as she divested herself of considerable amounts of property. Some shadowy notion still remained, it is true, of the inalienability of property once it had devolved upon the crown, for this surfaced in 1555 when members of the Commons argued that although Mary might do what she wished with the revenues of the crown during her own lifetime, she could not permanently alienate them,[29] but Mary was none the less permitted to give away almost all the property confiscated during her reign. An account drawn up at the beginning of Elizabeth's reign suggests that something in the region of £49,000 per annum was surrendered: £15,000 with the loss of first fruits and tenths, £10,000 with the surrender of the impropriated parsonages and tithes in the queen's hands, nearly £10,000 in gifts to those whose attainders had been reversed (this included over two thousand pounds to the Howards) and so on.[30] So generous was she that the memory of her donations lingered for sixty years after her death: in 1610 Salisbury reminded parliament of her gifts to the church, and, in particular, to the see of York, and of how much she had given to 'the successors whose ancestors were attainted'.[31] Although an impoverished crown had serious consequences for its subjects, parliament did not intervene except, briefly, during the discussion of the first fruits bill.

Moreover, in 1558 Mary pushed her powers over non-parliamentary taxes to the limit without causing any uproar in parliament itself. In March 1558 she forbade by proclamation the import of French wines, although an order in council decreed that such imports might be allowed on payment of an

---

[29] B. P. Wolffe, *The Royal Demesne in English History* (London, 1971), 51; *CSP Ven.* VI. i. 251; see above 136.

[30] SP 12/1/64.

[31] *Proceedings in Parliament, 1610*, ed. E. R. Foster (New Haven and London, 1966) I. 5–6; II. 23–4.

impost of forty shillings a tun.[32] A London merchant, Germaine Ciol, brought a case against the crown in the exchequer, arguing that he had already been granted a licence to bring in French wine provided that the normal custom had been paid, that he had paid three shillings a tun, which was 'all that was due and accustomed to be paid', and that he could not be forced to pay more. Judgment was given in the first year of Elizabeth's reign, against the crown.[33]

Mary did not stop here. In the new Book of Rates of May 1558 she increased the impost on a whole range of goods, including cloth, by an unprecedented amount.[34] The impact on the royal income was enormous,[35] but the constitutional importance of what had been done was even greater, for Mary had not consulted either parliament or the merchants. The London merchants complained bitterly, saying that the grant had not been sanctioned by parliament but imposed by the queen of her 'absolute power'.[36] However, the judges, when consulted, sanctioned the queen's actions. It is easy to sympathize with the merchants, whose relations with the crown had been embittered by Mary's reversal of her predecessor's policy towards the Hanse, and whose trade was disrupted by war. But those in parliament did nothing to support them: no mention seems to have been made of what Mary had done, or how she had done it, in either the brief session of November 1558 or in the first of Elizabeth's parliaments. The first parliamentary debate on the constitutional implications of Mary's actions appears to have been that of 1610, when one member argued that Mary

---

[32] Hughes and Larkin, *Tudor Royal Proclamations* II, no. 434, 439. It is not strictly correct to say, as does Professor Loades, that 'Parliament had refused to place a statutory prohibition on the trade' (*The Reign of Mary Tudor*, 416). Both Commons and Lords read bills to this effect, on 14 and 16 Feb., and the Commons abandoned their own bill when that passed by the Lords came down. This was read in the Commons on 19 and 21 Feb., and was committed to Petre. After a third reading on 26 Feb. it disappeared.

[33] Dyer, *Reports of Cases*, 165a; W. Hakewil, *The Libertie of the Subject; against the pretended power of impositions* ... (London, 1641), 96–7; G. D. G. Hall, 'Impositions and the Courts, 1554–1606', *Law Quarterly Review* LXIX (1953), 210–18. See also *APC* VII. 13, 19.

[34] T. S. Willan, *A Tudor Book of Rates* (Manchester, 1962).

[35] G. D. Ramsay, *The City of London in International Politics at the Accession of Queen Elizabeth* (Manchester, 1975), 50.

[36] Dyer, *Reports of Cases*, 165b.

'marrying with a stranger, began a strange and new course of imposition in some one thing, being seduced by foreign advice'.[37] Salisbury, trying to prove the legality of the 1608 Book of Rates, pointed out that Mary had raised the rate on cloth from five pence and five shillings and on Bordeaux wine from fourteen pence to sixteen shillings and eightpence without any complaint being heard in parliament.[38] It is certainly an interesting reflection on the state of the relationship between the Commons and the monarch at the two periods that despite the presence in the Commons in 1558 and 1559 of a number of members with trading interests—John Marshe sat for London both times, for instance—no complaint was voiced about the method used by Mary to improve her financial position.

If parliament was remarkably quiescent about the crown's financial exactions and their legal basis, and even about Mary's religious policy provided that the future of secularized property was safeguarded, it was persistently suspicious of Spain, and anxious about Philip's power and constitutional position. Although many of the Commons delegation of November 1553 seem to have felt that the queen would be unwise to marry any foreigner, it is possible that a particular hostility to a Spanish prince also existed. If this is so, it is more difficult to explain than historians have traditionally acknowledged. France, not Spain, was England's ancient enemy, and the by now orthodox foreign policy of Tudor monarchs, exemplified in the marriage of Mary's parents, was alliance with the Habsburgs. Under Catherine of Aragon a considerable interest existed in Spanish culture, both at court, where the king himself, Lord Berners, Lady Elizabeth Carew, the earls of Surrey and Bedford, John Skelton, and John Leland all had some sprinkling of the language,[39] and amongst the merchant community Roger Barlow, who travelled with Cabot in 1526, and the Bristol merchants Nicholas and Robert Thorne could speak Spanish.[40] It was perhaps from his trading friends that John

[37] *Proceedings in Parliament, 1610*, ed. Foster, I. 164.

[38] W. Notestein, *The House of Commons, 1604–10* (New Haven and London, 1971), 274.

[39] G. Ungerer, *Anglo-Spanish Relations in Tudor Literature* (Bern, 1956), 32.

[40] Ibid. 30.

Rastell also picked up a little of the language. It was, however, through translations from the French and Italian that most Englishmen came to know something of Spanish literature; Rastell, who published the first English edition of Celestina, used the Italian version of Alfonso Ordóñez,[41] and the popular work by Antonio de Guevara, *The golden boke of Marcus Aurelius*, published in London in 1535, was translated by Lord Berners from the *Livre dore de Marc Aurele*.[42] De Guevara's other well-known work, *A dispraise of the life of a courtier*, which appeared in 1548, was translated by Sir Francis Bryan from a French version.[43] The interest in Spanish culture reflected by the translation of these works seems to have encouraged some aspiring young men to take up the language: men such as Richard Eden, the translator of Peter Martyr Anglería,[44] Cecil, who was later to possess 'the largest private library of Spanish books in Tudor England',[45] and two of Princess Elizabeth's tutors, Roger Ascham and John Fortescue.[46] Thomas Smith later owned some Spanish books and may have learnt the language at this period.[47] An effort was indeed made to teach the young Edward VI some Spanish.[48]

However, the translating of Spanish works tailed off in the 1540s, and the young Cambridge graduates of the 1530s were unpromising soil in which to plant the seed of Anglo-Hispanic friendship in the 1550s, since most had been inclined towards protestantism. But a number of geographical and navigational works were published in translation during Mary's reign, as well as Luis de Zúñiga y Ávila's *The comentaries . . . which treateth of the wars in Germany*,[49] Juan de Flores's *The history of Aurelio and*

[41] *A new com(m)odye . . .* (London, n.d.), *RSTC* 20721: J. G. Underhill, *Spanish Literature in the England of the Tudors* (New York, 1892), 375.

[42] *STC* 12436; Underhill, op. cit. 66. Diego de San Pedro's *The Castell of Love* (London, n.d.), *RSTC* 21739. 5, was also translated by Berners from a French edition.

[43] London, 1548; *STC* 12431.

[44] Eden had been at Christ's, and in 1551 became private secretary to Cecil (DNB). See also D. Gwyn, 'Richard Eden, Cosmographer and Alchemist', *The Sixteenth Century Journal*, XV (1984), 13–36.

[45] C. Read, *Mr Secretary Cecil and Queen Elizabeth* (London, 1965), 114; Ungerer, op. cit. 222–9.

[46] G. Ungerer, 'The Printing of Spanish Books in Elizabethan England', *Library*, Fifth Series, XX (1965), 178, 194.

[47] Ibid. 178.

[48] Ibid. 179.

[49] London, 1555; *STC* 987.

of Isabell,[50] and Sir Thomas North's translation of de Guevara's *The Diall of Princes*.[51] Undoubtedly the most influential
of the works that appeared at this time was Eden's translation
from the Latin of Peter Martyr Anglería's *The Decades of the
newe world*.[52] Here was a story that revealed America for the
first time to a general English public, and revealed it as a land
of the noble savage, of 'that goulden worlde of the whiche
owlde wryters speake so much; wherein men lyued simplye and
innocentlye without inforcement of lawes, without quarelling
Iudges and libelles, contente onely to satisfie nature, without
further vexation for knowledge of thinges to come.'[53] This
ideal civilization, the author argued, had been shattered by the
conquistadores, the Spaniards. One copy of this work was
owned by Sir Peter Carew,[54] who may have lent it to a fellow
exile, John Ponet, since Ponet wrote in his *A Short Treatise of
politike power* of the tyrannical behaviour of the Spaniards in the
New World, of the suffering of the Indians, and of the possibility that Philip and his countrymen might treat the English in
the same way.[55] Thus, although the 'black legend',[56] exemplified in works such as this and Bartolomé de Las Casas's *Brevi-
ssima relación de la destruyción de las Indias*, published in Seville in
1552, played no great part in English attitudes to Spain in the
1550s, it did have some small propaganda value.

The prime importance at this time, however, of what was
known of Spanish ill-treatment of the Indians lay in the fact
that it fitted in with what was already believed about Spanish
colonialism in the Old World. When the Constable of France
talked to the English ambassador, Nicholas Wotton, about the
disasters that would result if Mary were to marry Philip he
pointed out that Wotton, as a well-travelled man, must know
'. . . what state all countreys ar, when Spaignardes beare anye
rule. Sicile, Naples, Lombardy, Siena, when they had it, and all

[50] Antwerp, 1556.
[51] London, 1557.
[52] London, 1555.
[53] Op. cit., fo. 8.
[54] C. Garrett, *The Marian Exiles* (Cambridge, 1938), 108, 256–7.
[55] N.p., 1556, sig. F 7ᵛ, L 4.
[56] W. S. Maltby, *The Black Legend in England* (Durham, NC, 1971).

other places where they haue had anye auctorite. Do yow not know, how they ar oppressid by the Spaignardes, yn what a bondage and myserye they lyve?'[57] He went on to describe the Spanish monopoly of office in Naples and other places, and the whole French court backed him up with tales of 'the intoller-able pryde, and the unsaciable covetousnesse of Spaignardes'. Although this sort of thing was no doubt to be expected from the French it certainly struck a responsive chord in English minds. Knox, in his *A faythful admonition vnto the professours of Gods truth in England*, published in 1554, declared that the bringing in of 'a proude Spaniarde' as king would be 'to the shame dishonoure and destruccion of the nobilitie, to the spoyle from them and theirs of their honoures, landes, possessions, chiefe offices and promocions, to the vtter decaye of the treasures, commodities, Nauie and fortifications of the realme to the abasyng of the yomanry, to the slauery of the communaltyie.'[58]

A supplicacyo[n] to the quenes maiestie, published in 1555, declared that Philip would bring the kingdom into 'bondage and slauerye, lyke as the emproure hath done Naples, Myland, and his nether contres of flanders, Holand, Seland, Brabant and Lyzelburg'. The writer went on to explain that in Naples the nobles had been expelled and Spaniards put in their places, while 'unreasonable excyses and tolles of corne, wyne, salte and frutes' had been charged on the province. In Milan these taxes had been levied as well as a chimney tax, and the heaviness of Spanish taxation in the Netherlands was, the author said, well-known.[59] Perhaps the most interesting of the works which re-flect contemporary views of Spanish colonization—if Professor Loades is correct in his argument that this is a catholic tract and not a protestant one[60]—is *The copye of a letter sent to the erles of Arundel, Darbie* ...[61] In this, the author, John Bradford, refers to those vanished works. *The Lamentation of Naples* and *The Mourning of Milan*, declaring that without even reading the

---

[57] SP 69/2/110.
[58] Kalykow, July 1554, sig. E 3ᵛ–4.
[59] N.p., n.d., fos. 21, 22.
[60] 'The Authorship and Publication of "*The copye of a letter*"', *Transactions of the Cambridge Bibliographical Society*, III (1960), 155–60.
[61] N.p., n.d., *STC*. 3480.

tracts he knows that in Naples and Milan the inhabitants pay taxes on chimneys and fires, and on food, as well as tithes.[62] Noailles reported as early as September 1553 that an anonymous tract, discussing Spanish rule in Naples, Milan, Julich, Constance, Cambrai, and Florence, declared that English liberties would likewise disappear 'et les parlements, qui se tiennent, ausquelz chascun des estatz de ce pays aveques liberté de pouvoir dire et alléguer toutes choses à l'utillité de Royaulme, seroit entirrement supprimé'.[63] Goodman later asked, 'do you think that Philip will be crowned kinge of Englande, and retayne in honor Englishe counsellors . . . Shall his nobilitie be Spaniardes, with out your land and possessions?'[64]

It is interesting to speculate on the origin of these views. The translator of Rudolph Walther (Gaulter)'s work, *Antichrist*, said in his preface that the work, which had appeared in Latin nine years earlier, had been written at a time when the 'Bishop of Rome bestowed the treasures of his blessing wyth fyre and sweorde (by Italianes and Spanyardes) vpon certayne partes of Germanye', and in the body of the work Walther exclaimed: 'what malicious heartes the Italianes and Spanyardes beare to all Germanie . . . they thinke it lawful for them to exercice all kynde of wickedness, tyrannie, and merciles crueltie vpon the Germaynes, as though they thought the Germaynes not worth to be counted among the nombre of men.'[65]

However, although Charles V's conduct towards German protestants was familiar to the English reformers it is noteworthy that Germany played little part in this particular myth, and the Low Countries, with the Spanish possessions in Italy, were far more important. There were refugees from Charles V's interim using the Austin Friars Church in London, and Walloon weavers at Glastonbury.[66] Of the seventy or so foreigners active in the printing trade in Edward's reign the majority were Dutch, and many of these retained a close con-

---

[62] Ibid. sig. F 1, 2.
[63] Arch. Étr. XII. fo. 79 (Vertot, II. 183).
[64] *How Svperior powers oght to be obeyd* (Geneva, 1558), 100.
[65] Southwark, 1556, sig. A 1ᵛ, fo. 166ᵛ. The translator was John Olde.
[66] W. Cunningham, *Alien Immigrants to England* (London, 1969 edn), 145, 147.

nection with their homeland.[67] English intercourse with the
Netherlands was substantial, moreover, and this led to occasional encounters with the Spanish: John Mason told the
privy council in November 1553 that 'our young men at
Antwerp' had had a 'byckering withe the Spanyardes as hath
so tykled them as they let not in all places to declare this discon-
tentacion *withe* the hole nac*io*n'.[68] It was said to be 'in his
travell and services in other partes afore' that Sir Thomas
Wyatt 'had observed bothe the meanes of the Spaniard for his
creepinge by all kindes of practizes into the governmentes of
sundrie states, and his greatnes therebie, and also his manner of
holding them in slaverie, by all kinds of crueltie and pride.'[69]
Refugees from the Spanish possessions in Italy such as Bernar-
dino Ochino and Peter Martyr Vermigli may also have confirmed the belief that the Spaniards were particularly
oppressive overlords.

This view of Spanish rule was not, however, very evident
before the late 1540s. When William Thomas wrote his guidebook he mentioned Spanish oppression only briefly in connection with Naples, which he said was peaceful—'sauying that
now of late is begonne a little striefe betwene the Vicare Don
Diego di Tolledo, and the barons of the realme, for the
makying of certain lawes, and some bickering and slaughter
hath haped betwene the Spaniardes and theim, and manie gen-
tilmen are fledde to Rome and other place for feare of punish-
mente'.[70] In 1547 there had been trouble over an attempt to
introduce the Spanish Inquisition into the realm, and in 1548
the viceroy, Tolledo, had reduced the freedom of the Neopoli-
tans to elect their own officials.[71] (Thomas also remarks of
Milan that the emperor 'draweth more money yerely to his
purse out of that onely estate, than out of some of his realmes'.[72])
The notion of Spanish oppression was subsequently to become

[67] A. D. M. Pettegree, 'The Strangers and their Churches in London, 1550–1580'
(Oxford Univ. D. Phil. thesis, 1983), Ch. 4.
[68] SP 69/2/84.
[69] *The Papers of George Wyatt Esquire*, ed. D. M. Loades (Camden Fourth Series, V,
1968), 202.
[70] *The historie of Italie* (London, 1549) fo. 136ᵛ, *RSTC. 24018*.
[71] R. Villari, 'The Insurrection in Naples of 1585', in *The Late Italian Renaissance
1525–1630*, ed. E. Chochrane (London, 1970), 307, 313–14.
[72] Thomas, *The historie of Italie*, fo. 183.

commonplace in England, however. When John Stubbs wrote *The discoverie of a gaping gvlf where into England is like to be swallowed by an other French marriage* he cited as the consequences of foreign domination the examples of 'the viceroys and Luogotenenti of Spayn in Naples, Cicil and here nere in the low countryes, [who] like boares in a fat new broken vp ground, by sowing first some seeds of dissentions to breed partialities in the countrye, doe roote out the auncient home growing nobilitie, and turne vnder perpetuall slauery, as doddes, the country people'.[73] He also argued, anticipating the critics of James I's financial exactions by three decades, that Philip had 'made Queene Mary to aske more extra ordinary and frequent subsidies and taskes, then had bene seene in so short a raigne: further causing her to borrow more loanes of hundred pounds, and ten poundes of her subiectes, then were euer payd agayn by a great sort' in order to fight a war for the benefit only of Spain, and one that resulted in the loss of Calais.[74] By 1579, then, Spain was universally regarded as a particularly oppressive colonial power: in the 1550s this was still a comparatively new image.

Outside the small circle of those who could read a little Spanish, or were at least interested in Spanish culture, most Englishmen were very ignorant about Spain. Educated men did not travel to Spain as they did to France and Italy, and it is significant that there existed no guidebook equivalent to that produced for Italy by Thomas.[75] Moreover, no substantial Spanish community existed in England that might have enabled the English to form a truer impression of the Spanish chracter.[76] Paget noted that the popular response to most foreigners was aggressive,[77] and Philip's train did not escape insults and blows.[78] Prejudice abounded at this social level. One of the participants in Wyatt's rebellion, a carpenter called John Toppylow, told a weaver friend that the object of the rising had been to prevent Mary's marriage, since, he said, if it oc-

---

[73] London, 1579, sog. D iv; *RSTC* 23400.

[74] Ibid. sig. C 7ᵛ.

[75] In 1550 he also published an Italian grammar (*RSTC* 24020).

[76] T. Wyatt, 'Aliens in England before the Huguenots', *Proceedings of the Huguenot Society*, XIX (1953).

[77] *CSP Sp.* XIII. 88–9.

[78] M. A. S. Hume, 'The Visit of Philip II, 1554', *EHR* VII (1892), 278. Spanish nationals had also been attacked in the riots of 1517.

curred, 'we shuld lye in swynestyes in caves and the spanyerd*es* shud haue o*u*r houses: and we should lyue lyke slaves, and be gladd to drynke a potte w*ith* water'.[79] Another report of this conversation declared that Toppylow had said that if the rebellion failed 'all we [in] Ingland shuld repent it and suche as I was shuld lye in the strete for defalte of loddgying and the Spanyerd*es* shuld haue our houses ... we shuld drynke noo drynke but water and paye a peny for a quarte pott full'.[80] William Isley, another of the participants in Wyatt's rebellion, said that 'the Spanyard*es* was com*m*ynge in to the Realme w*ith* harnes *and* handgonnes and would make vs Inglishe men wourse then dowges and viler / for this Realme should be brought to suche bondage by them as yt was neu*er* afore but should be vtterly conquered.'[81] There was also a great deal of anxiety about the financial, economic, and military consequences of a link with Spain: one pamphleteer declared that Mary had a Spanish heart, and gave Spaniards licences 'whereby they do cary and convoy away ... without paieng any custome therfore, our goudly and best commodites, as well, tin, leade, lether etc to the great decay and ympouerishment off the pour commons off this realm, by reaison wheroff the said comodites be now at doble pryces that they wer before.'[82] John Bradford complained that the Spaniards were taking treasure out of the realm.[83] A proclamation supposedly issued during Wyatt's rebellion declared: 'Spaniardes be nowe already arriued at Dover, at one passage to the nombre of an hundredth passing upwards to London, in companies of ten, foure and vj, with harnes, harquebusses, and morians with matchlight, the formest company wherof be alreadie at Rochester.'[84] The queen acknowledged the emotive force of this proclamation in her letter to the county of Gloucestershire explaining that the rebels were 'pretending upon false promises that the Prince of Spain and the Spaniards should come over to conquer this said realm' and pointing out that the articles of

---

[79] Norfolk and Norwich RO, Interrogatories and Depositions, 12a (i) fo. 135.
[80] Ibid, fo. 136.
[81] SP 11/2/10.
[82] *The Lame[n]taction of England* (n.p., 1557), 5; *STC* 10014.
[83] *The copye of a letter sent to the erles of Arundel, Darbie* ... sig. A 3ᵛ.
[84] J. Proctor, *The historie of Wyatts rebellion* (London, Jan. 1555), fo. 9.

marriage to which the nobility had given its consent proved how far from the truth was the proclamation.[85]

Anxieties such as these, and in particular those about the Spaniards' cruelty and acquisitiveness, should have been especially strong amongst the west country trading communities, whose members had frequently clashed with Spanish seamen and who had found themselves too often the quarry of the Inquisition.[86] In 1540 Thomas Cromwell sent one of his agents, Roger Basing, to Spain to investigate reports of ill-treatment of English merchants there.[87] Basing was informed by the merchants at San Lucar that if any Englishmen trading in Spain said or wrote that Henry VIII was a good Christian they were 'with moche creweltye put in pryson and their goodis lost forever and theyr lyfe in gret daunger'. However, the merchants were reporting in a period in which Anglo-Spanish relations were unusually bad, and may also have exaggerated somewhat, since most of those signing the letter to Basing continued to live in Spain, apparently without molestation.[88] Despite the seizure of a Spanish treasure ship coming from the Indies by a Southampton merchant, Robert Reneger, in 1545, and privateering by both nations, relations did not break down entirely in the 1540s and trade continued, albeit on a smaller scale.[89] None the less, it is surprising that pamphlets written against the Spanish marriage make no mention of incidents such as the arrest in 1539 of Thomas Pery, a wealthy London merchant residing in Ayamonte,[90] and that fewer men were found to support the rebellion of 1554 amongst the seafaring people of the west country than could be raised in the inland areas of Kent.[91]

There was, therefore, hostility to all foreigners at a popular

---

[85] *HMC Fourth Report* (Fitzhardinge), 365.

[86] G. Connell-Smith, *Forerunners of Drake* (London, 1954), 188.

[87] Ibid. 119–22, quoting SP, Henry VIII, CLXI, fos. 76–8.

[88] Ibid. 122–3.

[89] Ibid., chs. 7 and 8.

[90] Ibid. 111–18.

[91] It is interesting that it was Wyatt's father who, as ambassador to Charles V, protested in 1540 about the bad treatment of Englishmen in Spain (Connell-Smith, 110). On the other hand, Bonner, who followed him as ambassador, did not later seem to nurture anti-Spanish feelings.

level in the mid-sixteenth century, and a belief amongst the literate that the Spanish were far from liberal in their treatment of subject peoples. Such feelings were, however, probably still somewhat ameliorated in Mary's reign by happier memories of sympathetic Spanish figures such as Catherine of Aragon and the highly influential Vives: attitudes towards Spain in the 1550s were very different from what they were to become under the twin influences of the counter-reformation and the war at sea.

It was Philip's position as king consort that worried the English far more than his nationality. Although the accession and reign of a female occurred in practice without the difficulties that Henry VIII, in his search for a male heir, seems to have anticipated, the problem of Mary's marriage was an overwhelming one. Because all the rival contenders for the throne also happened to be women, little use was made of Mary's sex as a weapon of opposition. It is true that in the rising of 1554 one rebel said 'we ought not [to] haue a Woman to bere the sworde', but the reply was 'if a woman bere the swerde my lady Elyzabethe ought to bere hit fyrste'.[92] Those who disliked Mary's government tended, as this comment implies, to put their faith in her sister and could not, therefore, take a stand against female rule *per se*.[93] None the less the situation was unprecedented, fraught with difficulties and uncertainties. Did a queen regnant, for example, transfer some part of her regalian rights to her husband on marriage? The Constable of France clearly believed that she would, telling Wotton that 'when the prince hath maried the queene, he shall be kyng hym self and then what counsellour will or dare counseel against his kynges pleasure and will?'.[94] The French were not, of course, experts on the English constitution, but the fact is that no firm answer to this question emerged in the course of the reign. The whole matter had to be considered, therefore, *ab initio* in 1857 when Queen Victoria suggested that Prince Albert should be made king consort.[95] The Cabinet, after considerable discussion, declared that it was usual in England for the wife to take

[92] SP 11/2/2.
[93] J. Loach, 'Pamphlets and Politics, 1553-8', *BIHR* XLVIII (1975), 41.
[94] *PRO* SP 69/2/110.
[95] C. Woodham-Smith, *Queen Victoria; Her Life and Times* (London, 1972), I. 377.

her husband's rank, and not the reverse: to permit it in this instance would be to introduce a new principle. Moreover, if such
a principle were accepted, a king consort might, after the
queen's own death, marry again: would he then communicate
his rank to his new wife? Philip was of higher rank than Albert,
and his father bestowed the kingdoms of Naples and Jerusalem
on him just before his wedding, so that 'it might well appeare to
all men that the quenes highnes was then maried, not only to a
prince, but also unto a King',[96] but his position in England
was, presumably, analogous. Certainly the fact that parliament
was dissolved immediately on Mary's death proved, as one
commentator pointed out in the reign of William and Mary,
that Philip's title was determined by that of his wife, rather
than the reverse.[97]

In practice, Philip's position was very different from that of
his successors, Prince George and Prince Albert. The only consort in English history to be credited with 'regnal years', his
image appeared with that of Mary on queen's bench rolls and
on seals as well as on coins.[98] The latter caused deep offence to
at least one protestant pamphleteer, who asked about those
coins that showed the two monarchs with a crown over their
heads and the inscription 'Philip. et Maria Dei Gratia Rex et
Regina Anglie Francie et Neapolis Princeps Hispanic': 'who
seith not playnly that the prince off spain hath obtained to
haue the name of the king of England and also is permitted in
our english coine, to join his fisnamy with the quenes, the
croune of Englandde being ouer both ther heds in the midest?'[99]
When he was in England Philip signed formal documents with Mary, although in his absence she signed them

<hr>

[96] John Elder's 'Letter', in *Queen Jane and Queen Mary*, 141.

[97] BL Lansdowne MS 515, fo. 167.

[98] R. Ruding, *Annals of the Coinage of Great Britain* (London, 1840), I. 331. The disap-
pearance of any reference to Spain or Naples on later coins has sometimes been seen as
a response to anti-Spanish feeling (H. Symonds, 'The Coinage of Queen Mary Tudor,
1553–1558', *British Numismatic Journal*, VIII (1911), 188–9).

[99] *The Lame[n]tacion of England*, 10. The pamphleteer's claim that one English coin
even depicted Philip alone is correct, for a coin circulated in the Low Countries at this
time had the arms of Philip and Mary under a crown on one side and a device of
Charles V on the other: the inscription read 'Phi. Rex Ang. etc' (Ruding, op. cit. 332
and Plate in III. ii. III).

alone. This had been a difficult point to settle, and the lawyers had turned to a foreign precedent to guide them, that of Isabella of Castile, Mary's grandmother.[100] She was not necessarily a reassuring example, however, since despite a restrictive early agreement her regnal rights had gradually been extended to her husband.[101] The English tried to define Philip's position by the marriage treaty and this was, unusually, turned into a statute of the realm.[102] By this, Philip relinquished all claim to the disposal of offices in England and agreed to observe the laws of the realm. Further provisions of June 1554 forbade him from removing jewels or English artillery or from taking the queen out of the realm without her consent; Philip also promised to ensure that fortresses were well guarded by natives and that England should not be drawn into the existing war between the Empire and France.[103] Finally, he agreed that if the queen were to die childless he would lay no claim to the throne. However, treaties could be broken, as the Duke of Norfolk and Lord Windsor were both to point out, and 'who should suertie for the perfourmaunce thereof, and who should sue the forfaite?'.[104] The insistence of the English on the strict interpretation of the marriage treaty was a great source of chagrin to Philip, whose ambitions obviously extended beyond those of merely being a prop and support to his wife. The reports of the Imperial ambassadors and Charles V's own letters make it clear that the Habsburgs hoped that Philip would acquire a great deal more influence over English affairs than had ever been admitted. In November 1554, for example, Renard wrote to his master that

The arguments adduced by Paget and many other reasons combine to show how important it is that the King should take over the task of government and make it his especial care, for the object of the mar-

---

[100] *CSP Sp.* XII. 202. In fact Ferdinand and Isabella had agreed that the signature of either alone was valid in each kingdom, whereas Philip's signature alone was never sufficient in England.

[101] J. M. Bastista I Roca, 'The Hispanic Kingdoms and the Catholic Kings', *New Cambridge Modern History*, I. 320–1.

[102] HLRO, Original Acts, 1 Mary, sess. 3, 2: T. Rymer, *Foedera, Conventiones, Litterae etc.* (London, 1704–35), XV. 394–8. See also 1 & 2 Philip and Mary, c. 1, 'touching letters patents, and other writings to be signed by the queen'.

[103] *CSP Sp.* XII. 286–8.

[104] SP 46/124/215ᵛ.

riage is that he should, so fulfilling his duty towards the Queen in the manner provided for by the articles ... No better advice could be given to him than to follow the example set by the late Catholic King in his attitude towards Queen Isabella, for the circumstances are the same; his aim should be so to act that whilst he in reality does everything the initiative should always seem to proceed from the Queen and her Council. It would greatly help the King if the Queen were to assist, whenever able to do so, at the Council meetings at which he also is present, in order that the nobility and people may understand that all decisions are adopted with her and her Council's approval.[105]

Charles V and his advisers seem to have believed that Philip's position in England would be much enhanced if he were crowned. Renard constantly urged the queen to crown her husband; in October 1554 he thought that it might be possible to bring up such a proposal in parliament, 'though without giving him any right to the succession',[106] and a month later he believed, wrongly, that a formal scheme would be introduced.[107] In 1555 the Venetian ambassador with the Emperor reported that Charles V had decided to abdicate in favour of his son because Mary had told Philip that many Englishmen thought that any discussion of a coronation was premature, since he had not yet come into possession of his patrimony.[108] Later that same year a rumour was current that Philip was urging his wife to crown him on her own initiative, dispensing with the consent of parliament, 'in virtue of a law of the realm purporting that any king may of his own authority crown his consort': interestingly it was thought that Mary had refused to do so because another statute compelled 'all Englishmen to obey their kings in all military matters, after they have been crowned'.[109] Indeed, there may have been some substance in these reports of Mary's plans, since at the end of December she sent the Abbot of San Salute to Philip to apologize for her failure to persuade her subjects to agree either to a war with France or to Philip's coronation; to urge either further would,

---

[105] *CSP Sp.* XIII. 90–1.
[106] Ibid. 65.
[107] Ibid. 84.
[108] *CSP Ven.* VI. i. 200.
[109] Ibid. 281.

she believed, endanger her own position.[110] Philip in his turn
sent Don Juan de Fuguera to explain his own arguments to the
Privy Council.[111] The council remained opposed to the
scheme.[112] Throughout the early part of 1556 Philip urged his
case through Figuera, with the same result.[113]

Although Renard urged Mary to crown Philip in terms that
suggested that the ceremony was of no more significance than
her own mother's coronation,[114] he actually believed that the
coronation was peculiarly significant in England, since it confirmed and recognized title.[115] The Imperialists' belief in the
symbolic importance of the coronation was certainly shared by
many of those who opposed the Spanish match, for almost
every account of unrest contains some avowal that the speaker
wishes to prevent Philip being crowned. Indeed, this was a
major motive amongst the plotters of 1556: Sir Henry Dudley
asked Sir Nicholas Arnold, for instance, if he had heard that
'they goo abowtt a coronacyon', news which Arnold described
as 'worthe the hearyng'.[116] A London bricklayer, William
Crowe, heard that 'the earle of pembroke shold goo to fetche
the crowne from the Earle of Shrewsbury to crown the kyng
with', and declared that many others would 'spend ther lyves in
kepyng the crown in Inglyshe mens handes and that the
strangers shoold never haue yt'—if 'a paynter . . . woold make a
flagg ther woold be v c, ye and v c more that woold dye in this
quarrell that no stranger shuld haue the crowne'.[117] William
Oldnall, one of the queen's guards, was accused of saying that
Mary 'entendyth to haue a kynge to be crownyd here in this
Realme whyche thynge he sayd she shuld neuer bryng to passe
more then in other Realmes whyche he rehersed'—these were
Naples, Jerusalem, and Spain, of which Philip had become
king in 1555—'wher he sayde the kynge was neuer crownyd

[110] Ibid. 299.
[111] SP 11/7/5.
[112] SP 11/7/10. The bishop of Ely and the lord privy seal were sent to Philip to
explain the reasons for the council's decision.
[113] SP 11/7/20, 11/7/22, 11/8/43, 11/8/44.
[114] *CSP Sp.* XIII. 76.
[115] Ibid. 102.
[116] SP 11/8/49.
[117] SP 11/8/70.

nether shuld be wythe vs for he sayd ytt wald coste many A man hys lyff before he shuld be crownyd'.[118]

Why both Philip's adherents and his opponents attached such weight to his coronation is uncertain. Some shadowy notion existed, as we have seen, that treason against an uncrowned king was different from treason against a crowned one: John Bradford, the pamphleteer, argued that 'so long as he is not crowned, that manne is no traitour that speaketh agaynst his coronacion, but after his maiestie hath the crown the best of you all, that speaketh agaynst the Spaniardes proceedings, shalbe proued and ponished, lyke a rancke traitor'.[119] Once the king were crowned, he went on, 'who dare withstand his doings, doe not the lawes of Englande bind all men to obeie him?'[120]

Whatever the motive that lay behind the interest taken in the coronation, it seems to have been agreed by both sides that Philip could not be crowned without the consent of parliament. Mary defiantly declared in the autumn of 1555 that if it proved impossible to raise the subject in parliament she would go ahead on her own initiative,[121] and Renard reported that the proposal was not being laid before parliament out of constitutional necessity 'but merely to find out how opinion stands'.[122] In fact, both ultimately accepted that parliament's reluctance to see Philip crowned was an insuperable obstacle. Because parliament was so clearly averse to the scheme no formal proposal was laid before it: despite Mary's bold words she never attempted to crown her consort without parliamentary approval. This was a considerable check on royal power.

Attitudes towards the Spanish marriage and towards Philip's constitutional position were complicated, both in parliament and amongst the nation as a whole, by a widespread belief that the succession was a thing that could not be altered, even by the queen herself. It may be that the abortive attempt of Edward VI to leave the throne away from his sisters, with all the threat of strife and civil war that had been involved, had strengthened the idea of an inviolable succession: John Bradford, for

[118] PRO KB 27/1184, 12 Rex r (July, 1557).
[119] *The copye of a letter sent to the erles of Arundel, Darbie* . . ., sig. C 7ᵛ.
[120] Ibid. sig. F 3.
[121] *CSP Ven.* VI. i. 227.
[122] *CSP Sp.* XIII. 102.

example, said that if Mary were the last heir to the throne she could leave it as she wished, but 'if it belong to the heires of the realme, after her death, and if ther be any heires in England liuing after her, to whom the crowne oughte to come by iuste and lawefull discente' it would be a 'deadlye and damnable sinne' to attempt to change such descent.[123] Certainly an idea existed that Henry VIII's will, and the order of the succession therein contained, could not be altered. In Dudley's attempted coup Sir Anthony Kingston asked Henry Peckham to find a copy of the will, 'for ther ys suffycyent matter for ower purpose'.[124] Peckham replied that the copy of the will in the rolls could not be obtained, 'but yff I coold by any other means get yt than I schuld do yt'. He did in fact obtain his father's copy, which he then kept in the dirty linen basket in his room. So far had Henry's will permeated the conscience of the nation that a Kentish yeoman accused the queen in November 1554 of having broken the will 'for the duke of Nor*folk*, the lorde courtney, and the Bysshope of Wynche*ster* should haue remaynid in the Towre'.[125]

By the will, of course, Elizabeth was the next heir to the throne. Those who were attached to her might have been particularly suspicious of Philip, whilst those who were suspicious of Philip may have asserted the claims of the princess only in order to block any attempt by Philip to claim the throne for himself. Contemporaries believed that Elizabeth had a number of adherents in parliament. Renard reported, for example in December 1554 when the regency bill was under discussion, that the news that the Lords had passed the bill led to intrigue between 'certain persons' and some members of the Commons with the notion of dividing opinion in parliament and thus preventing Elizabeth from being declared a bastard.[126] In fact the French envoy had predicted just such behaviour a year earlier, when he wrote 'on estime que cedict parlement n'y consentira jamais, ne vouland permettre que la dicte dame Elizabeth soit excluse de la succession de la couronne et du droict qu'elle y peult esperer part le testament du feu roy

---

[123] *The copye of a letter sent vnto the erles of Arundel, Darbie . . .*, sig. F 4ᵛ–5.
[124] SP 11/8/52. See also L. B. Smith, 'The Last Will and Testament of Henry VIII: a Question of Perspective', *Journal of British Studies*, II (1962–3), 26.
[125] KB 9/559, fo. 7.
[126] *CSP Sp*. XIII. 130.

Henry son père, qu'ilz desirent ensuyvre.'[127] Elizabeth did indeed have some close associates in both Houses. In the Lords
these included Lord William Howard; in the Commons, her
cousin, Henry Carey, who sat for Buckinghamshire in both the
parliaments of 1554, her cofferer, Thomas Parry, who represented Wallingford in 1555, and John Astley, who also sat in
1555 as one of the burgesses for St Albans.[128]

None of these men committed any major act of opposition
during Mary's reign, either outside or within the parliament
chamber. Fuller, writing later of the gifts bestowed on Carey by
Elizabeth, declared that what he received was 'rather restitution than liberality . . . seeing that he had spent as great an
estate . . . in her service, or rather relief, during her persecution
under Queen Mary',[129] but although he was ordered after
Wyatt's rebellion to report regularly to the council,[130] Carey's
behaviour seems to have been more circumspect than might
have been expected of one characterized by Naunton as fond of
'sword and buckler men'.[131] Astley had his name on the Loseley
list, and William Cecil, who served Elizabeth in some unknown
capacity at this period,[132] admitted to having offended the
government in some way during the parliament of 1555.[133]
However, Parry, despite keeping suspicious company during
his time with Elizabeth at Woodstock,[134] did not leave any
mark on parliamentary history.

Thus association with Elizabeth does not seem to have led
these men into open defiance of the crown in parliament, nor
even outside it. Elizabeth was not, of course, ignorant of the
plots of the time, for after she had become queen she said that
she had in her time been 'a second person'

---

[127] PRO Transcripts 31/3/21. 4 Nov. 1553.

[128] The difficulty of distinguishing this man from his half-brother of the same name
is considerable. However, it seems probable that it was Elizabeth's servant who sat in
parliament rather than his half-brother, who had no political experience.

[129] T. Fuller, *The Worthies of England* (London, 1662), I. 432.

[130] *APC* IV. 25.

[131] R. Naunton, *Fragmenta Regalia* (London, 1870), 47.

[132] Read, *Mr Secretary Cecil and Queen Elizabeth*, 116.

[133] See above, 154.

[134] 'State Papers relating to the Custody of the Princess Elizabeth at Woodstock in
1554', ed. C. R. Manning, *Transactions of the Norfolk and Norwich Archaeological Society*, IV
(1855), 177.

... and haue tasted of the practizes against my sister who I would to God weare aliue againe. I had great occationes to harken to ther motsiones of whom some of them ar in the Common house but when frind*e*s fall out the truth doth appeare accordinge to the ould prouarbe and wear yt not for my honor ther knauery should be knowne. Ther wer occasione in me that tyme I stoode Indaunger of my lyfe my sister was so insensed against me I did diferr from her in R*e*ligione and I was sought for diu*e*rse wayes so shall neu*e*r my Successor be.[135]

During her stay at Ashridge James Croft had visited her and, almost certainly, told her of the rising planned for Easter 1554;[136] other plotters may also have taken her into their confidence. However, it appears that Elizabeth was protected less by any especial friends she might have than by the fact that parliament as a whole seems to have believed that the throne should pass to the princess if Mary were to die childless: despite frequent suggestions that she was to be prosecuted for treason,[137] declared illegitimate or barred from the throne[138] she remained the heir presumptive.

There existed, therefore, certain fundamental principles that the crown could not threaten in parliament with impunity: these concerned the succession, the sovereign rights of the crown, and the importance of the coronation. A belief that foreigners, whether Philip or the pope, should not interfere in English affairs was also frequently asserted. These principles caused the monarch to pause before attempting to exclude Elizabeth from the throne, or crown Philip, and produced changes and emendations in the treason laws and the statute covering the guardianship of any child Mary might have. However, it would be an error to see these principles as peculiar to a small group or 'parliamentary opposition', since they were shared by almost all those sitting in parliament and probably by the governing class as a whole. Thus these principles mark a

---

[135] BL Stowe MS 354, fo. 18ᵛ.
[136] C. A. Mackwell, 'The early career of Sir James Croft, 1570–1576' (Oxford Univ. B. Litt. thesis, 1970).
[137] *CSP Sp.* XII. 197, 201.
[138] Ibid. 220.

real limit to royal power in the mid-sixteenth century, for the crown could violate them only at the expense of that tacit compact with the property-owning classes on which the whole structure of Tudor government rested.

10

An Opposition Party?

THE evidence of the preceding chapters suggests that long-held theories about parliamentary conflict in the reign of Mary require considerable modification. One of these theories is that in the reign of Mary a formed, organized opposition emerged in the House of Commons with leaders and the capacity for subtle tactical manœuvre which sought to wrest domination of the House from the council. This theory is most clearly set out in the introduction to Sir John Neale's work on *Elizabeth I and her Parliaments*. Another theory is that opposition in parliament came at this time to be regarded as an alternative to rebellion, a new option for potential rebels.[1] The meagre evidence that is available runs counter to both these interpretations. The decision taken by individual men to plot or to participate in rebellion appears to have had little to do with events in parliament, whilst what seems at first glance to be formed opposition turns on closer scrutiny into an ephemeral and largely coincidental association.

The parliaments of Mary's reign, Neale claimed, mark an important stage in the development of parliamentary opposition, and, more particularly, in the development of opposition within the House of Commons. Yet the evidence set out above shows that conflict in Marian parliaments was infrequent, and that when conflict did arise it was more often because the whole body of those in parliament was hostile to what the monarch desired than because 'a party' within parliament was opposed to the crown: this is most obviously the case in discussions of the Spanish marriage and Philip's position, and in debates over taxation. Moreover, the direct achievements of parliament in frustrating measures proposed by the crown were achievements of the House of Lords as much as those of the Commons. For Mary, indeed, the failure of the heresy bill and of the bill

---

[1] Loades, *Two Tudor Conspiracies*, 242–3.

extending the protection of the treason law to Philip in the second of her parliaments was a worse blow than the loss of the exiles bill in the more famous parliament of 1555: for her, the grave wound came from the Lords, not the Commons.

None the less, it is easy to understand why accounts of opposition in parliament during this period have concentrated on events in the House of Commons. Leaving aside the tendency for parliamentary historians to become peculiarly influenced by 'Whig' historiography, the fact remains that what went on in the House of Commons is more obviously exciting than the rather ponderous doings of the Upper House. The sources, although still meagre, are better for the Commons than they are for the Lords, and, in particular, the accounts of the Venetian and Imperial ambassadors have provided generations of historians with vivid accounts of the more stirring scenes. Neither man was present at any of the scenes he so graphically described, of course, and since neither could speak English, each had access to only a limited range of informants:[2] none the less, in the absence of other information, the historian must turn with gratitude to their dispatches. There is no parallel for the House of Lords to the dramatic occasion, described by Michieli, when Kingston locked the doors of the Chamber and forced the speaker to take a vote: historians have, therefore, tended to believe that the House of Lords rarely opposed the crown, that it was almost a rubber stamp for government policy.

This was not the case. With the exception of the subsidy bills, which were merely approved by the Upper House, any proposal involving property rights was likely to receive close scrutiny by the Lords. Thus, for example, the bill for the attainder of the duke of Suffolk and his associates was lost in May 1554 because of some difficulty over the exact nature of the lands to be confiscated, and when it was finally passed in January 1555 seven peers still protested against it.[3] Peers always seem to have given careful consideration to the clauses in treason legislation relating to confiscation, as well as to the protection of their own pri-

---

[2] On this, see E. H. Harbison, 'French Intrigue at the Court of Queen Mary', *American Historical Review*, XLV (1940), 533–51.

[3] See above, 103–4 and 182.

vileges:[4] even the reversal of an act of attainder might involve considerable expenditure of time, as the example of the duke of Norfolk's case indicates,[5] since peers cared very much about the way in which landed estates were handled.

Yet, although it was by no means the mere pawn of the crown, the House of Lords did not provide the government with as many difficult moments as did the Commons. The reason for this was, perhaps, not only that any individual peer was likely to have a great deal more in common with his monarch than many members of the Lower House, but also that he had very frequently had some opportunity of influencing government policy before it reached the stage of a draft bill. Obviously, a far higher proportion of the Upper House were members of the privy council. Obviously, too, the individual peer had greater access to the queen and her advisers than did most of the Commons. Above all, he had a right and, indeed, a duty to advise his monarch. This duty was discussed in the course of the 1559 debates on the church settlement, most notably by Viscount Montagu—who, of course, owed his elevation to the peerage to Mary.[6] Montagu pointed out that the peers were summoned to sit in parliament, the highest council of the realm, 'wherin all men are bounde to discharge themselves, not only by yea and naye, but also as occasion serveth to further and advaunce all those thinges that sounde to the honour of god and wealth of the Realme'.[7] He went on to say that this was the reason 'wherfore hath God placed Noble men to be in dignitie before others', and that peers should therefore be particularly ready to sacrifice themselves for the good of their prince and country.[8]

The right of the peers to advise their monarch was recognized on various occasions during Mary's reign. Before her first parliament, some of her counsellors suggested that she should

---

[4] 1 & 2 Philip & Mary, c. 3.

[5] See above, 64–71.

[6] See above, 22.

[7] T. J. McCann, 'The Parliamentary Speech of Viscount Montagu against the Act of the Supremacy, 1559', *Sussex Archaeological Collections*, CVIII (1970), 52–3. The document quoted is wrongly cited in this article. It is Bodley MS Eng. th. b.12, II, fos. 840–843. This point is on fo. 841.

[8] Ibid. 55 (Bodley MS Eng. th. b.12, II, fo. 842ᵛ).

rather call a meeting of 'notables and private individuals chosen to represent Parliament':[9] although she rejected this advice, the day after the dissolution of parliament Mary broke the news of her betrothal to what was described by Renard as 'the Great Council and foremost members of the parliament'.[10] The notion still lingered of an assembly of 'notables' as an alternative consent-giving body to parliament: in 1555 Mary was said to have thought of crowning Philip after the dissolution of parliament with the approval of 'a number of peers and other personages of the kingdom',[11] and in the following spring she was reportedly attempting to win the consent of Shrewsbury, Derby, Westmorland, and others to the coronation, presumably again with the idea that a Great Council might give her the approval that parliament would not.[12] In December 1557 Michieli alleged that Mary intended to summon in Epiphany what he called 'half a parliament', consisting of knights, lords, pensioners, and officials.[13] All these were rumours, and their origins may have rested in no more than the ambassadors' failure fully to understand English constitutional niceties, but the frequency with which the notion of meetings of peers and other notables is mentioned suggests that the monarch was as aware as her noble subjects of their customary role as advisers.

Certainly opposition to the crown in the Lords by any individual peer was often an indication that he felt that his advice was being ignored. Opposition in the Lords thus differed very considerably from opposition in the Commons, for it could be merely tactical, an attempt to alter the balance of power at court. It is such 'tactical' opposition that explains, at least in part, the loss of the heresy and treason bills in the spring of 1554.

Before the parliament began it was obvious that a serious split existed amongst the council. Paget and Pembroke were known to be opposed to the religious measures that Gardiner proposed to lay before the assembly.[14] The queen herself recognized this and seems to have attempted to win over Pem-

[9] *CSP Sp.* XI. 171.
[10] Ibid. 428.
[11] *CSP Ven.* VI. i. 227.
[12] Ibid. 415–16.
[13] Ibid. VI. ii. 848.
[14] *CSP Sp.* XII. 168. See above, 97.

broke by open expressions of favour to him and to his wife.[15] However, her attempts to smooth things over failed, and not only the heresy bill was lost but also the bill extending the treason law to Philip. This last came as a shock, since Paget appears earlier to have approved the proposal.[16] Paget's opposition was supported by Rich, by Pembroke, and by Arundel, as well as by a substantial majority of the other peers. Rich was apparently obsessed by anxiety about the future of his substantial landholdings[17] and Arundel may have hoped that his son might marry Elizabeth,[18] but the actions of Paget and Pembroke seem to have stemmed entirely from disappointed ambition.[19] Paget, after all, was not in principle opposed to the heresy laws, although he thought that Gardiner was introducing them at a politically inept moment. Similarly, he had been one of the chief architects of the Spanish marriage. Neither Pembroke nor Rich nor Arundel was an opponent of catholicism or of Philip as such. What they were trying to do was to force the queen to listen to their advice rather than to that of Gardiner and the 'old catholics'. Like some of the so-called 'opposition MPs' of the Jacobean period, the peers were demonstrating their nuisance value: they hoped, by showing the queen how difficult they could be, to persuade her that she would be well-advised to pay more attention to them. In this they eventually succeeded, for although they never became intimate confidants of the queen they played a prominent part in subsequent policy-making: Paget, in particular, was much esteemed by Philip.

The spilling over of conciliar conflict into the House of Lords was, then, a source of great embarrassment and annoyance to the queen in 1554. However, the council soon resolved its difficulties and the episode was not repeated.[20] Although individual councillors and, indeed, individual lay peers and bishops,

---

[15] Ibid. 202.

[16] Ibid. 230.

[17] See above, 101.

[18] *CSP Sp.* XII. 231, 308–9.

[19] Renard frequently refers to Pembroke's sense of grievance. See *CSP Sp.* XII. 152, 198.

[20] On the council at this period, see A. Weikel, 'The Marian Council Revisited', in *The Mid-Tudor Polity c. 1540–1560*, 52–73.

were at times very critical of the crown's policy, no concerted acts of defiance took place in any of the subsequent parliaments of the reign.[21]

Opposition in the House of Lords was, therefore, very often an indication of tension at court, whereas opposition in the House of Commons might, much more ominously, indicate that a substantial portion of the governing class disliked some part of the crown's policy. The 'individualistic' nature of opposition in the House of Lords stemmed in part from, and in part reflected, one privilege enjoyed by a peer which was not open to members of the House of Commons. This was the right to register a formal protest when a measure had been passed to which he objected: in 1555, for example, Walter Devereux, Viscount Hereford, and Lord Cobham, registered protests against the bill allowing the queen to alienate first fruits and tenths.[22] Their action could have no impact on the bill's progress, but they felt it necessary to make their position known. It may be that this privilege acted as a useful safety-valve, allowing the discontented—and neither Hereford nor Cobham was in favour at this time[23]—to believe that their protests might at least persuade the monarch to reconsider the broad lines of her policy. The protest had no short-term impact, for the bill was still passed, but it perhaps had some cumulative effect. Certainly, as we have seen, peers took protests seriously and made frequent use of them.[24]

Having protested, peers do not seem at this period to have taken their opposition any further. There is no clear evidence suggesting that a peer who disliked a bill but had been unable to stop it in the Upper House would then attempt to organize opposition to it in the Commons. Certainly one or two of the members of the Lower House who can be identified as critical of government proposals were attached to a particular peer— Robert Farrar, for instance, was a client of the earl of

---

[21] For a different view, see above, 47 and 119–22.

[22] *LJ*, 23 Nov. 1555.

[23] This and the previous session were the only Marian parliaments Hereford attended. He had been imprisoned and fined in 1553 for his support of Jane Grey (Machyn, 43). Cobham was in disgrace because of the part played by his sons in Wyatt's rebellion (Loades, *Two Tudor Conspiracies*, 60–2, 110–11).

[24] See above, 60.

Rutland[25]—but there is no proof that their activities in the Chamber were dictated by their patrons. Indeed, the actions in the parliament of 1555 of some of Pembroke's clients suggest that the chains of patronage might easily be disregarded if matters of conscience were at stake.[26] Opposition to the crown in the House of Lords, although more frequent and more annoying to the crown than is sometimes suggested, could be contained. Peers were, in general, not given in Mary's time to the kind of factiousness in the Chamber that had marked Edward's reign; they were primarily concerned about their own personal affairs and about the rights and privileges of their estate.

Was the House of Commons any different? As we have already seen, there is much evidence to suggest that those sitting in the Lower House were concerned primarily with the affairs of their locality, their trade or their family. They did not attend daily, and grew impatient if a session went on too long. Is it possible to find, amongst these preoccupied but often idle burgesses and country gentlemen, the men thinking critically 'on issues of transcendent importance to their consciences' of whom Neale speaks? Was Mary's reign, for the House of Commons in general, and for the development of a constitutional opposition in particular, a stage in its 'apprencticeship to future greatness'?

Can we speak of 'an opposition party' in the House of Commons during the reign of Mary? Sir John Neale, although he expressed himself with great caution, clearly believed that one could, for he writes of 'the opposition' as being 'Protestant, or inclined, for political and other reasons, to sympathise with Protestants'; he also declared that this 'opposition' had both a need and an inclination 'to exploit freedom of speech within the limits of Sir Thomas More's definition of the privilege'. The concept of such an 'opposition' implies, as Neale recognized, continuity of personnel. It also involves consistent principles. Did such a 'platform' of opposition ideas exist in these parliaments? Did those who criticized government policy do so for the same reasons? And were they always the same people—were the men who opposed the crown's policy over first fruits

---

[25] See below, 209.
[26] See above, 139.

and the exiles in 1555, for instance, the same as those who had withstood some aspect of the crown's religious policy in 1553?

On two occasions lists were drawn up of men who opposed some measure put forward by the crown in parliament.[27] In neither case can we be certain what the issue was, and neither list includes members of the Upper House, although, as we have seen, the crown did meet with difficulties in the House of Lords. The first list is the Bodley list, which refers to the parliament of 1553, and the second the Loseley list, which probably refers to the parliament of 1555. Both lists were drawn up as a result of opposition to some measure that had to do with religion, yet the overlap betwen the names on the list is not great. Of those members whose names were marked on the Bodley list and also sat in the parliament of 1555 five are not on the Loseley list—Creed, Henry Hussey, Leweston, Henry Stafford, John Throckmorton—and ten are—Dyer, Farrar, Hopton, Marshe, More, Peckham, Perrot, Skinner, Smethwick, and Strangways. Of the men on the Loseley list who had sat in the parliament of 1553 twelve appear on the Bodley list with no mark by their names: Blount, Caryll,[28] Chiverton, Reginald Corbet, Drury, John Holmes, Sir Henry Jones, Mohun, Peyton, Randall, Wingfield, and possibly Nowell. Although these calculations must be tentative because of the difficulty of identifying some of the names on the Loseley list, it is clear that opposition to the crown's policy in one parliament did not necessarily lead to opposition in another, even if the issue were similar. This in itself must throw doubt on the concept of an opposition party.

None the less, the ten men who are on both lists form, if anything does, a basis for considering the notion of 'an opposition' in these years. Is it possible to speculate about the motives that pushed Dyer, Farrar, Hopton, Marshe, More, Peckham, Perrot, Skinner, Smethwick, and Strangways towards their criticisms of the crown's policy, and do they have enough in common to make the concept of a 'party' a reasonable one? Six of the group were substantial country gentlemen, but Marshe

[27] See Appendices B and D.
[28] The History of Parliament Trust believes that this name reads 'Cavell' and identifies the member with Humphrey Cavell, who in 1555 sat for Bodmin.

was a London business man and Skinner an academic. Robert Farrar was the earl of Rutland's secretary. In January 1553 Rutland had asked for, and obtained, the nomination to one parliamentary seat from the corporation at Lincoln,[29] and it is likely that Farrar represented the borough in Edward's second parliament:[30] he sat for the town in all Mary's parliaments save the last, as well as in 1559 and 1563—indeed, he had been nominated for the seat in December 1557 before Rutland suddenly put in Francis Kempe, Heath's mace-bearer, perhaps because he wanted his secretary with him for the campaigns in France. Little is known of Farrar himself but his patron, Rutland, appears to have been a protestant sympathizer;[31] he was briefly imprisoned at the beginning of Mary's reign, and both he and members of his household fell under suspicion in later years.[32] The other member of the group of whom little is known is William Smethwick. He had been in the royal household from the mid 1530s and became one of Catherine Parr's chamber servants.[33] He sat for the Seymour seat of Penryn in 1547 and was involved in the plots of Thomas Seymour.[34] In October 1553 he represented Grampound, but he fell under suspicion at the time of Wyatt's rebellion and was imprisoned briefly in the Tower and then the Fleet.[35] However, in 1555, when both he and his fellow-member, John Vaughan, appear on the Loseley list, he was sitting for Sir Thomas Cawarden's borough of Bletchingley. In that year Smethwick, with Sir Thomas Smith, obtained a papal indulgence allowing him to eat flesh in Lent.[36] The link with Smith, who had been his colleague when he represented Grampound, like the association with the Parr–Seymour group, perhaps suggests protestant leanings, but his court service is all that is definitely known of him.

Most of the rest of the group had in fact also improved their

---

[29] *HMC Lincoln Corporation* XIV. viii. 47, 48, 49.

[30] The returns for Lincoln are lost for this parliament.

[31] He was present at the debates on the sacraments that took place in 1551 (C. Read, *Mr Secretary Cecil and Queen Elizabeth*, 84–5) and his reading included Latimer's sermons and the works of Calvin (*HMC Rutland* XII. i. 55, 73).

[32] Machyn, 38; *HMC Rutland* XII. i. 64.

[33] PRO E 179/69/47, 48.

[34] Haynes, *A Collection of State Papers*, 2.

[35] *Queen Jane and Queen Mary*, 53, 71.

[36] Dewar, *Sir Thomas Smith*, 78.

position by royal service in the 1530s and 1540s. Thomas Dyer, who sat for Bridgewater in 1545, 1547, both the parliaments of 1553, probably in 1555, and in 1559, had built up a considerable estate in this way, acquiring, for instance, some of the attainted Somerset's lands as well as a quantity of former ecclesiastical property.[37] He was perhaps under a shadow in Mary's reign: summoned before the privy council after Wyatt's rebellion,[38] he subsequently disappeared from public life until, at Elizabeth's accession, he became sheriff of his county.[39] It is not without interest that Sir Anthony Kingston granted Dyer some of his Gloucestershire land in 1555[40] and that he was granted land in 1558 by Thomas Marrow, another of those marked on the Bodley list.[41] Sir Ralph Hopton, knight for Somerset in both the parliaments of 1553, member for an unknown constituency in 1555, and burgess for Heytesbury in 1559, is an even more substantial figure. He rose through the service of Thomas Cromwell to become in 1542 knight-marshal of the household.[42] He served under Russell and Herbert at the time of the Western Rising, and then attached himself to the Dudleys, receiving presents from Northumberland's heir[43] and becoming, in 1551, surveyor for augmentations in Somerset. His position as knight-marshal became of particular significance and for a time he was in control both of the Tower and the Marshalsea,[44] for which he received the not inconsiderable sum of 6s. 4d. per day.[45] In August 1553 he was ordered to bring to court the patent of 'his late office', a summons he appears to have ignored.[46] He was suspected—according to the Spanish ambassador, arrested[47]—at the time of Wyatt's rebellion, when he was reported to have asked his servants, 'how leke

---

[37] *CPR*, Edward VI, V. 27.
[38] *APC* IV. 402.
[39] *The House of Commons, 1509–1558*.
[40] *CPR*, Philip and Mary, III. 93.
[41] Ibid. IV. 327.
[42] *Letters and Papers* XIII. ii. 1184: PRO LC 2/2, fo. 80.
[43] Bodley Additional MS c. 94, fos. 3, 4.
[44] *APC* II. 326, 406; III. 44, 52, 88, 268, 278, 283, 293, 322, etc.
[45] Ibid. III. 52.
[46] Ibid. IV. 329.
[47] *CSP Sp.* XII. 126.

yow the cumynge off the kynge off Spayne and Spanyrd*e*s whycche wylle ocupy yowar wyffes beffore yowr fac*e*s', and was heard to 'invey and make Ressons agayne the cumynge in off the the kynge off Spayne and Spanyard*e*s'.[48] No action seems to have been taken against him and it was not until after Mary's fourth parliament, in which he had been critical of some aspect of royal policy, that he was sent a letter 'streightly commaunding him to make his indelaied repairs to the Courte, taunswere suche matter as at his coming shalbe objected unto hym by the Lords of the Counsaill'.[49] On 16 February 1556 Hopton was ordered to 'declare what he can alleage whie he shuld not be removed from the office of Knight marshal for his contynuall absence from the same';[50] in May he surrendered his patent into the exchequer and handed over his office to Sir Thomas Holcroft, who appears to have been carrying out many of his duties already.[51] Hopton was restored in December 1558.[52]

Hopton's dissatisfaction in Mary's reign can be explained in a variety of ways. He may have disliked Mary's religious policy: in 1554 he was accused of eating 'Flesshe [on] the Fastyng Days',[53] he was to be recommended by his bishop in 1564 as a favourer of the established church[54] and there was a sermon at his funeral in 1571.[55] But these are only tenuous indicators of religious beliefs. He may have been anxious about his office as knight-marshal, although it seems that, despite his laxness, he was given considerable leeway.

The most considerable of this group of men who had risen through royal favour was Sir John Perrott, although his position was a slightly different one since he was said to be a bastard of Henry VIII himself.[56] He received a number of favours from the king, and became a substantial Pembrokeshire land-

[48] SP 11/2/33.
[49] *APC* V. 203 (16 Dec. 1555).
[50] Ibid. 236.
[51] Ibid. 279.
[52] Ibid. VII. 25: *CPR* Elizabeth, I. 35.
[53] SP 11/2/33.
[54] *Camden Miscellany IX*, 63.
[55] See Glover's certificate: Bodley MS Ashmole 836, fo. 403.
[56] E. L. Barnwell, 'Notes on the Perrot family', *Archaeologia Cambrensis*, III. xi (1865), 108–29.

owner. He was briefly imprisoned on Mary's accession, but his period out of favour did not last long and he was rewarded for his services against Wyatt.[57] He was entrusted in March 1554 with the welcome of the Imperial envoy, Count d'Egmont, and Philip later gave him a gold chain worth 200 marks, in company with such men as the earl of Ormonde and Mary's trusted household servant, Sir Henry Jerningham.[58] In Edward's first parliament Perrott had sat for Carmarthenshire, but in Mary's reign he sat for Sandwich as a result of the good offices of his father-in-law, Sir Thomas Cheyne, the warden of the Cinque Ports: Cheyne intruded Perrott in 1553 in place of a townsman, Thomas Menys, and in 1555 another townsman, Roger Manwood, was displaced for him.[59] It was in the course of this parliament that Perrott quarrelled with his patron, the earl of Pembroke, over the exiles bill and was reportedly dismissed from his service.[60] He was one of the discontented members of parliament who met at Arundel's Tavern during the session.[61] Arrested at the time of Dudley's conspiracy, Perrott was soon released as there was no firm evidence against him.[62] He served the queen at St-Quentin the following year.

It is possible that Perrott held protestant opinions. According to later family tradition he angered Pembroke by a refusal to carry out the heresy commission in Wales[63] and he was said to have sheltered a number of protestants, including Laurence Nowell.[64] However, there is no contemporary evidence for these activities, and the violence of his opposition in 1555 may have sprung from a naturally bellicose temperament rather than from religious conviction: Perrot had quarrelled with Lord Abergavenny during the period when both were in the service of Paulet, and in 1554 he was put in the Fleet because of

[57] *Queen Jane and Queen Mary*, 187.
[58] *CSP Sp*. XII. 136, 315.
[59] See *The House of Commons, 1509–1558*, under Cinque Ports, and above, 32.
[60] Above, 139.
[61] SP 11/8/35.
[62] Machyn, 104, Loades, *Two Tudor Conspiracies*, 233.
[63] Barnwell, 'Notes on the Perot family', 110.
[64] R. Churton, *The Life of Alexander Nowell* (Oxford, 1809), 253–6. Perrott was also said to have sheltered his uncle Robert, described as a reader in Greek during the reign of Edward VI—was this Robert Berkeley, later bishop of Bath and Wells?—and 'a gentleman by the name of Banister'.

an argument with the earl of Worcester's servants.[65] Later, he was to be on extremely bad terms with his Pembrokeshire neighbours. In short, although Perrot may well have opposed Mary's policies from conviction, the resolute stand he took could have stemmed from a choleric temperament as well as conscience.

Despite the importance of court service to men such as Hopton and Perrott, it was not a characteristic of the whole group. Neither More nor Strangways, for instance, seems to have spent time in the royal household. Sir Giles Strangways of Melbury Sampford, Dorset, had been sought as a ward by no less a person than Sir Richard Rich.[66] In 1553, April 1554, 1555, 1558, and 1559 he served as knight of the shire for Dorset. He does not appear to have come under suspicion at the time of Wyatt's rebellion, although Wyatt shook hands with him on the scaffold:[67] indeed, he was at that time first put onto the commission of the peace.[68] Although he was a rich man, he was outlawed briefly in 1555 for non-appearance in the court of common pleas over a debt of £104.[69] According to the Venetian ambassador, who reported that 'they have sent into the country to seize Sir Giles Strangways, a wealthy knight and a person of account', Strangways was questioned during the investigation into Dudley's conspiracy.[70] If this were so, he did not remain under a cloud for long, since he served with the army in Scotland in 1557.[71]

William More also came from a successful family: his father had been knight of the shire for Surrey in 1539 and 1537. The younger More represented Reigate in 1547, but sat for Guildford in October 1553, November 1554, and 1555. He served on various commissions in the reign of Edward VI, and became provost-marshal in Surrey in 1552.[72] Under Mary he took little part in local government, but his position improved markedly

---

[65] *APC* IV. 388.
[66] J. Hurstfield, *Freedom, Corruption and Government in Elizabethan England* (London, 1973), 180.
[67] *Queen Jane and Queen Mary*, 74.
[68] *CPR* Mary, I. 18.
[69] *CPR* Philip and Mary, II. 259.
[70] *CSP Ven.* VI. i. 440. Loades conflates Sir Giles and Strangways the pirate.
[71] *HMC Foljambe*, 5.
[72] Guildford RO, LM Correspondence, 3/1.

when Elizabeth came to the throne: he was chosen sheriff and was involved therefore in the complicated negotiations that marked the subsequent elections.[73] He became, in fact, an 'old parliament man', sitting in thirteen or fourteen parliaments in the course of his life,[74] although it was not until the latter part of his life that he took any large part in parliamentary affairs.[75]

More is one of the very few members of a Marian parliament about whom a great deal is known, because he left a large quantity of papers. However, his personal papers are inextricably mixed up with those of his intimate friend, Sir Thomas Cawarden, who had been Master of the Revels under Henry VIII and Edward VI, and it is therefore only too easy to associate More with his friend's opinions. Cawarden had fallen foul of Gardiner as early as 1543,[76] and he was an object of suspicion under Mary: he was put in the Tower at the time of Wyatt's rebellion and was arrested again at the period when Dudley's conspiracy was being investigated.[77] More may have shared Cawarden's interest in protestantism—he was to be described by his bishop in 1564 as a 'favourer' of religion[78]—but there can be no certainty about his inclinations during Mary's reign. In 1569 the Master of Guildford Grammar School, in dedicating to More a treatise on the sacrament of the altar, declared that he knew More's judgement 'to haue been longe sence soundly settled', and that he had a 'good and godly disposicion to be suche, as well liketh and accepteth matters of learninge, speciallie if thei favor and sound to the setting furthe of trewe Religion',[79] but 'long since' may in this context mean no more than a decade. However, we do know that in 1556 (contrary to the proclamation of June 1555) he still possessed one book by the reformer Justas Jonas, Peter Martyr's *A Discourse* (an account of the famous 1549 Oxford disputation), Cranmer's *An Answer* (a reply to Gardiner published in 1551), and Erasmus's

---

[73] J. E. Neale, *The Elizabethan House of Commons*, 40–4.
[74] *The House of Commons, 1509–1558*, argues that he sat for an unknown constituency in 1539. See also *The House of Commons, 1558–1603*.
[75] J. E. Neale, *Elizabeth I and Her Parliaments, 1584–1601* (London, 1957), 49, 182, 303.
[76] J. K. McConica, *English Humanists and Reformation Politics* (Oxford, 1965), 221–2.
[77] Loades, *Two Tudor Conspiracies*, 57, 190.
[78] *Camden Miscellany IX*, 56.
[79] Guildford RO, LM 1085/3.

Praise of Folly, probably in the 1549 English translation of his fellow member of parliament, Sir Thomas Chaloner.[80] More was in fact a prolific buyer of books: in 1557, when his income from land was £147, he paid such sums as 3s. 4d. for Machiavelli in Italian, 1s. 8d. for a French New Testament, and 8d. for More's *Utopia*.[81] He seems to have been a man of some considerable culture, for he possessed Thucydides, Ptolemy, and a number of works associated with the spread of humanism, such as Sir Thomas Elyot's Latin–English dictionary, Vives's . . . *the instructio[n] of a cyristen woma[n]* and William Thomas's *The historie of Italie*. His constitutional and political interests are suggested by the possession of a large number of chronicles, including Froissart and Fabyan, as well as collections of statutes. He also owned works by Gower and Lydgate, ballads, prognostications, and other ephemera, whilst his wife owned several prayer books.[82] It is interesting to find that in 1557 More bought 'a pedigree of the king', which was probably that published to show that Philip was descended from John of Gaunt.[83]

From this reading it is possible to suggest that More may have been opposed on political and religious grounds to various aspects of Mary's rule. But we must be careful not to make too much of the ownership of particular books: Cardinal Pole, for example, left a large collection of the works of Erasmus, and his vicar-general, David Pole, bequeathed to All Souls, Oxford, a library that included Melanchthon, the Augsburg Confession, and a book by Luther.[84] For a layman, and one who, as far as we know, did not attend a university, More seems to have been highly cultivated, but whether his learning and intellectual interests had any bearing on the way in which he behaved in parliament is impossible to decide.

We can be far more certain about the reasons for Henry Peckham's disaffection. He felt that he had not been treated with the generosity he deserved. The son of Sir Edmund Peck-

[80] Guildford RO, Loseley MS 1109. This is an inventory of *c.*1556.

[81] John Evans, 'The Private Account Book of William More', *Archaeologia*, XXXVI (1855), 284–310. This book is thought now to be in America.

[82] Loseley MS 1109.

[83] Evans, op. cit. For this pedigree, see *CSP Sp.* XII. 242.

[84] A. B. Emden, *A Biographical Dictionary of the University of Oxford AD 1501 to 1540* (Oxford, 1974), 730–4.

ham, a wealthy Buckinghamshire landowner who had been cofferer to Henry VIII,[85] Henry seems to have been favoured by Dudley.[86] He married into another family with influence in Buckinghamshire, the Verneys,[87] and sat in parliament for the first time in March 1553, when he represented the family borough of High Wycombe. He sat for Wycombe in October 1553, April 1554—when he was also elected for Aylesbury—and 1555. In the course of the 1555 parliament Peckham was one of those who met in Arundel's Tavern to plot:[88] he was clearly implicated in Dudley's conspiracy[89] and was executed in July 1556.[90]

Why did a young man who might have expected a profitable career in the service of the crown throw his life away in this manner? Henry was not Edmund Peckham's eldest son—his elder brother Robert served, like his father, on Mary's privy council—and he may well have had financial difficulties. In September 1554 he was summoned before the privy council,[91] probably about a debt he owed the crown, and he died still owing minor sums.[92] On the other hand, he had been rewarded by Mary in April 1554 for his services against Wyatt,[93] and received grants from the queen in July 1555.[94] After the discovery of Dudley's conspiracy Sir Robert Peckham explained his brother's treason by recounting a conversation he had had with him, in which Henry had declared that he was not 'well handled, to haue my Landes to be takene awaye that I purchased of my L. Clinton, and were sometime the old duke of Nofolkes'.[95] Peckham was here referring to the manor of Ches-

---

[85] *DNB.*

[86] Longleat, Thynne Papers, I, fo. 11.

[87] *Letters and Papers of the Verney Family*, ed. J. Bruce (Camden Society, os, LVI 1853), 58.

[88] SP 11/8/35.

[89] Loades, *Two Tudor Conspiracies, passim.*

[90] Wriothesley, 136.

[91] *APC* V. 77. He was summoned with Sir Edmund Rous and Richard Bunney. The latter owed the crown nearly £3,000, and Sir Anthony Rous had died in 1546 owing £6,000. (Richardson, *History of the Court of Augmentations 1536–1554*, 262, 264.)

[92] He owed £10 to Ralph Perne, citizen and grocer of London. (*CPR* Philip and Mary, III. 255.)

[93] *CPR* Mary, I. 9. I owe this reference to Mr Hill, who has very kindly provided me with a great deal of information about Henry Peckham.

[94] Ibid. II, 141, 175, 295.

[95] SP 11/8/46.

worth, Sussex, that he bought from Lord Clinton in 1550: with Norfolk's restoration Peckham had been forced to surrender Chesworth without adequate compensation, according to the 1555 petition, in which he is specifically named.[96] It was to this that another conspirator, Christopher Ashton, was also referring when he told Peckham that he had served 'the unthankffullest mysteres on *the* earth', who had given him 'but one hundred merks A year & hathe taken from the foer': the Lady Elizabeth, Ashton went on to argue, was 'a Lyberall dame'.[97] Peckham himself admitted that he had had a conversation with Sir Anthony Kingston about Henry VIII's will, and that in the course of this conversation he had been told of the discontent of Lord Williams of Thame, who was 'fayent to brake up hys howse and to lyue at becon̄ffeld' because of the queen's lack of generosity;[98] Peckham would have sympathized heartily with Williams. It is clear that Peckham, whether justifiably or not, felt that he had been done down in the course of these land transactions.

Ralph Skinner's opposition to Mary's policies may, on the other hand, have sprung from genuine religious zeal. Educated at Winchester and New College, Oxford, Skinner became New College's first married warden in 1551,[99] but he resigned when the college's visitor, Gardiner, was released in 1553.[100] (After Elizabeth's accession he was ordained and in 1561 became dean of Durham.) During Edward's reign Skinner, like a number of other young scholars, attracted the attention of the marquis of Dorset,[101] which may explain his election in 1547 for the city of Leicester. In 1553 Skinner sat for Penryn; he represented an unknown constituency in April 1554 and Bossiney in 1555. Skinner's main act of opposition to crown policies came in the parliament of April 1554, in which he spoke against the bill declaring that the regality of a queen was the same as that of a king,[102] arguing that the measure was unnecessary. When William Fleetwood wrote his account of Skinner's speech

---

[96] See above, 69.
[97] SP 11/8/52.
[98] Ibid.
[99] J. Buxton and P. H. Williams, eds., *New College 1379–1979* (Oxford, 1979), 48.
[100] A. H. Smith, *New College, Oxford, and its Buildings* (Oxford, 1952), 63–4.
[101] J. Strype, *Annals of the Reformation* (Oxford, 1820), II. ii. 497.
[102] HLRO, Original Acts, 1 Mary, sess. 3, 1.

twenty years later he noted that in 1554 Skinner was not over-much concerned about offending the crown, for he had 'little too loose, and much lesse to care for':[103] Skinner was undoubtedly at a low ebb in Mary's reign, with his career blighted by Gardiner, Visitor of New College and the possible originator of the bill that Skinner opposed.

An interesting and important member of this group is John Marshe, who sat for Reading in 1547, and for London in both the parliaments of 1553, in April 1554, 1558 and 1559, 1563, 1571, and 1572. He also sat for Old Sarum in 1555. Marshe is in some respects a shadowy figure because of the commonness of his name,[104] but his standing in the London mercantile world there can be no doubt: one historian has described him as 'a link between the bourgeois world and the royal court' as important in his own way as Thomas Gresham.[105] (Marshe in fact married the daughter of William Gresham in 1543.) He combined legal and mercantile interests, as his monument in St Michael's, Cripplegate, was later to record:[106] having attended Lincoln's Inn, he became common sergeant of London in 1547, a position he retained until pressure of other business forced him to give it up in 1563. A Merchant Adventurer, he became Governor of the Company briefly in 1555, and then again between 1559 and some date in the 1570s.[107] He was Warden of the Mercers' company in 1558 and 1565, and President of the Spanish Company in 1577, even though he was not personally engaged in the trade.[108]

A ship[109] and property owner[110] and a man of considerable

[103] BL Harley MS 6234, fos. 20–21ᵛ. See above, 96–7.

[104] On the difficulties of distinguishing Marshe from his namesake and uncle see F. F. Foster, *The Politics of Stability: A Portrait of the Rulers in Elizabethan London* (London, 1977), 107 n. 2.

[105] Ramsay, *The City of London in International Politics at the Accession of Elizabeth Tudor*, 55. I have benefited greatly from discussing Marshe's career with Dr Ramsay.

[106] J. Stow, *The Survey of London* (Everyman edn., 1965), 267.

[107] Ramsay, *The City of London in International Politics*, 53–4.

[108] T. S. Willan, *The Muscovy Merchants of 1555* (Manchester, 1953), 112.

[109] Ibid. 112.

[110] A John Marsh received grants in London and Northamptonshire from the last years of Henry VIII's reign onwards (*Letters and Papers*, XXI. ii. 245 etc.). Our Marshe certainly owned the manor of Sywell in Northamptonshire, and it was probably therefore he who became receiver of augmentations in that county (BL Stowe MS 571, fo. 11ᵛ) and he who was rewarded 'for his services' in 1559 with an appointment as receiver-general of Worcestershire and Shropshire (*CPR Elizabeth*, I. 40).

weight and substance, Marshe was frequently employed by other merchants as a land agent and trustee.[111] He was clearly a person of administrative and political experience, as his appointment in late 1558 to a commission 'to consider what points the realm hath sustained great loss during the late queen's reign' testifies.[112] Cecil and other members of Elizabeth's council seem to have had great trust in his judgement and he carried on a detailed correspondence with them.[113] Not surprisingly, the House of Commons made use of Marshe's skills, and he served on numerous committees. In April 1554 a bill 'touching cloth making in the city of Worcester' was committed to him[114] and in November 1558 he took charge of a bill 'touching tanners, shoe-makers and curriers, for tanned leather'.[115]

In the reign of Elizabeth Marshe emerged as a committed protestant. His bishop in 1564 described him as a 'favourer' of religion,[116] and two years later the Spanish ambassador, de Silva, told the duchess of Parma that 'los protestantes que tienen ay inteligiencias y correspondencia deste reyno' were Marshe, Lionel Duquet (Duckett), Richard Springham, Thomas Heton, and Aldresi Nidam.[117] Heton and Springham were amongst the London merchants who, according to Strype, assisted the Marian exiles with money, the group described by Miss Garrett as the 'sustainers':[118] both went into exile themselves later in the reign.[119] It is tempting to associate Marshe with this group, and to note that in the course of 1556 he was clearly under some sort of cloud: he lost the post of

---

[111] *CPR* Edward VI, III. 202, etc.

[112] Ramsay, *The City of London in International Politics*, 53.

[113] *Calendar of State Papers, Domestic*, I, ed. R. Lemon (London, 1856), 235–8, 241, 285, 308, etc.

[114] *CJ* 10 Apr. 1554.

[115] Ibid. 11 Nov. 1558. On 18 Feb. 1558 Marshe had complained to the House that one of the members for Worcester, Thomas Wyld, had slandered him before the London Drapers by claiming that Marshe had taken the burden of the search of cloths from the clothiers and put it on the buyers. The question of privilege thus raised was ordered to be examined by Sir John Baker and Mr Mason.

[116] *Camden Miscellany IX* 60.

[117] *Relations politiques des Pays-Bas et de L'Angleterre sous le règne de Philippe II*, ed. J. M. B. C. Baron Kervyn de Lettenhove (Brussels, 1882), IV. 276. Dr Ramsay very kindly provided me with this reference.

[118] Garrett, *The Manan Exiles*, 7–8.

[119] Ibid. 182–3, 292–3.

governor of the Merchant Adventurers to the less able Anthony Hussey,[120] he was summoned before the council and bound in a recognizance of £5,000.[121] (He was excused from daily attendance three weeks later on grounds of illness, but warned to keep himself in readiness.[122]) Perhaps he was thought to have been involved in Dudley's conspiracy. There is no hard evidence about his religious views during the 1550s, although it is possible that our man should be identified with the Marsh whom Edward Underhill described as joining him in the reign of Edward in a complaint to Cranmer about Henry Moore, formerly abbot of Tower Hill and at that time vicar of Stepney, who had his church bells rung so loudly whenever a reformer preached that no one could hear the sermon;[123] the area in which this 'mr march' lived is certainly close to that with which Marshe was later associated.

Marshe comes nearer than almost any other of this group to the concept of 'the opposition member', as described by Neale. He was an experienced member of the Commons who would not be overawed by privy councillors; he had served on a number of committees both in parliament and in the city and doubtless understood very clearly how they could be manipulated. He was a man of property, and a man with protestant leanings. However, we unfortunately know too little about his conduct in the reign of Mary to argue that he used this weight and experience to wrest control of the Commons from the government.

It is not easy to find a common thread linking these ten men. They all, of course, came from the propertied classes, and Perrot and Strangways were of such standing that their parliamentary misdeeds were forgotten when their service was required by the crown, but the mercantile background of John Marshe is quite different from that of the academic Skinner. Ralph Farrar, Rutland's secretary, occupied a different place in society from that of the country gentleman, Sir Thomas Dyer. Henry Peckham was labouring under a deep sense of grievance, and

---

[120] Willan, *The Muscovy Merchants*, 24.
[121] *APC* VI. 262.
[122] Ibid. 263, 267.
[123] *Narratives of the Days of the Reformation*, ed. J. G. Nichols (Camden Society, os, LXXVII, 1859), 157; Ridley, *Thomas Cranmer*, 320.

the career of Skinner and perhaps that of Marshe had received a check with the accession of a catholic monarch, but there is no serious sense in which the group can be described as consisting of 'outs'. What is known of the religious views of these ten men suggests a tendency towards protestantism, but it is probable that this was of prime importance only to Skinner. It is difficult to see them as a 'party', with coherent principles.

It is also difficult to believe that the group comprised a 'party' in any organized sense. Having, presumably, been critical of the crown's religious policy in 1553, Farrar and William More, along with others whose names are marked on the Bodley list, sat silent in parliament a year later, when the great bill reuniting England with Rome was passed. In that parliament, the burden of 'opposition' fell upon the shoulders of one man, Sir Ralph Bagnall, and—according to an Italian report—a silent ally: Farrar, More, and the others were presumably, with the rest of the assembly, kneeling in tears to beg Pole's forgiveness.

Bagnall's intervention in November 1554 complicates still further any attempt to trace the growth of an 'opposition party' in the reign of Mary. Bagnall's father was a mere merchant of Newcastle under Lyme, in Staffordshire, but Ralph and his brother seem to have come to court in the reign of Henry VIII: Nicholas became marshal of the army in Ireland under Edward and was to play an important part in Irish affairs in the reign of Elizabeth.[124] Ralph seems also to have been a military man, for he was granted Dieulacres Abbey, Staffordshire, in recognition of his services in France, Scotland, Ireland, and elsewhere.[125] In the parliament of 1547 Ralph Bagnall sat as one of the knights of the shire, but in November 1554 he was reduced to representing Newcastle, the seat for which his brother sat the following year. It was in this parliament that Bagnall made his only recorded speech.[126] Declaring that he had sworn the contrary in the time of Henry VIII, Bagnall at first refused to admit once more the supremacy of the see of Rome. Perhaps religious conviction led him into this—he was thought suitable

---

[124] *DNB.*
[125] *CPR* Edward VI, IV. 440.
[126] See above, 107–8.

to remain a justice of the peace by his bishop in 1564[127]—but it seems more likely that he retained an attachment to the memory of Henry VIII and his own youth.[128] Having failed to prevent the restoration of catholicism, and perhaps in financial difficulties,[129] Bagnall became involved in *émigré* politics. He was indicted of treason in December 1556, accused of plotting and of having declared in Dieppe that

> if the kinge were ones come into this realm ... he would and durste come yn and lande here if he had but one hundred men for they shulde have men inought here that wolde take there partes and goe withe them. But untyll the kynge were come there was noe medlinge for unles the Spanyerd were here ... people of the realme here wolde not so redely take there partes.[130]

However, despite this, and a short period in a French gaol under suspicion of spying,[131] Bagnall was pardoned in June 1557.[132] By October of that year he was trusted sufficiently to be sent to interrogate a French prisoner.[133] The whole episode is a curious one, and it may be that Bagnall was acting as an *agent provocateur* or was, indeed, an English spy. He is certainly an unlikely person to find in the company of the first Marian martyr, John Rogers who, in the course of his interrogation, told Gardiner that those who altered the policies of Henry VIII were traitors, predicting that if the king rose from the dead and perceived 'that his actes were chaunged, there wold be no small hurly-burly'.[134]

The unfriendly response that Bagnall's speech encountered

---

[127] *Camden Miscellany IX*, 41–2.
[128] Edward Underhill said that Bagnall was one of a number of young roués at court in Henry's reign (*Narratives of the Days of the Reformation*, 158).
[129] One reporter told Sir Edward Hastings that Bagnall was in France 'for dett only as far as ever I could lerne' (SP 11/8/19). Despite a further land grant in 1560 (*CPR* Elizabeth, I. 308), Bagnall began disposing of his property piecemeal to his tenants a year later ('The Chartulary of Dieulacres Abbey', ed. G. Wrottesley, *William Salt Archaeological Society*, ns, IX (1906), 302).
[130] *CPR* Mary, III. 318–19.
[131] SRP 11/8/55.
[132] *CPR* Mary, III. 318–19.
[133] *APC* VI. 181.
[134] J. L. Chester, *John Rogers* (London, 1861), 319. Gardiner mentioned Bagnall to Rogers, in very dismissive terms (ibid. 295).

and, indeed, the absence in the parliament of 1554 of any other resistance to the reconciliation with Rome militates strongly against the notion that parliamentary opposition steadily grew and developed in the reign of Mary. Some sixty to eighty members of the Lower House had, after all, been willing to resist the repeal of the Edwardian religious legislation when that was proposed in 1553, yet only one, or at the most two, members were ready a year later to oppose the repeal of Henry's religious legislation. Six of those whose names are marked on the Bodley list, including Farrar and More, sat in the 1554 parliament, and yet the defence of Henrician policy was left to the 'gamester, dicer and whoremonger', Bagnall.

Thus the parliaments of Mary's reign witnessed no sudden and spectacular change in the nature of parliamentary opposition. This was because the issues raised by the accession of a female and catholic ruler—the problem of a king consort, the security of secularized property, and so on—were a matter of concern to the whole parliament, and not the preoccupation of a small clique which would have found it necessary for success to learn the arts of political management. Only on very rare occasions did the House of Commons split in such a way as to leave a path for the development of 'party': because the principles and the personnel involved in each of these episodes were different, no coherent 'opposition group' was born.

A second theory about the events of the parliaments of Mary's reign is that they reflect a growing realization on the part of the governing classes that, as a political weapon, rebellion was useless. Professor Loades, in particular, has argued that the plots and conspiracies of the period convincingly demonstrated the limitations of violence as a means of persuading the monarch to change her mind: 'the shrewder and more far-sighted', he argues, therefore sought in the House of Commons an alternative means of influencing the crown.[135] Whereas the 'opposition leaders' of 1553 were quick to despair of the effectiveness of parliament as a means of checking the queen, the attitude of their successors in 1555 was, he writes, quite different. Indeed, he suggests that although it would be an anachronism to speak of a

[135] Loades, *Two Tudor Conspiracies*, 242.

'country party' in the 1550s, 'the country gentry had undoubtedly begun by 1558 to use the House of Commons as a forum for their views, and a vehicle for their influence at the national level'.[136]

Although this theory ignores the way in which the country gentry of the late fourteenth and early fifteenth century had constantly used parliament as a forum for their own views, it has its attractions. Most historians would agree that in the sixteenth century Englishmen became less rebellious than they had been, and it is tempting to find in the simultaneous growth in size and importance of the House of Commons a causal factor. However, on close examination it is apparent that the evidence of Mary's reign does not suggest that any clear connection can be made between parliamentary opposition and rebellion, or parliamentary opposition and the absence of rebellion.

There is, for example, little evidence that 'opposition leaders' changed their views about the effectiveness of rebellion. From the very beginning of Mary's reign those who sat in parliament were unwilling to become involved in active disobedience. The members of the Lower House in 1553 were almost uniformly opposed to the Spanish marriage, and at least sixty of them—those whose names were marked on the Bodley list—were also critical of some aspect of the crown's religious policy, but only four of them attended the meeting on 26 November at which the first plans for rebellion were laid.[137] After the rising had failed, the government thought it necessary to question only three other former members of the Commons, and their involvement had clearly been slight.[138] The reluctance to rebel shown by members of the parliament of 1553 was shared by their successors in 1555, for only Peckham, Kingston, and Francis Verney were certainly involved in the Treasury plot, whilst the others appear to have been guilty of little more than indiscretion. Contrary to Professor Loades's argument, slightly more of the discontented appear to have been ready to rebel in 1555 than in 1553, but the proportion of the whole parliament involved remained very small.

[136] Ibid. 243.
[137] Ibid. 15–16.
[138] See above, nn. 38, 47, and 35.

The relationship between the development of a parliamentary opposition and the decline of rebellion cannot, therefore, be seen as one that evolved in a simple and coherent form. Moreover, a study of the few members of parliament who became involved in rebellion does not throw up any clear answers as to why they, and not their colleagues, turned to violence. The only obvious feature shared by the four members of the Commons known to have been present at the meeting of 26 November 1553, for example, is their social position and the self-confidence it apparently engendered. Sir Peter Carew, a Devon man, had become a substantial landowner in Lincolnshire by his marriage to Lady Tallboys.[139] Sir Edward Rogers had been an esquire of the body to Henry VIII and a member of Edward's privy chamber: in these positions he had been able to accumulate monastic property in the west.[140] Sir Nicholas Throckmorton had also been a member of Edward's privy chamber,[141] as well as an under-treasurer at the Mint;[142] he received a large grant of land in 1551.[143] Sir Edward Warner had been a member of the royal household from 1537, being knighted in the Scottish campaign of 1544.[144] He acquired considerable estates, by gift and by purchase,[145] and in 1552 became lieutenant of the Tower, a position he lost at Mary's accession although he was then given some property 'in consideration of his service unto the queen'.[146] He appears to have been a client of the earl of Rutland, for it was at the nobleman's 'special suit' that he sat for Grantham in March 1553:[147] he had already represented the borough in 1545 and 1547 and did so again in the first of Mary's parliaments.

The motives pushing these men towards rebellion appear diverse. Carew may well have been moved by a deep hatred of Spain that perhaps originated with the time he spent in France

---

[139] J. Hooker, *The Life and Times of Sir Peter Carew*, ed. J. Maclean (London, 1857), 46–8.

[140] *DNB; The House of Commons, 1509–1558*.

[141] BL Stowe MS 571, fo. 29ᵛ.

[142] *CPR* Edward VI, III. 137; V, 9: *APC* IV. 76, 84.

[143] *CPR* Edward VI, IV. 104–5.

[144] *The House of Commons, 1509–1558*; W. A. Shaw, *The Knights of England* (London, 1906), I. 56.

[145] *CPR* Edward VI, I. 272: II. 215, 267–73: IV. 300.

[146] Ibid. Mary, I. 394.

[147] BL Lansdowne MS 3, fo. 75.

as a child;[148] he was, according to his biographer, 'perfect in the French tongue', and was reported to have said to the Constable of France after his abortive rising that he had become involved because he could 'not abyde to see the oppressings of his countrey by them, who were the French kinges mortal enemyes'.[149] This was perhaps a comment meant to please his hearer, but Carew was also recorded as having said to his companions when they arrived in Normandy: 'what auncient howse is there here or in Fraunce, but we claim by them, and they by us why should we not rather embrace theier Love, then submit ourselfes to this servitude of Spain?'.[150] Renard believed that Carew was also a protestant, describing him as 'the greatest heretic and rebel in England', as someone who had plotted in parliament for Courtenay and who was opposed to the restoration of catholicism.[151] Certainly Hooker later declared that Carew was 'an earnest promoter of God's true religion', a man who maintained a preacher to instruct his family and 'to preach elsewhere in the countries around him',[152] but the only certain evidence for Carew's early religious views comes from the fact that in 1545 he, along with a number of the other young bloods at court, was in possession of a suspicious book.[153] For Carew's involvement in the rebellion of early 1554 the best guide would seem to be his own claim: 'If the quene wold forbeare this mariage with the Spanyardes and Vse a moderacion in the matter of Religion I wold dye at her foote but otherwyse I wyll doe the best to place the ladye Elizabeth in her steade.'[154]

The motives of Sir Edward Rogers are less clear, perhaps because he played no serious part in the rising: although he was not released from the Tower until January 1555,[155] he was never tried and does not appear to have paid any fine.[156] Indeed, in February 1558 he even petitioned the privy council for compensation for losses he had suffered as a result of his imprison-

---

[148] Hooker, *Life and Times of Sir Peter Carew*, 7–42.
[149] Ibid. 115: SP 69/4/187.
[150] SP 69/3/172.
[151] *CSP Sp.* XII. 16.
[152] Hooker, *Life and Times of Sir Peter Carew*, 111–12.
[153] *Letters and Papers*, XX. ii. 995.
[154] PRO KB 27/1176, Rex III.
[155] Machyn, 80.
[156] Loades, *Two Tudor Conspiracies*, 96.

ment.[157] He sat as knight of the shire for Somerset again in 1558 and went on to play an active role in politics under Elizabeth, as a privy councillor and vice-chamberlain, and later as comptroller of the household:[158] as Neale's narrative shows, he also became a useful servant of the crown in the Lower Chamber. Whilst all this suggests that he was not, in religious terms, out of sympathy with the Elizabethan regime, it does not prove that he was an ardent protestant, and his participation in the plotting may have been the consequence of his friendship with some of those also involved.

The other two men indicted for their presence at the meeting, Throckmorton and Warner, were great friends. It was Warner who heard Throckmorton's complaints, early in Mary's reign, about 'his own estate, and the tyranny of the time extended upon divers honest persons for religion'.[159] Throckmorton's justification of his involvement in the discussions that led to the rebellion, and his stout assertion that he had done no more than talk, were set out clearly at his trial, which took place in April 1554. In the course of this trial, in which he showed himself an eloquent and learned orator, he admitted that he 'did mislike the Queen's marriage with Spain and also the coming of the Spaniards thither', although, he went on to say, in so doing he was not alone for 'I did learn reasons for my misliking of you master Hare, master Southwell, and others in the parliament house; there I did see the whole consent of the realm against it.'[160] This is so much the authentic voice of opposition pamphlets that it seems likely that the account has been embellished, but it must none the less represent the general drift of Throckmorton's comments. He had, after all, also told the francophile Carew, who talked of bringing in foreign assistance, that he could 'as evil abide the Frenchmen after that sort as the Spaniards'.[161] It would seem that a mixture of nationalistic pride and religious fervour—Throckmorton was, in the next reign, constantly to urge further reform of the church—led him

[157] *APC* VI. 270.
[158] *DNB; The House of Commons, 1558–1603.*
[159] Howell, *A Complete Collection of State Trials*, 883.
[160] Howell, op. cit. 875. Hare was not elected to the 1553 parliament, although as master of the rolls he would have been present in the House of Lords. Robert Southwell, who had been master of the rolls from 1541 to 1550, sat for Kent.
[161] Ibid. 883.

into conspiracy. But he was not so resolutely opposed to the Marian government that he did not petition the queen for pardon after Dudley's revolt,[162] and persuade his friend Sir Nicholas Wootton, the English ambassador to France, to plead his case further.[163] He was pardoned in May 1557.[164]

Warner was almost certainly included in the conspiracy because of his friendship with Throckmorton, and perhaps also because of his close family connection with some of the Kentish rebels: his wife was the daughter of Lord Cobham, and the widow of the elder Sir Thomas Wyatt.[165] In 1546 he and Lord Thomas Howard had been questioned about their 'indiscreet talking of Scripture matters';[166] Warner perhaps shared Howard's dislike of the sermons that had recently been preached at court.[167] Neither these incidents nor his subsequent prosperity under Elizabeth[168] are sufficient evidence for us to label Warner a protestant in Mary's reign, and his conduct may have stemmed from anxiety about the future of the very substantial quantities of church land that he had accumulated. He may also have been worried about the future of former Howard land since his tenure of Castleacre contributed substantially to his income.[169]

These four men have in common, therefore, an established social position, a profitable career at court in the reigns of Henry and Edward, and, more tentatively, an inclination towards protestantism. Although they might well have feared for their standing under a catholic queen—in Warner's case, apparently with some justification—they could probably have conformed and prospered as other men did: they were all to be pardoned later in the reign despite their conduct in 1553 and

---

[162] BL Stowe MS 280, fos. 104–6. His letter was regarded as so elegant that it is included in this collection of models for all occasions as an example of 'the supplication'.

[163] *CSP For.* Mary, 543.

[164] *CRR* Philip and Mary, III. 476.

[165] Machyn, 382.

[166] *Letters and Papers*, XXI. ii. 768.

[167] *APC* I. 408, 411.

[168] He regained his position at the Tower (SP 12/1/3) and later became Master of St Katherine's by the Tower (C. Jamison, *The History of the Royal Hospital of St Katherine by the Tower of London* (Oxford 1952), 62).

[169] See ch. 3 n. 131.

1554.[170] Many others with a similar background made the transition from Edward to Mary without difficulty, and only individual factors of temperament and conscience can explain why these four were prepared to contemplate taking their hostility to some of the queen's policies to the point of rebellion. They cannot be regarded as feudal throw-backs, nor as political anachronisms who did not understand that the way forward was no longer by recourse to arms but through debate in parliament: such men would not have flourished in the stormy days of the 1540s. Perhaps those involved in the conspiracy of 1555 conform better to this backward-looking stereotype, for Kingston was a bluff country squire, not a courtier, and Henry Peckham a discontented and unsuccessful younger son. But the others who were questioned were men who had known how to turn the circumstances of sixteenth-century political life to their advantage. Perrott had risen through the favour of Henry VIII, as had Sir Nicholas Arnold, whose talents had, indeed, first been spotted by Thomas Cromwell—hardly the pedigree of a feudal relic.[171] Chichester had also been a servant of Cromwell.[172] It is difficult, then, to see even the men who became involved in the 1555 plot as inherently less 'shrewd and far-sighted'[173] than their colleagues who had confined their opposition to the parliament chamber; it is also difficult to accept that they had less commitment to the parliamentary process, since Arnold, Chichester, Perrott, and Pollard all successfully sought election to later parliaments. (Courtenay died in 1557.)

Whether a member of parliament who had been critical of the crown in the Chamber subsequently became involved in unconstitutional opposition seems, therefore, to be largely a matter of temperament and, perhaps, of association with others of like mind: it is difficult to prove that it had anything to do with different expectations from parliament. The relationship

---

[170] Two versions of Carew's pardon exist, one restoring all his lands and forfeited goods, the other only his goods (*APC* Philip and Mary, III 45–6). This might suggest that there is some truth in Miss Garrett's assertion that the price of Carew's pardon was involvement in the plot to kidnap Sir John Cheke, which was carried out in 1556 (Garrett, *The Marian Exiles*, 105–6). Rogers and Warner were pardoned in July 1555 (*CPR* Philip and Mary, II. 293).

[171] *DNB Supplement; The House of Commons, 1509–1558.*

[172] Ibid.

[173] Loades, *Two Tudor Conspiracies*, 242.

between the decline of violence and the rise of constitutional opposition is clearly, therefore, not a simple one.

Although the House of Commons became more self-confident and its members more assertive in the course of the next three reigns rebellion did not, after all, become extinct. Many of the gentlemen involved in the Northern Rising and in Essex's revolt of 1601, for example, had had an opportunity to express their grievances in parliament—Leonard Dacre had represented Cumberland in 1558, 1559, and 1563, for example, and of Essex's followers Charles Danvers, George Devereux, Ferdinando Gorges, Christopher Heydon, and John Lyttleton had all sat in the Commons. Although, then, there is something in Professor Loades's belief that the opportunities offered in parliament 'for protest and obstruction' relieved the property-owning classes 'from the excruciating dilemma of rebellion' they were not finally convinced of this until after the Great Rebellion or perhaps even the Revolution: Mary's reign was not for them a turning point.

In the sixteenth century—and, indeed, the early seventeenth century—crown and subjects alike expected to find in parliament agreement and compromise. Professor Lehmberg has commented that the story of the Reformation Parliament should be read 'in terms of partnership and co-operation rather than antagonism and opposition',[174] and the history of the legislation of this century, especially in the sphere of economic and social policy, reveals the give and take of parliamentary business. The parliaments of the Tudors were, of course, very much more productive than those of their late medieval predecessors or their Stuart descendants, partly because they were not marred by the bitter attacks on royal ministers characterized by the process of impeachment. But even judged by these high standards, Mary's parliaments were far from unsuccessful: she never found it necessary, for instance, to veto a bill, and in this was unlike her father and brother, and very unlike her sister, whose relationship with parliament is usually considered so much more amicable than Mary's own.

None the less, there were issues that produced conflict

---

[174] S. E. Lehmberg, *The Reformation Parliament, 1529–1536* (Cambridge, 1970), 255–6.

between her and her parliaments. The most common of these concerned property rights, but matters touching the succession to and powers of the crown also produced considerable debate. Thus, although Mary wished to crown Philip and to exclude Elizabeth from the throne she did not raise either proposal in a formal government bill: given the importance that the Imperialists attached to the coronation as a symbol, given the focus for discontent that Elizabeth could have provided, a focus that she herself recognized when she later refused to name her own successor, the significance of such passive parliamentary resistance should not be underestimated.

However, the reign was marked by far less resistance to formal proposals put forward by the government than has traditionally been supposed: the concord at the time of the great bill of repeal is particularly striking. The government seems to have secured almost all the legislation that it planned, and some of the concessions that it made in the face of criticism of its original proposals—for instance, reductions in the rate of taxation—may be seen as part of a normal process of negotiation. In terms of legislation passed, therefore, these were for the crown productive parliaments.

There was not, then, much resistance to the greater part of the government's legislative programme: when there was such resistance it was not very successful. Opposition in the Lords to a government proposal, it is true, often stifled it, but such action was unusual. The House of Commons, on the other hand, rarely succeeded in blocking important pieces of government legislation: even the turbulent events of 1555 did not bring about the loss in the Commons of any bill about which the queen minded passionately. The procedure of the House, the lack of experience of many of those who sat in it, and the weighty combination of speaker and councillors made it difficult for individuals or small groups to resist government proposals. Opposition in the Commons was to be a little more successful in the next reign for two, linked, reasons. One was the impact of dissatisfaction with the Elizabethan church settlement, a dissatisfaction that brought members together and led them to plan their tactics before and during the sessions. The other was the fact that some of Elizabeth's councillors shared that dissatisfaction. Protestantism in Mary's reign was not the force in parliament that dissatisfaction with the 1559 settlement was to be, partly because of the threat of severe ecclesiastical censure that hung over it, and partly because the driving force of the movement was not in parliament but in Geneva and Frankfurt, where it was using much of its energy in internal struggles and feuds. Whilst there were convinced protestants, such as Ralph Skinner, sitting in the parliaments of Mary's reign, those who felt strongly were not generally in a position to appear in parliament: those who cared most chose exile or martyrdom. Whatever the success of the Marian reaction in purely religious terms, the policy of persecution probably helped to produce amenable parliaments. To achieve anything in parliament, therefore, those who opposed the crown on religious grounds had to find support from broader interests, the most common alliance—if anything so fluid may be called an alliance—being with those who feared for the future of their former church lands: it is significant that the one real success of a sectional interest, the defeat of the exiles bill, lay in a field in which concern for property also operated.

The theory that Mary's parliaments witnessed the 'apprenticeship to future greatness' of the House of Commons will not, therefore, stand up, for the foundation on which it rests—the presence in the Commons of an organized, articulate, and above all protestant opposition—is demonstrably false. There were no significant developments in procedure during the reign, although the details of the process of 'dividing' the House may have been refined, and there is no evidence that those critical of the crown's policies evolved any original methods of opposing them. Far from providing any answer to the questions about why and how the House of Commons came to oppose the crown in the 1640s, and oppose it successfully, the history of parliament in the reign of Mary reveals the continuing importance of the House of Lords and the relative lack of sophistication of the Commons.

None the less, even the Upper House was in general very willing to see the queen's business done. Professor Loades has argued that Mary ruled by faction, and thus lost the 'middle ground' of 'noblemen, gentlemen, and clergy, whose principal characteristics were social and religious conservatism, insular-

ity' and loyalty to the monarch.[175] However, a study of the behaviour of the men involved in parliament during Mary's reign
does not support this conclusion. Those who in her first parliament opposed the marriage with Philip later helped to defeat
Wyatt when he rose to prevent the marriage from taking place,
whilst those who attacked the crown's policies in the parliament of 1555, including men who came under suspicion when
the Treasury plot was discovered, rallied to the monarch in
1557. Sir William Courtenay went off to France,[176] Sir Francis
Fleming and Sir Giles Strangways to Scotland,[177] Sir John
Chichester, recently released from prison, was sent to the
Scilly Isles[178] whilst Sir Ralph Bagnall, who had opposed the
presentation to Pole of the petition for reunion with Rome,
played some role in what might be called the intelligence service.[179] In 1557 and 1558 the parliamentary classes and the
crown presented a united front. It is not difficult to understand
why this should be. To a conviction that obedience and order
were pleasing to God, the property-owning classes were forced
to add at this time a profound anxiety about social unrest, for
the combination of high corn prices and viral disease produced
in the last years of the decade one of the worst demographic
crises between 1540 and 1870. (The epidemic hit the upper
classes as well as the lower and it is therefore hardly surprising
that 'during 1558 attendance at both council and court was
low'[180]: to interpret absence from London at such a time as evidence for disaffection with the regime is to perceive in narrowly
political terms what was a crisis second only to the Black Death
in its intensity.) In such circumstances the upper classes,
warned by the events of Edward's reign, were unwilling to
threaten the stability of the regime.

They had, in any case, little desire to do so. Those who argue
that Mary's foreign policy, for example, alienated the governing classes are blinded by subsequent events: in Elizabeth's
reign, it is true, Spain became England's main rival and enemy,

---

[175] Loades, *The Reign of Mary Tudor*, 471.
[176] Machyn, 144.
[177] *HMC Foljambe*, 5.
[178] *APC* VI. 118, 134.
[179] Ibid. 181.
[180] *The Reign of Mary Tudor*, 469.

but this was not the case in the 1550s. Although most Englishmen, both inside and outside parliament, disliked the idea of a female English monarch marrying a foreign prince, there is no reason to believe that their hostility was aimed especially at Philip, or that they would have regarded with any greater favour a marriage with French or Italian: it must be remembered that at this time Philip was not 'the hammer of the counter-reformation' that he subsequently became, but a young man with a taste for Titian's nudes and a deep hatred for Pope Paul IV. Mary, conservative in this as in all other things, simply followed the policy of her father and grandfather by allying herself with the Habsburgs: it was Elizabeth, not Mary, who changed what had become traditional Tudor foreign policy. Thus, it was not Mary's marriage that produced war with France in 1557—although it may possibly have dictated the timing of the outbreak of hostilities—but the grievances and enmity that had remained after the Hundred Years War. These grievances had led to sporadic fighting throughout the century, providing the nobility with a *raison d'être* and the upper classes in general with a chance of booty and social advancement: although they were reluctant in 1558 to pay war taxation, many men appear to have been willing to see if they could advance their fortunes on the battlefield. The readiness of members of the parliamentary class to become involved in the war thus throws doubt on Professor Loades's description of the conflict as the 'final disaster' of the reign.

Indeed, his whole theory that 'by 1557 the momentum of the regime had run down' needs to be set against both the evidence for demographic disaster and the smooth conduct of parliamentary affairs in the two sessions of 1558. Like most recent historians Loades accepts, at least for the latter part of the reign, Pollard's verdict of sterility and failure. That verdict has always been applied to Mary's parliaments: see, for instance, Michael Graves's conclusion that Mary's controversial policies 'undermined the very function and purpose of parliament'.[181] But the purpose of a meeting of parliament was, primarily, to secure the passing of legislation, and this was achieved: the crown's business was done, even in the difficult circumstances

---

[181] Graves, *The House of Lords*, 199.

of 1558, and many private interest-groups secured the passage of important bills. Looking at events in parliament, and the behaviour of the men who attended these sessions, it is difficult to accept that Mary had alienated her natural supporters. Her marriage does not appear to have permanently antagonized those who sat in parliament and her religious policy seems to have been a matter of indifference to many, provided that they could keep their secularized property. Most of those who sat in parliament were, after all, preoccupied by the problems of their families, localities, and trades. It is an anachronism to see such men as ranged in groups 'for' or 'against' the crown: a man might dislike the restoration of the pope's authority, for example, but approve of the government legislation on weaving, and to assume that the first mattered to him more than the second is unwarranted. Mary's parliaments were very like those of her father: antagonism and opposition occasionally surfaced, but partnership and co-operation were more common. Since the men who sat in parliament were in a real— although not, of course, technical—sense representative of the governing classes from which they came it is difficult to believe that the relationship of monarch and property-owners outside parliament was antagonistic and hostile. What is meant by a judgement on a reign of 'success' or 'failure' is not clear: what is clear, however, is that compared with the parliaments of Henry VI or Charles I, the parliaments of Mary's reign were highly successful.

Appendix A

Members of Mary's third parliament against whom legal proceedings were taken (PRO KB 29/1188, fo. 48^{r-v}).

Constituency	*Name*
Worcester	Edward Brogden
Droitwich	George Newport
Warwickshire	William Wigston
Warwick	Ralph Broune
Coventry	John Harford
Canterbury	{ Nicholas Fish { Richard Railton
Lichfield	Marc Wyrley
Hull	Walter Jobson
Southampton	James Brande
Hastings	John Peyton
Winchelsea	John Cheyne
Romney	William Oxenden
Hythe	Thomas Keys
Dover	William Hannington
Sandwich	{ John Tyser { Nicholas Crispe
Montgomeryshire	Edward Herbert
Montgomery	Richard Lloyd
Radnorshire	John Knill
Carmarthanshire	Henry Jones
Brecon	Meredydd Games
Anglesey	Richard Bulkeley
Grimsby	Thomas Constable
Stamford	Henry Lee
Leicester	Francis Farnham
Lancashire	John Holcroft
Liverpool	William Bromley
Monmouthshire	Thomas Somerset
Brackley	George Ferrers
Nottingham	Nicholas Powtrell
King's Lynn	{ Thomas Moyle { Thomas Waters
Oxford	William Tylcock

Constituency	*Name*
Surrey	Thomas Cawarden
Stafford	Matthew Cradock
Shrewsbury	George Leigh (Lye)
Bridgenorth	John Horde
Ludlow	John Allsop
Winchester	William Lawrence Robert Hodson
Dunwich	Edmund Rous Robert Coppyn
Oxford	John Harman
Bath	William Crowche
Wells	Thomas Lewis William Godwin
Sussex	John Ashburnam
Chichester	Walter Roynan
Shoreham	William Mody
Steyning	John Roberts William Pellatt
Arundel	Richard Bowyer
Appleby	William Danby
Salisbury	Robert Griffith John Hooper
Wilton	William Clerke
Westbury	Griffin Curteys
Devizes	Thomas Hull
Malmesbury	Edmund Unton
Cricklade	Thomas Parker John Rede
Ludgershall	Arthur Allen
Wootton Bassett	Giles Payne William Hampshire
Marlborough	Peter Taylor
Buckinghamshire	Thomas Denton
Buckingham	Henry Carey
Windsor	Richard Ward
Reading	Edmund Plowden
Cornwall	Henry Chiverton
Newport	Robert Browne
Liskeard	John Connock John Pethebridge
Truro	John Melhuish

Constituency	*Name*
Bodmin	{ John Courtenay { Ralph Michell
Penryn	Thomas Mathew
Cambridge	Richard Brasshey
Chester	Thomas Massey
Derbyshire	{ Peter Frescheville { Henry Vernon
Derby	{ William More { William Bainbridge
Tavistock	John Evelegh
Dartmouth	Nicholas Adams
Dorset	Richard Phelips
Poole	{ Anthony Dillington { Andrew Horde
Dorchester	Christopher Hole
Lyme	John Mallock
Melcombe	{ Thomas Phelips { John Hannam
Weymouth	{ John Phelips { William Randall
Bridport	John Moynes
Wareham	{ Hugo Smith { Roger Gerard
Knaresborough	Ralph Scrope
Ripon	Thomas More
Gloucestershire	William Rede
Huntingdonshire	Henry Mannock
St Albans	John Maynard
Leominster	Nicholas Depden
Lincolnshire	Philip Tyrwhitt
Truro	Thomas Royden (added)

Appendix B

Members of the House of Commons whose names are marked with a cross on Bodley MS e Museo 17, with their constituencies.

The list probably came to the Library in 1658 at the death of Gerard Langbaine (*Summary Catalogue*: MS 3706). The list is written on eight narrow oblong sheets, sewn together in a paper cover to make a book. It is clearly a crown office List (on which see N. Fuidge, 'Some Sixteenth Century Crown Office Lists at the Public Record Office', *BIHR* XLII (1969), 200–11). Although this is the only list known to exist for the first of Mary's parliaments, the fact that two have survived for the parliament of 1558 (PRO C 193/32/2, and List of Knights and Burgesses in the William Salt Library, Stafford) suggests that the office was prepared to draw up more than the one list which was given to the clerk of the Commons as a record of Members returned; the Bodleian list may not, therefore, be the clerk's own copy. Probably the constituencies and their order were copied from a list prepared for the proposed third parliament of Edward's reign, and the names of the members from yet another list, for when copying out the names of the burgesses for Dunheved the scribe at first repeated the name of one of the members for Lostwithiel, the constituency immediately above it on the list, as if he had lost his place (fo. 2ᵛ), and at various points he had difficulty in making out the names. Some effort was taken to keep the list up to date: the name of Alexander Nowell, a burgess for Looe, is erased, presumably after a committee of the House had reported on 13 October that, as a member of convocation, he was not eligible to sit in the Commons. However, the name of John Forster, burgess for Plympton, whose case was referred to the same committee as that of Nowell, and then to another on 27 October, is left standing; there is no evidence about the decision of this second committee. The Bodley list was, therefore, still being worked on in mid-October, if not later.

Henry Peckham, Wycombe	Richard Blackwell, Derbyshire
John Gayer, Launceston	Sir Peter Carew, Devon
William Smethwick, Grampound	William Hawkins, Plymouth
Ralph Skinner, Penryn	Nicholas Adams, Dartmouth
Robert Beverley, Trevena	Sir Giles Strangways, Dorset
Francis Goldsmith, Mitchell	John Leweston, Melcombe

Owen Reynolds, Melcombe[1]
Sir Edmund Brydges,
  Gloucestershire
Humphrey Coningsby,
  Herefordshire
George Heneage, Grimsby
Thomas Heneage, Stamford
Sir Edward Warner, Grantham
Thomas Farnham, Leicester
Sir Walter Mildmay, Peterborough
William Fitzwilliam, Peterborough
Robert Saunders, Brackley
Sir John Hercy, Nottinghamshire
Thomas Markham, Nottingham
John Walpole, Lyme Regis
Robert Eyre, Yarmouth
William Hunston, Thetford
Sir Edward Bray, Surrey
Matthew Colthurst, Bletchingley
William More, Guildford
Sir Thomas Cornwallis, Gatton
Henry Stafford, Stafford
Edward Leighton, Shropshire
George Rithe, Petersfield
John Gosnold, Ipswich
Sir Edward Rogers, Somerset

Sir Ralph Hopton, Somerset
John Godwin, Wells
Sir Thomas Dyer, Bridgewater
Sir Henry Hussey, Lewes
Thomas Gawdy, Arundel
Henry Creed, Wilton
Richard Fulmerston, Bedwyn
William Badger, Cricklade
Sir Nicholas Throckmorton, Old
  Sarum
John Throckmorton, Old Sarum
Sir Thomas Russell, Worcestershire
John Lyttelton, Worcestershire
Thomas Marrow, Worcester
Clement Throckmorton, Warwick
John Marshe, London
John Blundell, London
Robert Farrar, Lincoln
Thomas Gawdy, Norwich
John Nethermill, Coventry
Sir Francis Fleming, Southampton
Thomas Jekyn, Hythe
Sir John Perrot, Sandwich
Simon Linch, Sandwich
Charles Vaughan, Radnorshire

---

[1] The cross by this name is a little obscure.

Appendix C

Bodley MS Tanner 391, fo. 37[1]

Part of this document relates how, supposedly in 1555, a bill was preferred

> entailing ... the Crown to K.Ph and Qu.M. & to the heirs of the body of Qu.Ma: it being discovered to the house by Serjeant Pollard that if the Queen should die without issue K.Ph: should be tenant in tail of the Crown after possibility of Issue Extinct by that bill as it was penned Desires to know whether it was the pleasure of the House to have it so, who presently called for the bill to put it to Question, thereby to dash it, but the Speaker having his instructions beforehand, feigned himself Sick & upon request the passing of the bill was deferred for that time, but ordered to Sit in the afternoon for debate thereof. The Speaker deferred his coming til 4 of the Clock in the afternoon & then some principle men having been dealt withall by the Queen no man durst move it [the bill] until it began to be dark, whereupon Sir Anthony Kingston resolved to move it, but first caused torches to be sent for. Upon his motion the House called for the Question, the Speaker refused to put it. They threaten to choose a new Speaker. At last the question was made & the bill was dashed. The Queen committed Sir Anthony Kingston hereupon to the Tower.

The account goes on to say that the House refused to sit in Kingston's absence and that he 'was delivered and sent to them again'. There is an obvious problem about the dating of this episode. The author attributed it to 1555 and Kingston, who plays such an important part in the affair, was a member of the Commons in 1555 but not in the preceding year. None the less, it seems likely that the incident occurred during Mary's third parliament, when the future of the unborn heir was under discussion, rather than in the fourth, when it had tacitly been accepted that no heir was immediately forthcoming.

---

[1] This is a manuscript dealing with parliamentary procedure: one chapter of it, on the passing of bills, was printed as William Hakewil's *The Manner how Statutes are enacted in Parliament by Passing of Bills* (London, 1659)—the entire manuscript may, therefore, be a draft of the large work on parliament that Hakewill was planning to write. I am most grateful to Lady de Villiers for the reference, and for information on the manuscript.

Moreover, the distinction drawn between 'serjeant Pollard' and 'the Speaker' makes it improbable that the incident occurred in 1555, when Pollard was serving his second term as speaker. (It is interesting that Renard had mentioned Pollard specifically as someone who was critical of the earlier draft, complaining that the obscure phrasing was unsatisfactory in a measure relating to Philip, to whom the realm owed a debt of gratitude.[2]) The episode almost certainly, therefore, relates to the third of Mary's parliaments.

There is another account of what appears to be the same incident in a manuscript in the British Library (BL Add. MS 36,856, fos. 48–54: printed by E. R. Foster, 'Speaking in the House of Commons', *BIHR* XLIII (1970), 47–8). This relates how 'In the beginning of the reign of King Philip and Queen Mary, when it was desired by the King and the Queen that the crown might be entailed to them and the heirs of their bodies, that bill being earnestly spoken against by Sir Anthony Kingston, he was the next day sent for by the Queen and committed to the Tower, but being justified by the House in the manner of his speech as being in no way unfitting (although it were very free) they did refuse any longer to sit until their Member might again be restored to them, which was accordingly yielded to by the King and Queen.' The episode was cited as a precedent in the parliament of 1621 (*Commons Debates in 1621*, ed. W. Notestein, F. H. Relf, and H. Simpson (New Haven, 1935), VI. 345).

There are too many problems about this evidence for it to be cited with anything other than extreme caution, but it does tend to reinforce the suggestion that some proposal to extend Philip's power was made in the course of this parliament.

---

[2] See above, 119.

Appendix D

Guildford Museum, Loseley MS 1331/2[1]

'Al theys in quene marys tyme were in *the* parliament fyrst holden ageynste the general repele of al treasens etc whereby the statute of *the* supremisy was repelyd'.

Sr anthony ky(n)gston
Sr John Sentloo
Sr Thomas diere
Sr Raphe hopton
Sr John Rogers
Sr Nicholas poyns
Sr george hawood
Sr Thomas gargrave
Sr John parret
Sr Willi(ia)m Courtney
Sr John pollarde
Sr John Chammon
Sr arthur chamburne
Sr giles Stranguyshe
Sr Nicholas Arnolde
Sr Will(ia)m Cobham
Sr george blunt
Sr Thomas Throckmerton
Sr Nicholas Strange
Sr humfrey Ratclife
Sr Roger North
Sr geams Stumpe
Sr Lawrens Smythe
Sr Andro Corbet
Mr Coks
Mr Rastwolde
Mr Mone
Mr Smythwyke
Mr Mathew Arru(n)del
Mr bynge
Mr Marshe
Mr younge
Mr bullar
Mr Morgayne
Mr Jones
Mr Jones

Mr Wyllyams
Mr Raphe Skynner
Mr Clyfforde
Mr Portor of greysin
Mr Porter of glositer
Mr Messenger
Mr baseley
Mr Erbye
Mr bolde
Mr Chune
Mr More
Mr Vagh(a)n
Mr John Chaliner
Mr Carel[1]
Mr Varney
Mr Varney
Mr John Asheley
Mr Bowyere
Mr Knyght
Mr Nowel
Mr Sakforde
Mr Carye
Mr Holmes
Mr Drurye
Mr Thom(a)s huggon
Mr perne
Mr dennys
Mr Robothim
Mr Appleyearde
Mr T(?i)dloo
Mr fowlar
Mr b(?a)dnam
Mr peyton
Mr pleydall
Mr Rande

Mr Smythe
Mr huntley
Mr Devenishe
Mr Randoll
My Lyght
Mr fillips
Mr hodgskyns
Mr pekham
Mr Chiuerton
Mr Crouche
Mr fludkyn
Mr Rydley
Mr Acton
Mr Dauid Seymer
Mr Thornef
Mr Bolton
the baron of birport[3]
Mr Thom(a)s fillips
Mr fulks
Mr clement hiet
Mr george Willi(a)ms
Mr farrar
Mr Semar
Mr fissher
Mr Malery
Thom(a)s Maria Wynkfild
Mr Jobson of hayle
Mr spiser
Mr Fenne
Mr balgye
Mr Sturton
Mr Corbyt
Mr Kemptorne
Mr Tyrrell
Mr George Cobh(a)m

[1] There is a copy of this list, with some small variants of transcription and an attempt at identification, in *The House of Commons, 1509–1558*, 20–3.

[2] Or 'Cavel'. See above, Ch. 10 n. 28.

[3] Richard Cornwall of Burford, Salop.

Bibliography

MANUSCRIPT SOURCES

London

British Library

Additional 15388, 36856, 41577
Cotton Titus B. II, C. VII, Vespasian D. xv (i)
Harley 419, 2143, 6069, 6234
Lansdowne 3, 156, 515
Royal 17 C. 3, 18 C. 24
Stowe 280, 354, 571

City of London Record Office

Repertory Book 13
Journal 16, 17

House of Lords Record Office

Original Acts: Mary, Philip and Mary
House of Commons Journal, 1553–1558
House of Lords Journal, 1554–1558

Inner Temple Library

Petyt 538, vol. XLVII

Lambeth Palace Library

Microfilm of Douai MS 922: Pole's Legatine Register

Public Record Office

Account of Henry VIII's funeral LC 2/2
Controllment Roll 29/1188
Crown Office Lists C 193/32
Exchequer Accounts 101/424
Parliament Rolls C 65/162–5
Placita coram Rege KB 27/1176–1187
Star Chamber 4/3, 4/7, 4/8, 4/9
State Papers, Mary (11), Elizabeth (12)
State Papers, Foreign SP 69/1–5
State Papers, Supplementary 46/8, 46/124
Subsidy Rolls E 179/69
Transcripts 31/3, 31/14
Writs and Returns C 219/21–5

Outside London

California, Henry E. Huntingdon Library
Hastings MSS: Parliamentary Papers—List of knights and burgesses
    for the parliament of November 1554 (available as a xerox copy)

Exeter City Record Office
Act Book II, V
Book 60h: J. Hooker, 'The order of kepinge of a p[ar]lament yn these
    dayes'

Guildford Museum and Muniment Room
Loseley MS 1085, 1109, 1331; Loseley Correspondence 3

Longleat House, Wiltshire
Thynne Papers, I–III

New Haven, Connecticut, Beinecke Rare Book and Manuscript Library
Osborn Shelves f a 23 (copy of the Commons Journal for the reign of
    Mary)

Norfolk and Norwich Record Office
Fitzwilliam (Molton) MSS, Paget Letter Book

Oxford, Bodleian Library
Additional c 94
Ashmole 836
Bodley 53
e Museo 17
Eng. th. b. 12, II
Rawlinson B. 102, D. 68
Tanner 90, 391

Paris, Archives du Ministère des Affaires Étrangères
English Correspondence: vols. IX, XII

Plas Newydd, Anglesey
Paget Papers, Boxes I, II, III, Miscellaneous

Rome, Vatican Library
MSS 5968, 5987 (available as Bodley Film 33)

Stafford, William Salt Library
MS 264: List of Knights and Burgesses for the parliament of 1558

PRINTED SOURCES
(Primary sources and books first printed before 1642)

Acts of the Privy Council, ed. J. R. Dasent, vols. I–VII (London, 1890–1907).

Anglería, P. Martyr, *The Decades of the newe world* (London, 1555; *STC* 645).

Aylmer, J., *An harborowe for faithfvll and trew subiectes* (n.p., 1559; *STC* 1005).

Bradford, J., *The copye of a letter sent to the erles of Arundel, Darbie . . .* (n.p., n.d; *STC* 3480).

Calendar of the Patent Rolls, Edward VI, Mary, Elizabeth (London, 1924–39).

Calendar of the Shrewsbury Papers in the Lambeth Palace Library, ed. E. G. W. Bill (Derbyshire Archaeological Society, 1966).

Calendar of State Paper, Domestic, vol. I, ed. R. Lemon (London, 1856).

Calendar of State Papers Domestic, 1601–3, with Addenda, 1547–1565, ed. M. A. E. Green (London, 1870).

Calendar of State Papers, Spanish, vols. XI–XIII, ed. Royall Tyler (London, 1916–54).

Calendar of State Papers, Venetian, vols. IV–VI ed. R. Brown, C. Bentinck, and H. Brown (London, 1864–98).

Catalogue of MSS in the Library of the Honourable Society of the Inner Temple, ed. J. Conway Davies (Oxford, 1972).

Celestina, *A new com[m]odye . . .* (London, n.d; *RSTC* 20721).

'The chartulary of Dieulacres Abbey', ed. G. Wrottesley, *William Salt Archaeological Society*, NS, IX (1906).

A Chronicle of the Grey Friars of London, ed. J. G. Nichols (Camden Society, OS, LIII, 1852).

The Chronicle of Queen Jane and of two years of Queen Mary, ed. J. G. Nichols (Camden Society, OS, XLVIII, 1850).

Coke, E., *The first part of the institute . . .* (London, 1628).

—— *The Third Part of the Institutes of the Laws of England* (London, 1671).

—— *The Reports of Sir Edward Coke* (London, 1776).

—— *Fourth Part of the Institutes* (London, 1644).

'A Collection of Original Letters from the Bishops to the Privy Council 1564', ed. M. Bateson (*Camden Miscellany IX*, 1895).

Commons Debates in 1621, ed. W. Notestein, F. H. Relf, and H. Simpson (New Haven, 1935).

Copia d'una Lettera d'Inghilterra quale narra l'entrata del Rever[endissimo] Cardinale Polo . . . in Inghilterra (Milan, 1554).

Cooper, C. H., *Annals of Cambridge* (Cambridge, 1853).

Cranmer, T., *A confutatio[n] of vnwritte[n] verities* (n.p., n.d; *STC* 5996).
D'Ewes, S. P., *The Journals of All the Parliaments during the Reign of Queen Elizabeth* (London, 1682; Shannon reprint, 1973).
'Descriptio reductionis Angliae ad Catholicam unitatem', in *Epistolae Reginaldi Poli* (below).
A Discourse of the Common Weal, ed. E. Lamond (Cambridge, 1893; 1929).
Dyer, J., *Reports of Cases in the Reigns of Henry VIII, Edward VI, Queen Mary and Queen Elizabeth* (Dublin, 1794).
Dugdale, W., *A Perfect Copy of all the Summons of the Nobility ...* (London, 1685).
Evans, J., 'The Private Account Book of William More', *Archaeologia*, XXXVI (1855).
An Exhortation to the carienge of Chrystes crosse (n.p., n.d.; *STC* 5890).
'The Count of Feria's Despatch to Philip II of 14 November 1558', ed. M. J. Rodríguez-Salgado and S. Adams, *Camden Miscellany XXVIII* (Camden Fourth Series, XXIX, 1984).
Flores, J. de, *The history of Aurelio and of Isabell* (Antwerp, 1556; *STC* 11092).
Foxe, J., *Acts and Monuments*, 6 vols. (London, 1841).
The Letters of Stephen Gardiner, ed. J. A. Muller (Cambridge, 1933).
Goodman, C., *How Svperior powers oght to be obeyed* (Geneva, 1558; *STC* 12020).
Guaras, A. de, *The Accession of Queen Mary*, ed. R. Garnett (London, 1892).
Guevara, A. de *The golden boke of Marcus Aurelius* (London, 1535; *STC* 12436).
—— *A dispraise of the life of a courtier* (London, 1548; *STC* 12431).
—— *The Diall of Princes* (London, 1557; *STC* 12427).
Guilding, J. M., *Reading Records* (London, 1892).
Hakewil, W., *The Libertie of the Subject: against the pretended power of impositions ...* (London, 1641).
—— *Modus tenendi parliamentum, or the manner of holding parliaments in England* (London, 1641).
—— *The order and course of passing bills in Parliament* (London, 1641).
—— *The Manner how Statutes are enacted in Parliament by Passing of Bills* (London, 1659).
Haynes, S., *A Collection of State Papers ... left by William Cecil, Lord Burghley* (London, 1740).
Historical Manuscripts Commission:
    Third (Duke of Devonshire at Bolton Abbey, Bedingfield), 1872.
    Fourth (Fitzhardinge), 1874.
    Seventh (More-Molyneux), 1879.

Thirteenth, IV (Rye and Hereford Corporations), 1892.
Fourteenth Reports, VIII (Lincoln, Bury St Edmunds and Grimsby Corporations), 1895.
Salisbury, II, 1888.
Rutland, I and II, 1888.
Foljambe, 1897.

Hooker, J., *The order and vsage of the keeping of a Parliament in England* (n.p., n.d; *RSTC* 24886.7)

—— *The Life and Times of Sir Peter Carew*, ed. J. Maclean (London, 1857).

Howell, T. B., *A Complete Collection of State Trials*, vol. I (London, 1816).

Hughes P. L., and Larkin, J. F., *Tudor Royal Proclamations*, vol. II (New Haven and London, 1969).

Journals of the House of Commons, The, vol. I (London, 1852).

Journals of the House of Lords, The, vol. I (London, 1846).

Knox, J., *A faythful admonition vnto the professours of Gods truth in England* (Kalykow, 1554; *RSTC* 15069).

—— *The first blast . . .* (n.p., 1558; *RSTC* 15079).

Lame[n]tacion of England, The (n.p., 1557; *STC* 10014).

Las Casas, Bartolomé de, *Brevíssima relación de la destruyción de las Indias* (Seville, 1552).

Letters and Papers, Foreign and Domestic, of the Reign of Henry VIII, ed. J. S. Brewer, J. Gairdner and R. H. Brodie (London, 1864–1932).

'Letters, illustrating the Reign of Queen Jane', ed. J. More-Molyneux, *Archaeological Journal*, XXX (1873).

Life of Henry Fitz Allan, last Earle of Arundell, The', ed. J. G. Nichols, *Gentleman's Magazine*, CIV (1833).

Lodge, E., *Illustrations of British History* (London, 1791).

Machyn, H., *The Diary of Henry Machyn*, ed. J. G. Nichols (Camden Society, os, XLII, 1850).

'Narrative of Richard Troughton, The', ed. F. Madden, *Archaeologia*, XXIII (1831).

Narratives of the Days of the Reformation, ed. J. G. Nicols (Camden Society, os, LXXVII, 1859).

Naunton, R., *Fragmenta Regalia* (London, 1870).

Original Letters Relative to the English Reformation, 2 vols. ed. H. Robinson (Parker Society, 1846–7).

'Parkyn's Narrative of the Reformation', ed. A. G. Dickens, *English Historical Review*, LXII (1947).

Peck, F., *Desiderata Curiosa* (London, 1732).

'Perrot Papers', ed. C. McNeill, *Analecta Hibernica*, XII (1943).

Philpot, J., *The trew report of the dvsputacyon in the conuocacyo[n] hows* (Basil, n.d.; *RSTC* 19890).

Plowden, E., *The Commentaries or Reports of Edmund Plowden* (London, 1816).

Pole, R., *Epistolae Reginaldi Poli*, ed. A. M. Quirini, 5 vols. (Brescia, 1744–57).

Ponet, J., *A Short Treatise of politike power* (n.p., 1556; *RSTC* 20178).

Proceedings in the Parliaments of Elizabeth I, vol. I, ed. T. E. Hartley (Leicester, 1981).

Proceedings in Parliament, 1610 ed. E. R. Foster (New Haven and London, 1966).

Proclamation of Queen Jane (London, 1553; *STC* 7846).

Proctor, J., *The historie of Wyatts rebellion* (London, Jan. 1555; *RSTC* 20407).

Relations politiques des Pays-Bas et de l'Angleterre sous le règne de Philippe II, ed. J. M. B. C. Baron Kervyn de Lettenhove (Brussels, 1882).

Rymer, T., *Foedera, Conventiones, Litterae, etc.* (London, 1704–35).

'Dr Nicholas Sander's Report to Cardinal Morone', ed. J. H. Pollen, *Miscellanea*, vol. I (Catholic Record Society, 1905).

San Pedro, D. de, *The Castell of Love* (London, n.d.; *RSTC* 21739.5).

Smith, T., *De Republica Anglorum*, ed. M. Dewar (Cambridge, 1982).

Speciall grace ... vpo[n] the good nues and Proclamation, A (n.p., 1558; *STC* 7559).

'State Papers relating to the Custody of the Princess Elizabeth at Woodstock in 1554', ed. C. R. Manning, *Transactions of the Norfolk and Norwich Archaeological Society*, IV (1855).

Stow, J., *The Survey of London* (Everyman edn., 1965).

Stubbs, J., *The discoverie of a gapin gvlf where into England is like to be swallowed by an other French marriage* (London, 1579; *RSTC* 23400).

Supplicacyo[n] to the quenes maiestie, A (n.p., 1555; *RSTC* 17562).

Thomas, W., *The historie of Italie* (London, 1549; *RSTC* 24018).

—— *Principal rules of the Italian grammar* (London, 1550; *RSTC* 24020).

—— *The Pilgrim*, ed. J. A. Froude (London, 1861).

Throckmorton, Sir Nicholas, 'Sir Nicholas Throckmorton's Advice to Queen Elizabeth on her Accession to the Throne', ed. J. E. Neale, *English Historical Review*, LXV (1950).

Tytler, P. F., *England under the Reigns of Edward VI and Mary* (London, 1839).

Letters and Papers of the Verney Family, ed. J. Bruce (Camden Society, os, LVI, 1853).

Vertot, R. A., de, *Ambassades de Messieurs de Noailles en Angleterre*, 5 vol. (Leiden, 1763).

'The "Vita Mariae Angliae Reginae" of Robert Wingfield of Brantham', ed. D. MacCulloch, *Camden Miscellany* XXVIII (Camden Fourth Series, 29, 1984).

Walther, R., *Antichrist* (Southwark, 1556; *RSTC* 25009).

Willan, T. S., *A Tudor Book of Rates* (Manchester, 1962).
Wriothesley, C., *A Chronicle of England during the Reigns of the Tudors*, ed. W. D. Hamilton (Camden Society, NS, XX, 1877).
Wyatt, G., *The Papers of George Wyatt Esquire*, ed. D. M. Loades (Camden Fourth Series, V, 1968).
Zúñiga y Ávila, Luis de, *The commentaries . . . which treateth of the wars in Germany* (London, 1555; *STC* 987).
Zurich Letters, The, ed. H. Robinson, 2 vols. (Parker Society, 1842–5).
York Civic Records, vol. v, ed. A. Raine (Yorkshire Archaeological Society, CX, 1946).

SECONDARY WORKS

Abbott, L., 'Public Office and Private Profit: The Legal Establishment in the Reign of Queen Mary', in *The Mid-Tudor Polity c.1540–1560*, ed. J. Loach and R. Tittler (London, 1980).
Adair, E. R., and Evans, F. M., 'Writs of Assistance, 1558–1700', *English Historical Review*, XXVI (1921).
Alexander, G., 'Bonner and the Marian Persecutions', *History*, LX (1975).
—— 'Victim or Spendthrift? The Bishop of London and his Income in the Sixteenth Century', in *Wealth and Power in Tudor England: Essays presented to S. T. Bindoff*, ed. E. W. Ives, R. J. Knecht and J. J. Scarisbrick (London, 1978).
Ancel, D. R., 'La Réconciliation de l'Angleterre avec le Saint-Siège', *Revue d'histoire ecclésiastique*, X (1909).
Andrew, A. E., 'Henry, Lord Stafford (1501–63) in Local and Central Government', *English Historical Review*, LXXVIII (1963).
Barnwell, E. L., 'Notes on the Perrot family', *Archaeologia Cambrensis*, III, xi (1865).
Bartlett, K., '"The misfortune that is wished for him": the Exile and Death of Edward Courtenay, Eighth Earl of Devon', *Canadian Journal of History*, XIV (1979).
Baskerville, G., 'The Dispossessed Religious of Gloucestershire', *Transactions of the Bristol and Gloucestershire Archaeological Society*, XLIX (1927).
Batista I Roca, J. M., 'The Hispanic Kingdoms and the Catholic Kings', *New Cambridge Modern History*, I (Cambridge, 1957).
Ballamy, J., *The Tudor Law of Treason* (London and Toronto, 1979).
Bindoff, S. T., ed., *The House of Commons, 1509–1558* (London, 1982).
Boynton, L., *The Elizabethan Militia, 1558–1638* (London, 1967).

Burnet, G., *History of the Church of England*, 7 vols. (Oxford, 1865).

Buxton, J., and Williams, P. H., eds., *New College 1379–1979* (Oxford, 1979).

Chaplais, P., 'The Original Charters of Herbert and Gervase Abbots of Westminster (1121–1157)', in *A Mediaeval Miscellany for Doris Mary Stenton*, ed. P. M. Barnes and C. F. Slade (Pipe Roll Society, NS, XXXVI, 1960).

Chester, J. L., *John Rogers* (London, 1861).

Churton, R., *The Life of Alexander Nowell* (Oxford, 1809).

Collinson, P., *The Elizabethan Puritan Movement* (London, 1967).

Connell-Smith, G., *Forerunners of Drake* (London, 1954).

C(orbet), A. E., *The Family of Corbet* (n.p., n.d.).

Crehan, J. H., 'The Return to Obedience', *The Month*, NS, XIV (1955).

Cross, C., *The Royal Supremacy in the Elizabethan Church* (London, 1969).

Cunningham, W., *Alien Immigrants to England* (London, 1897, 1969).

Davies, C. S. L., 'England and the French War, 1557–9', in *The Mid-Tudor Polity c.1540–1560*, ed. J. Loach and R. Tittler (London, 1980).

Dewar, M., *Sir Thomas Smith* (London, 1964).

Dickens, A. G., 'The Edwardian Arrears in Augmentation Payments and the Problem of the ex-Religious', *English Historical Review*, LV (1940).

Dixon, R. W., *History of the Church of England*, 6 vols. (London, 1891).

Dunham, W. H., 'Regal Power and the Rule of Law', *Journal of British Studies*, III (1963–4).

Edwards, J. G., *The Commons in Mediaeval English Parliaments* (Creighton Lecture for 1957, London, 1958).

—— 'The Emergence of Majority Rule in English Parliamentary Elections', *Transactions of the Royal Historical Society*, Fifth Series, XIV (1964).

—— 'The Emergence of Majority Rule in the Procedure of the House of Commons', ibid. XV (1965).

Edwards, P. S., 'The Parliamentary History of Anglesey in the Mid-Sixteenth Century', *Welsh Historical Review*, X (1980).

Elton, G. R., *The Tudor Revolution in Government* (Cambridge, 1952).

—— *Reform and Renewal* (Cambridge, 1973).

—— 'Tudor Government: the Points of Contact', *Transactions of the Royal Historical Society*, Fifth Series, XXIV (1974).

Emden, A. B., *A Biographical Dictionary of the University of Oxford* AD *1501 to 1540* (Oxford, 1974).

Emmison, F. G., *Tudor Secretary: Sir William Petre at Court and Home* (London, 1961).

Foster, E. R., *The House of Lords, 1603–1649* (Chapel Hill and London, 1983).

—— 'Speaking in the House of Commons', *Bulletin of the Institute of Historical Research*, XLIII (1970).

Foster, F. F., *The Politics of Stability: A Portrait of the Rulers in Elizabethan London* (London, 1977).

Fuidge, N., 'Some Sixteenth Century Crown Office Lists at the Public Record Office', *Bulletin of the Institute of Historical Research*, XLII (1969).

Fuller, T., *The Worthies of England* (London, 1662).

Furley, O. W., 'The Whig Exclusionists: Pamphlet Literature 1679–81', *Cambridge Historical Journal*, XIII (1957).

Garrett, C., *The Marian Exiles* (Cambridge, 1938).

Gilkes, R. G., *The Tudor Parliament* (London, 1969).

Graves, M. A. R., *The House of Lords in the Parliaments of Edward VI and Queen Mary I: An Institutional Study* (Cambridge, 1981).

—— 'Proctorial Representation in the House of Lords in the Reign of Edward VI: A Reassessment', *Journal of British Studies*, X (1971).

—— 'The House of Lords and the Politics of Opposition, April–May 1554', in *W. P. Morrell: A Tribute* ed. G. A. Wood and P. S. O'Connor (Dunedin, 1973).

—— 'Thomas Norton the Parliament Man', *Historical Journal*, XXIII (1980).

Gwyn, D., 'Richard Eden, Cosmographer and Alchemist', *The Sixteenth Century Journal*, XV (1984).

Habakkuk, H. J., 'Daniel Finch, 2nd Earl of Nottingham: His House and Estate', in *Studies in Social History: A Tribute to G. M. Trevelyan*, ed. J. H. Plumb (London, 1955).

Hall, G. D. G., 'Impositions and the Courts, 1554–1606', *Law Quarterly Review*, LXIX (1953).

Harbison, E. H., *Rival Ambassadors at the Court of Queen Mary* (Princeton, 1940).

—— 'French Intrigue at the Court of Queen Mary', *American Historical Review*, XLV (1940).

Hasler, P., ed., *The House of Commons, 1558–1603* (London, 1981).

Hassell Smith, A., *County and Court: Government and Politics in Norfolk, 1558–1603* (Oxford, 1974).

Heal, F., *Of Prelates and Princes* (Cambridge, 1980).

Hill, C., *Economic Problems of the Church* (London, pb. edn. 1971).

Hill, L. M., 'The Two-Witness Rule in English Treason Trials', *American Journal of Legal History*, XII (1968).

Hoak, D. E., *The King's Council in the Reign of Edward VI* (Cambridge, 1976).

Holdsworth, W. E. S., *A History of English Law*, vols. i, iv, v, vi, (London, 1922–52).

Houlbrooke, R. A., *Church Courts and the People during the English Reformation, 1520–1570* (Oxford, 1979).

Hughes, P., *The Reformation in England* (London, 1963).

Hume, M. A. S., 'The Visit of Philip II, 1554', *English Historical Review*, VII (1892).

Hurstfield, J., *Freedom, Corruption and Government in Elizabethan England* (London, 1973).

Jones, N. L., *Faith by Statute* (London, 1982).

Jamison, C., *The History of the Royal Hospital of St. Katherine by the Tower of London* (Oxford, 1952).

Lambert, S., 'Procedure in the House of Commons in the Early Stuart Period', *Historical Journal*, XXIII (1980).

Langbein, J. H., *Prosecuting Crimes in the Renaissance* (Cambridge, Mass., 1974).

Lehmberg, S. E., *The Reformation Parliament, 1529–1536* (Cambridge, 1970).

—— *The Later Parliaments of Henry VIII, 1536–1597* (Cambridge, 1977).

—— 'Early Tudor Parliamentary Procedures: Provisos in the Legislation of the Reformation Parliament', *English Historical Review*, LXXXV (1970).

Loach, J., 'Pamphlets and Politics, 1553–8', *Bulletin of the Institute of Historical Research*, XLVIII (1975).

—— 'Parliament: A "New Air"?', in *Revolution Reassessed: Revisions in the History of Tudor Government and Administration*, ed. C. Coleman and D. Starkey (Oxford, forthcoming).

Loades, D. M., *Two Tudor Conspiracies* (Cambridge, 1965).

—— *The Reign of Mary Tudor* (London, 1979).

—— 'The Authorship and Publication of "The copye of a letter"', *Transactions of the Cambridge Bibliographical Society*, III (1960).

—— 'The Last Years of Cuthbert Tunstall, 1547–1559', *Durham University Journal*, XXXV (1973–4).

McCann, T. J., 'The Parliamentary Speech of Viscount Montagu against the Act of the Supremacy 1559, *Sussex Archaeological Collections*, CVIII (1970).

McConica, J. K., *English Humanists and Reformation Politics* (Oxford, 1965).

Maltby, W. S., *The Black Legend in England* (Durham, NC, 1971).

'Members of Parliament for Newcastle on Tyne, 1377–1558', *Archaeologia Aeliana*, XLV (1937).

Miller, H., 'Attendance in the House of Lords during the Reign of Henry VIII', *Historical Journal*, X (1962).

—— 'Henry VIII's Unwritten Will: Grants of Land and Honours in 1547', in *Wealth and Power in Tudor England: Essays presented to S. T. Bindoff*, ed. E. W. Ives, R. J. Knecht, and J. J. Scarisbrick (London, 1978).

Muller, J. A., *Stephen Gardiner and the Tudor Reaction* (London, 1926).

Myers, A. R., 'Parliament, 1422–1509', in *The English Parliament in the Middle Ages*, ed. R. G. Davies and J. H. Denton (Manchester, 1981).

Neale, J. E., *The Elizabethan House of Commons* (London, 1949).

—— *Elizabeth I and her Parliaments, 1559–1581* (London, 1953).

—— *Elizabeth I and her Parliaments, 1584–1601* (London, 1957).

Notestein, W., *The House of Commons, 1604–1610* (New Haven and London, 1971).

Pogson, R., 'Revival and Reform in Mary Tudor's Church: A Question of Money', *Journal of Ecclesiastical History*, XXVI (1975).

Ramsay, G. D., *The City of London in International Politics at the Accession of Queen Elizabeth* (Manchester, 1975).

Read, C., *Mr Secretary Cecil and Queen Elizabeth* (London, 1955).

Richardson, W. C., *History of the Court of Augmentations 1534–1554* (Baton Rouge, 1961).

Ridley, J., *Thomas Cranmer* (Oxford, 1962).

Rose-Troup, F., *The Western Rebellion of 1549* (London, 1913).

Roskell, J. S., *The Commons and their Speakers in English Parliaments, 1376–1523* (Manchester, 1965).

Ruding, R., *Annals of the Coinage of Great Britain* (London, 1840).

Schenk, W., *Reginald Pole, Cardinal of England* (London, 1950).

Shaw, W. A., *The Knights of England* (London, 1906).

Simpson, A., *The Wealth of the Gentry* (Cambridge, 1961).

Smith, A. H., *New College, Oxford, and its Building* (Oxford, 1952).

Smith, L. B., 'The Last Will and Testament of Henry VIII: A Question of Perspective', *Journal of British Studies*, II (1962–3).

Snow, V. N., 'Proctorial Representation in the House of Lords during the Reign of Edward VI', *Journal of British Studies*, VIII (1969).

Somerville, R., *The History of the Duchy of Lancaster* (London, 1953).

Stanley, A. P., *Historical Memorials of Westminster Abbey* (London, 1876).

Stephens, W. E., 'Great Yarmouth under Queen Mary', *Norfolk Archaeology*, XXIX (1946).

Stone, L., *The Crisis of the Aristocracy* (Oxford, 1965).

Strype, J., *Ecclesiastical Memorials* (London, 1721).

—— *Annals of the Reformation* (Oxford, 1820–40).

Sturge, C., *Cuthbert Tunstal* (London, 1938).

Swales, T. H., 'The Redistribution of Monastic Lands in Norfolk at the Dissolution', *Norfolk Archaeology*, XXXIV (1966).

Symonds, H., 'The Coinage of Queen Mary Tudor, 1553–1558, *British Numismatic Journal*, VIII (1911).

Thirsk, J., ed., *The Agrarian History of England and Wales*, vol. iv (Cambridge, 1967).

Tittler, R., 'The Incorporation of Boroughs, 1540–1558', *History*, LXII (1977).

Underhill, J. G., *Spanish Literature in the England of the Tudors* (New York, 1892).

Ungerer, G., *Anglo-Spanish Relations in Tudor Literature* (Bern, 1956).

—— 'The Printing of Spanish Books in Elizabethan England', *Library*, Fifth Series, XX (1965).

Victoria History of the County of Warwickshire, 8 vols. (London, 1904–69).

Villari, R., 'The Insurrection in Naples of 1585', in *The Late Italian Renaissance, 1525–1630*, ed. E. Cochrane (London, 1970).

Weikel, A., 'The Marian Council revisited', in *The Mid-Tudor Polity c.1540–1560*, ed. J. Loach and R. Tittler (London, 1980).

Welford, R., *History of Newcastle and Gateshead* (London, 1885).

Willan, T. S., *The Muscovy Merchants of 1555* (Manchester, 1953).

Willen, D., *John Russell, First Earl of Bedford* (London, 1981).

Williamson, J. A., *Hawkins of Plymouth* (London, 1949).

Wolffe, B. P., *The Royal Demesne in English History* (London, 1971).

Woodham-Smith, C., *Queen Victoria: Her Life and Times* (London, 1972).

Wyatt, T., 'Aliens in England before the Huguenots', *Proceedings of the Huguenot Society*, XIX (1953).

UNPUBLISHED THESES

Ericson, C. G., 'Parliament as a Representative Institution in the Reigns of Edward VI and Mary' (University of London Ph.D. thesis, 1974).

Lemasters, G. A., 'The Privy Council in the Reign of Queen Mary I' (University of Cambridge Ph.D. thesis, 1971).

Loach, S. J., 'Opposition to the Crown in Parliament, 1553–1558' (University of Oxford D.Phil. thesis, 1974).

Mackwell, C. A., 'The Early Career of Sir James Croft, 1520–1570' (University of Oxford B.Litt. thesis, 1970).

Pettegree, D. M. A., 'The Strangers and their Churches in London, 1550–1580' (University of Oxford D.Phil. thesis, 1983).

Pogson, R. H., 'Cardinal Pole—Papal Legate to England in Mary Tudor's Reign' (University of Cambridge Ph.D. thesis, 1972).

Swales, R. J. W., 'Local Politics and the Parliamentary Representation of Sussex, 1529–1558' (University of Bristol D.Phil. thesis, 1964).

Weikel, A., 'Crown and Council: A Study of Mary Tudor and her Privy Council' (Yale Ph.D. thesis, 1966).

Index